T0320051

Framing the Economy of the Future

Framing the Economy of the Future

Six Socio-Economic Trends for Sustainability, Circularity and Inclusivity

Edited by

Niels Faber

Professor of Transition Towards a Circular Economy, Hanze University of Applied Sciences, and Researcher, University of Groningen, the Netherlands

Sjors Witjes

Associate Professor, Institute for Management Research, Radboud University Nijmegen, the Netherlands

Edward Elgar
PUBLISHING

Cheltenham, UK • Northampton, MA, USA

Published by
Edward Elgar Publishing Limited
The Lypiatts
15 Lansdown Road
Cheltenham
Glos GL50 2JA
UK

Edward Elgar Publishing, Inc.
William Pratt House
9 Dewey Court
Northampton
Massachusetts 01060
USA

A catalogue record for this book
is available from the British Library

Library of Congress Control Number: 2024941800

This book is available electronically in the **Elgar**online
Economics subject collection
https://dx.doi.org/10.4337/9781789900248

ISBN 978 1 78990 023 1 (cased)
ISBN 978 1 78990 024 8 (eBook)

Printed and bound in Great Britain by
TJ Books Limited, Padstow, Cornwall

Contents

Figures

Tables

Contributors

Egbert Dommerholt is Professor of Biobased Business Valorization at the Hanze University of Applied Sciences and is connected to the Hanze UAS International Business School. He studied economics at the University of Groningen and received his PhD in 2009 at the Free University Amsterdam for his dissertation 'Corporate Sustainability Performance: Constructs, Measures, and Investors' responses'. His areas of expertise are sustainable development, the circular economy, and new business models. Egbert has authored several books on these topics.

Niels Faber is Professor of Transition Towards a Circular Economy at the Hanze University of Applied Sciences and Assistant Professor of Circular Entrepreneurship at the University of Groningen. His research focuses on organizational aspects of sustainability and circular economy, in particular on sustainable and circular business models and the ensuing transition and assessment of the progress made towards a circular economy. He has published numerous papers and books on these topics.

Elizabeth Hodson de Jaramillo is Professor Emeritus at the School of Sciences of the Pontificia Universidad Javeriana and has a PhD in botany. She is an international consultant on bioeconomy, biodiversity, agro-biotechnologies and biosafety of GMOs, a Member of the Academia Colombiana de Ciencias Exactas, Físicas y Naturales, and an Honorary Fellow for the Scientific Committee in Fondazione Scuola Medica Salernitana (Italy). She is also a member of the Ad Hoc Technical Expert Group on Risk Assessment and Risk Management under the Cartagena Protocol on Biosafety (Convention on Biological Diversity), a member of UNESCO's World Commission on the Ethics of Scientific Knowledge and Technology (COMEST), and a member of the Inter-American Network of Academies of Sciences (IANAS). She also serves as the Chair of Bioeconomy and Sustainable Development of the IICA (Inter-American Institute for Cooperation on Agriculture).

Jan Jonker is Emeritus Professor at the Nijmegen School of Management (NSM) of the Radboud University Nijmegen, the Netherlands. His research concerns corporate responsibility in relation to new business concepts and business strategy. He is a highly qualified international lecturer and presenter. He is a visiting professor at institutions such as the Business Schools of

Toulouse, Kaunas and Barcelona. In addition to his research, teaching and academic entrepreneurial activities he is also a business consultant. In 2010 he was appointed one of Holland's Top 100 most influential 'green' people.

Dré Kampfraath was a partner at InterimIC, a virtual network of entrepreneurs, consultants and freelance digital professionals. Dré passed away in 2023.

Arnoud Lagendijk is Professor of Economic Geography at Radboud University, Nijmegen, the Netherlands. He has a long track record in the field of regional development and policy, and he has published widely on themes such as innovation, clustering, strategy-making, regional identities and the diffusion of socio-economic practices.

Paul Manwaring is the founder of the Internet of Things (IoT) Living Lab, a citizen engagement consultancy in Amsterdam (NL), and co-founder of the City Innovation Exchange Lab (CITIXL). He studied at Penn State University and holds a BA in Integrative Arts with a co-operating major in philosophy. In 2000 he created a multimedia and web design firm in Amsterdam where he continues to live and work on cutting-edge digital interactive experiences to bridge the gap between the city and citizens with participatory platforms.

Berber Pas's research interests have evolved around the impact of digitalization on interorganizational collaboration and professional practices, trying to integrate whatever can be learned from research studies into teaching and occasional consulting activities, and always aiming to contribute to enhancing understanding regarding the responsible use of digital technology.

Adrián G. Rodríguez is a member of the United Nations Economic Commission for Latin America and the Caribbean, Santiago, Chile. He is an experienced Chief of Development with a demonstrable history of working in the international affairs industry. Skilled in government, rural development, Spanish, non-governmental organizations (NGOs) and policy analysis, he is a strong community and social services professional with a Doctor of Philosophy (PhD) focused on agricultural economics from Penn State University.

Peter Troxler is Research Professor at Rotterdam University of Applied Sciences. He studies how digital technologies enable new ways of designing and manufacturing and challenge and influence incumbent practices in industry and education. He has worked internationally in the energy industry, as a design consultant, and in higher education.

Jasper van den Berkmortel is a lawyer at the Wijn & Stael law firm. In 2020 he graduated with a Master's in both Law and Business Administration. For his master's thesis for BA, he conducted a literature study on different discourses in academic literature on big data in and for organizations.

Mark A. Wiering is Associate Professor of Environmental Governance and Politics at Radboud University in Nijmegen, the Netherlands. He studies the governance of socio-political transformations towards a sustainable society, especially the changing narratives and discourses in various policy domains, including water management, renewable energy policies and agriculture.

Sjors Witjes is Associate Professor of Organizational Sustainability and Circularity at Radboud University in the Netherlands and President of the International Sustainable Development Research Society. Sjors has been part of corporate sustainability and innovation processes applying TD approaches resulting in research and education that supports organizations to reflect on their contribution to a more sustainable society.

Introduction to *Framing the Economy of the Future*

Niels Faber and Sjors Witjes

We live in an exciting and contradictory, but also energetic and promising, society that is increasingly 'ramshackled' with a confusing number of developments reinforcing and simultaneously counteracting each other.

The corona pandemic and geopolitical conflicts have resulted in rapidly growing energy prices especially in continental Europe. The ever-growing worldwide electricity need (IEA, 2022) reflects an energy dependency that results in a state of urgency when energy prices rise. Whether it is for political reasons, growing awareness of the impact of current energy mixes on the environment or clean air, or because we are running out of energy resources, there is a growing need for changing the current energy system to fit demand and supply avoiding negative long-term effects.

The growing awareness of the use of resources has resulted in an urgency on the supply of sufficient resources to uphold our resource intensive society: whether it is as fuel or production material, the efficiency of the use of resources has grown over time but so also has the growth of the human population and, additionally, their consumption. With the latter being controlled, concepts like the circular economy are aiming for enhancing the efficient use of resources while being in the technosphere. An additional result of the efficiency in the use of resources is the reduction of extraction of natural resources or of untreated waste (e.g. in landfills or as plastics in the oceans).

These two examples of developments in resource and energy systems reinforce themselves while the change towards an alternative and more efficient resource system is only possible with a more sustainable energy system (Chen & Kim, 2019; Chishti et al., 2023; Koval et al., 2023).

Certainly, there are crises as well as profound and persisting problems leading to complicated issues and dilemmas; however, as a result of what? Cutbacks as a consequence of structural excessive spending in the past are justified and necessary, and the urge to engage in transitions finds increasing support. Against the backdrop of these observations, we deemed it relevant to identify and elaborate on a number of 'slow' and enduring economic and societal trends that have embodied the potential to shape our economy in the past and present and will most possibly do so in the near future. Underlying these trends, we observe various societal developments at all levels of society. In this light, we recognize a changing perspective on our relationship with things, in particular related to the issue of ownership. Current generations seem to adhere less to a sense of ownership when it comes to individual products (Tukker, 2004). Along with this comes a changing positioning of product responsibility to distributed responsibility that covers the entire product life cycle (European Commission, 2022). At the same time, increased transparency about the product life cycle leads to a generation that aims towards a sustainable society and is consequently increasingly worried about the impact of the products they acquire (Vezzoli et al., 2021).

This book is about six fundamental trends in socio-economic life that form the breeding ground for a new economy. Do we live in a society of crises, depletion and scarcity or in one of social, technological and economic inno- vation? If the latter, then where do we see the signs or even the substance for a movement of change? In this publication, seven innovative societal trends are emphasized that are contributing to societal transformations. These trends include: (1) digitization, (2) the circular economy, (3) the bio-based economy, (4) the sharing economy and collaborative economy, (5) the self-production economy, and (6) the Internet of Things and Internet of Services economy. If these trends develop further, they will allow the framing of an emerging economy. This has the propensity to establish an economic arena based on the principles of sustainability, circularity and inclusivity. This emerging economy questions the foundations of our present linear economy and, therefore, the established order of the economy and its actors. Out of these developments, a new logic of collectiveness arises which should ultimately solidify into a new generation of societal or business models. They give shape to the identified socio-economic trends.

After presenting more in-depth economic reflections in Chapter 1, each of the following chapters will elaborate the seven trends with analysis and criticism by various authors. Each chapter is structured roughly following a similar format. Chapters start with a further elaboration of the origins and background of the trend at hand. This may be followed by an exploration of the changing perspective on value-creation the trend has instigated, followed by a presentation of the implications for business models unfolding as part of the trend. Connections with the other trends are subsequently addressed. Next, a brief exposé of cases in which the trend materializes in practice is provided. Finally, each chapter finishes by making a more profound interpretation of the relationship of the trend with the larger topic of sustainability, and the devel- opment of a brief research agenda for the trend at hand.

In its entirety, this volume should be considered a 'conceptual toolbox' that provides an outlook of a future economy. At the finish, we provide a compre-

hensive discussion on the similarities and differences between the seven identified trends and how they reinforce and hinder each other. Also, we provide
an outlook towards upcoming developments that may influence the seven
economic trends either as catalysts, resistors, or even having the propensity to
develop into a trend of their own.

We wish you happy readings!

Zwolle, the Netherlands, 8 January 2024

REFERENCES

Chen, W. M. and Kim, H. (2019). Circular economy and energy transition: A nexus
focusing on the non-energy use of fuels. *Energy & Environment* 30(4): 586–600.
Chishti, M. Z., Dogan, E. and Zaman, U. (2023). Full-length effects of the circular
economy, environmental policy, energy transition, and geopolitical risk on sustaina-
ble electricity generation. *Utilities Policy* 82.
European Commission. (2022, 22 June). *Sustainable Products Initiative*. European
Commission.
IEA. (2022). *World Energy Outlook 2022*. Paris, France, International Energy Agency.
Koval, V., Arsawan, I. W. E., Suryantini, N. P. S., Kovbasenko, S., Fisunenko, N.
and Aloshyna, T. (2023). Circular economy and sustainability-oriented innovation:
Conceptual framework and energy future avenue. *Energies* 16(1): 1–19.
Tukker, A. (2004). Eight types of product–service system: Eight ways to sustainabil-
ity? Experiences from SusProNet. *Business Strategy and the Environment* 13(4):
246–260. https://doi.org/10.1002/bse.414.
Vezzoli, C., Ceschin, F. and Diehl, J. C. (2021). *Product-Service Systems Development
for Sustainability. A New Understanding*. In C. Vezzoli, B. Garcia Parra and C.
Kohtala (eds), *Designing Sustainability for All* (pp. 1–21). Springer International
Publishing. https://doi.org/10.1007/978-3-030-66300-1_1.

1. Sustainable development, degrowth and expressions of moral responsibility

Egbert Dommerholt

'Anyone who believes in indefinite growth in anything physical, on a physically finite planet, is either mad or an economist.'
Kenneth E. Boulding

1. INTRODUCTION

In 1972 Dennis Meadows and his team were among the first to model various factors affecting future human development, which were centred around five variables: technology, population growth, nutrition, natural resources, and environment, including factors such as resource depletion, illiteracy, damage to the natural environment and global income redistribution. These factors were combined in the model the Club of Rome used in making its case. The outcomes showed that a complete collapse of global society was to be expected in the early 21st century in case of a business-as-usual scenario. Only radical changes in population and economic growth could prevent this from happening. The Club of Rome report entitled *The Limits to Growth* (Meadows et al., 1972) was heavily criticized, but at the same time it had an enormous impact on political thinking and public opinion in those days, especially in Europe. It brought the finiteness of the earth's resources and human dependence on and vulnerability of the natural environment to the forefront of discussions at the institutional and the business-society level.

Some 40 years on, Australian physicist Graham Turner compared the report's projections with the actuality between 1970 and 2000, and he found that *The Limits to Growth* business-as-usual scenario was still highly accurate (Turner & Alexander, 2017).

In 2021 Gaya Herrington conducted a study based on new data and found that:

> The two scenarios aligning most closely with observed data indicate a halt in welfare, food, and industrial production over the next decade or so, which puts into

question the suitability of continuous economic growth as humanity's goal in the twenty-first century. (Herrington, 2020)

But also:

Results indicate a slowdown and eventual halt in growth within the next decade or so but leave open whether the subsequent decline will constitute a collapse.

In other words, predictions made some five decades ago appear to be still very accurate to date.

The report by Dennis Meadows' team, as well as Gaya Herrington's update study, focus on the limits to economic growth and seem to suggest that economic growth as such is not the cause of the problems we are currently facing, but that limits to growth are the problem.

In this chapter, I argue that it is not the limits to growth that are the root cause of the problems, but that economic growth is. Going beyond the limits brought us exactly where we are today, and to stay within the limits we need to degrow. That is, we need to reduce resource and energy consumption to bring the economy back into balance with the living world in a way that reduces inequality and improves human well-being (Hickel, 2020a,b). However, degrowth also entails a transition from the current market capitalist system towards a more egalitarian system.

I also argue that degrowth is an authentic interpretation of sustainable development, although this runs counter to how the UN, the Organisation for Economic Co-operation and Development (OECD) (Belmonte-Ureña et al., 2021; Hickel & Kallis, 2019) and the European Commission (*A European Green Deal*, 2019) interpret sustainable development. To these institutions, sustainable development coincides with green growth, which aims at greening capitalism whilst leaving established power and economic structures intact. Green growth proponents argue that economic growth and environmental preservation are compatible (Sandberg et al., 2019). However, the belief that growth is possible without having a severe and negative environmental impact rests on the yet unproven premise that technology can undo the harm done without causing further harm either in the longer future or in the form of externalities (Ossewaarde & Ossewaarde-Lowtoo, 2020). However, if economic growth is the root cause of negative environmental and related social problems as predicted by the Club of Rome and others, then economic growth has an existential dimension which calls for economic actors taking moral responsibilities.

This chapter consists of two sections. The first section focuses on the sustainable development concept, especially the intergenerational and intragenerational perspectives. At the end of the first section some conclusions will be formulated, which form the starting point for the second section, which concentrates on examples of expressions of moral responsibilities by economic actors in Global North countries with regard to the transition towards a degrowth economy.

2.   SUSTAINABLE DEVELOPMENT

The term 'sustainable development' was first coined in the mid-1980s and began trending through the publication 'Our Common Future' by the World Commission on Environment and Development (WCED). This UN committee, also referred to as the Brundtland Commission after its chairwoman – the former Norwegian Prime Minister Gro Harlem Brundtland, defined sustainable development as: 'a development that meets the needs of the present without compromising the ability of future generations to meet their own needs' (WCED, 1987). In this publication, the Commission urges governments to eradicate poverty to protect the ecological environment predominantly in what we have come to call 'developing countries' (Aguirre, 2002). According to some, the Brundtland definition lacks precision. Others disparagingly call it a slogan (Banerjee, 2002). Ever since the mid-1980s, the number of interpretations of the Brundtland Commission's sustainable development definition has soared. Despite the ambiguity of the concept, the Commission's definition is seen as leading and ground-breaking.

What the definition does show is that sustainable development goes beyond merely satisfying economic needs, as social and ecological needs need to be met as well. Also, an intergenerational and intragenerational perspective can be detected; the intergenerational perspective focusing primarily on tensions between current and future generations in satisfying their economic, social and environmental needs. The intragenerational perspective articulates tensions between (groups of) individuals satisfying their social, ecological and economic needs at a certain point in time. In other words, sustainable development is about the tension between the 'there' and 'here' (intragenerational) and the 'now and in the future' (intergenerational) (Steg et al., 2001).

However, we need to bear in mind the contextuality of the 'there and here' notions, as they may concern the divide between and within so-called developed and developing countries, but also the divide or tension between urban and rural areas, regions, inner cities and city districts. When talking about the intragenerational component, I will mainly focus on the North-South divide.

We need to be aware that the tension between the 'now' and 'in the future' is relatively difficult to quantify. We can estimate the needs of the current generation fairly well, but we cannot quantify the needs of future generations yet, because these generations do not yet exist, and their desires therefore cannot be identified. Despite this, it is obvious that if virgin resources are depleting at a rapid pace, future generations will bear the consequences. The same goes for emissions of harmful substances and greenhouse gases: if we continue to pollute the air, oceans and land, the generations that come after us will have to pay the price.

In addition, sustainable development can also be split up into three interrelated principles: an ecological, social and economic principle (Geissdoerfer et al., 2017; Bansal, 2002), which all have a quantitative and qualitative dimension.

2.1   Intergenerational Perspective of Sustainable Development

Figure 1.1 provides some quantitative insights into the 'now and in the future' perspective of sustainable development, and presents the social, environmental and economic principles in their mutual coherence for the 2000–2030 period. This figure is the graphical representation of the famous I = PAT formula by Ehrlich and Holdren (Ehrlich & Holdren, 1971), in which:

> I = Impact of human action on the ecological environment;
> P = Population (i.e., population size);
> A = Affluence (i.e., level of prosperity represented by income or consumption per capita);
> T = Technology (i.e., the technology required to produce consumer goods, including the political, social, and economic framework within which the production of goods and services takes place. (Ehrlich, 2014)

In Figure 1.1, the impact of human action on the ecological environment, population, affluence and technology factors is represented by the 'Planet', 'Population', 'GDP per capita' and the 'Planet/GDP' blocks respectively. The latter is to be interpreted as resource and energy consumption, CO_2 emissions et cetera, per unit of product, which are likely to slow down or drop as a result of technological innovation.

Compared to 2000, in 2030 the (negative) impact of human activity on the planet is estimated to increase substantially. Fossil fuel consumption increases from almost 64 per cent (coal) to more than 85 per cent (gas). In tandem, CO_2 emissions are expected to increase by almost 50 per cent, which is bad news as this means that global warming will continue to rise. This increase is mainly caused by Global North countries (i.e., United States and Canada, the European Union, Russia and the rest of Europe, Japan and Australia), which are historically responsible for 92 per cent of CO_2 emissions, whilst the Global South only contributes 8 per cent, with some 90 per cent of the negative impact resting on the shoulders of the world's poorest countries (Hickel, 2020c).

Furthermore, Oxfam International and the Stockholm Environment Institute estimated that in 2015, 49 per cent of the carbon emissions could be attributed

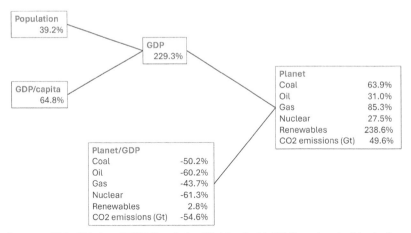

Source: United Nations DESA/Population Division (n.d.), US Department of Agriculture (2021), International Energy Agency (2018). Adapted by the author.

Figure 1.1   Sustainable Development 2000–2030 (based on the New Policies scenario of the International Energy Agency)

to the 10 per cent richest people on the planet, whilst the poorest 50 per cent were responsible for only 7 per cent (Oxfam International, 2020). In August 2021 the Intergovernmental Panel on Climate Change (IPCC) released an alarming report, which tracks five projected scenarios from very low to very high CO_2 emissions to estimate global warming in the coming century. In every scenario, the planet continues to warm until mid-century, and if emissions continue unchecked, warming of over 2°C will be reached by 2050 (Vigran, 2021).

Increasing CO_2 concentrations in the atmosphere cause temperatures on the planet to rise, with all due consequences, such as melting polar ice caps and rising sea levels. In some regions, extreme weather events and rainfall are becoming more common, whilst others will experience more extreme heatwaves and droughts. These impacts are expected to intensify in the coming decades (World Wildlife Fund, n.d.) and will have a dramatic impact on people's lives. The USA-based National Bureau of Economic Research estimated that by the end of this century, 75 out 100,000 world citizens will die annually because of the effects of climate change (Carleton et al., 2020). Based on a world population of 11 billion, this entails that approximately 8.3 million people will die annually, with death rates being highest in the poorest countries, making it painfully clear that economic growth not only creates prosperity (at least for some), but actually kills people, most notably the poor, who hardly contribute to the climate issue in the first place. On top of that, globally, some 90 per cent of the people breathe polluted air, resulting in 7 million deaths per year (WHO, 2018).

Although material resources are not included in Figure 1.1, the OECD estimates that material resource use will more than double in the 2011–2060 period (from 79 Gt to 167 Gt). However, the materials intensity of the global economy is projected to decline at a rate of – on average – 1.3 per cent per year (OECD, 2018). But then resource reserves will dry up in due course. Depletion of some critical resources, like iron ore, gold, zinc, etc., is merely a matter of decades (Dobbs et al., 2011; Copper Alliance, 2018). The same applies to fossil fuels. According to the oil company BP, based on the year 2016, reserve-to-production ratios are approximately 50 years for oil and natural gas and 150 years for coal. But even if these figures turn out to be inaccurate, we need to realize that the annual sustainable extraction mark of 50 billion tons was already transgressed more than two decades ago (Hickel, 2020b).

The European Environmental Bureau (EEB) and Friends of the Earth Europe found that:

- The EU material footprint is currently 14.5 tonnes per capita, about double what is considered a sustainable and just limit, and well over the global average.
- The EU alone already uses between 70 and 97 per cent of the global environmentally 'safe operating space' related to resource extraction impacts. Any resource extraction beyond this 'safe' threshold threatens the stable functioning of the earth's biophysical systems (Bolger et al., 2021).

According to the International Institute for Sustainable Development (IISD), extraction and processing of materials, fuels and food make up about half of total global greenhouse gas (GHG) emissions and more than 90 per cent of biodiversity loss and water stress across the globe (IISD, 2019).

Figure 1.1 also shows that an increasing production volume is the result of a growing population size and per capita income. In the 2000–2030 period, population is expected to increase by almost 40 per cent globally. However, growth rates are not evenly distributed across the globe. Particularly in low-income countries, population is projected to more than double (and in sub-Saharan countries even triple), whereas in high-income countries population increases by 'only' 15 per cent. In some high-income countries (e.g., Germany, Italy and Japan) current population growth rates are almost zero, or even negative.

On a global level income per capita, or prosperity, increases by almost 65 per cent. Here we also witness large regional differences. Income per capita growth is highest in low-income countries and lowest in Global North countries. However, we need to realize that average income in Global North countries is approximately 50 times higher than in Global South countries.

What I regularly hear people say, and also what Figure 1.1 might suggest, is that population growth is a main driver of resource consumption and climate change. However, we need to be very careful here. With some irony and a slight sense of overstatement we can even claim that people in low-income countries are born in a state of misery caused by overconsumption in high-income countries. It is not population growth that is the problem, it is the consumption of affluent households. Or as Wiedmann et al. (2020) formulate it:

> (…) consumption of affluent households worldwide is by far the strongest determinant and the strongest accelerator of increases of global environmental and social impacts.

2.1.1   Gross domestic product: measurement and flaws

Gross domestic product (GDP) growth is pivotal when it comes to the negative impact of human action on the earth and its inhabitants, but also to the debt creation volcano we created. But, so far, we have not discussed what GDP and GDP growth actually is. GDP refers to the monetary value of all final goods and services that are being produced in a country in a specific time period.

Gross national product and in its slipstream gross domestic product metrics were created by Simon Kuznets, Nobel Memorial Prize laureate, who was very much aware of the limitations of the metric, because it only takes monetized economic activities into account, whether these are useful or not. If pollution causes the number of hospital visits to increase, GDP increases. If irreplaceable wildlife habitats are being destroyed for the sake of economic development, GDP goes up. In contrast, looking after one's ageing parents, or helping out the neighbours, doing voluntary work for a charity, raising one's children as responsible citizens, has no economic meaning since it does not contribute to GDP. Just like enjoying a long walk in the forest with your loved ones on a Sunday afternoon has no effect on GDP at all, however precious or priceless these moments may be for the people involved.

The flawed-ness of the metric was also recognized by Bobby Kennedy[1] at the start of his presidential campaign back in 1968, addressing a Kansas University audience. This is what he said:

> [GDP]counts air pollution and cigarette advertising, and ambulances to clear our highways of carnage. It counts special locks for our doors and the jails for the

---

[1]   https://www.jfklibrary.org/learn/about-jfk/the-kennedy-family/robert-f-kennedy/robert-f-kennedy-speeches/remarks-at-the-university-of-kansas-march-18-1968

people who break them. It counts the destruction of the redwood and the loss of our natural wonder in chaotic sprawl. It counts napalm and counts nuclear warheads and armoured cars for the police to fight the riots in our cities. It counts Whitman's rifle and Speck's knife, and the television programs which glorify violence in order to sell toys to our children. Yet the gross national product does not allow for the health of our children, the quality of their education or the joy of their play. It does not include the beauty of our poetry or the strength of our marriages, the intelligence of our public debate or the integrity of our public officials. It measures neither our wit nor our courage, neither our wisdom nor our learning, neither our compassion nor our devotion to our country, it measures everything in short, except that which makes life worthwhile. (Remarks at the University of Kansas, March 18, 1968/JFK Library, 1968)

As Figure 1.1 shows, gross domestic product (GDP) is expected to grow substantially in the 2000–2030 timeframe. But why does the economy have to grow anyway? For Global South countries it is obvious that economic growth is a prerequisite, because of the relatively low living standard of people living in these counties. Almost half of the people living in low-income countries must make do with \$1.90 per day or less. In high-income countries this figure is no more than half a percentage point (World Bank Open Data, n.d.).

But why is GDP still growing in rich countries? There are at least four reasons.

Firstly, if labour productivity continuously rises, then economic growth is necessary to stabilize or increase employment. If the labour force increases and employment levels do not increase in tandem, then unemployment will increase with all due political and social consequences. The last thing we want is a recession and consequently a loss of jobs (Wiedmann et al., 2020).

Secondly, economic growth, partly driven by the substantial marketing efforts of firms, seems to be a panacea to all kinds of societal problems ranging from lowering government debt to financing covid-related support programmes et cetera (Wiedmann et al., 2020).

Thirdly, the so-called rebound effect plays a role. Because of more efficient production processes, the cost per unit of product decreases, causing prices to drop and the purchasing power of consumers and demand for goods and services to increase. But lower cost per unit can also result in higher profit margins incentivizing producers to boost sales of products and services to maximize profits (Schenderling, 2022).

Fourthly, there is also a systemic dimension to economic growth, which has to do with profit and capital accumulation (Hickel, 2020b). It is about buying resources at low prices and subsequently selling the products at high prices and making a profit. This profit is not just money to be used for buying goods to satisfy economic needs. It is reinvested to make even more money. Goods are not wanted for their use value, but to earn money that buys even more goods that can be sold at a profit.

Or as Hickel formulates: 'It (the process of accumulating exchange value) is fundamentally unhinged from any conception of human need.' So, the quest for ever higher profits drives economic growth.

Whatever the reason, economic growth clearly has a dual effect. On the one hand it supports employment and helps alleviate all sorts of societal issues, on the other hand it also has an impact on climate change and finite resource reserves. However, how has that worked out over time? Does economic growth really have a negative environmental and resource impact? This is what I will discuss now.

2.1.2   Relative and absolute decoupling

In Figure 1.1 the amount of environment per unit of product (Environment/GDP) is a non-autonomous factor, indicating that the negative impact on the environment as a result of an increasing production volume can be compensated by using resources and auxiliary materials more efficiently. But also by decreasing emissions of greenhouse gases, waste and water per unit of product. In the 2000–2030 timeframe, consumption of coal, oil and gas per unit of product is estimated to decrease by 50, 60 and 44 per cent respectively. We speak of relative resource or impact decoupling if resource consumption or greenhouse gas emissions per unit of product decrease. In other words: resources are used more efficiently, whilst production is also more CO_2 efficient. However, as Figure 1.1 shows, since CO_2 and resource efficiency rates are outpaced by economic growth, absolute CO_2 emissions and resource consumption is estimated to increase.

One could confer that higher efficiency rates should cause resource consumption and CO_2 emissions to drop, but the opposite may also happen. The reason is that because of efficiency gains, the cost of resources and materials per unit of product are likely to fall, causing prices of goods and services to drop as well, and consequently demand for these goods and services to rise, thus intensifying the negative impact on the planet. This is called the rebound, or take-back effect (Khazzoom, 1980). The rebound effect also manifests itself when people start generating their own electricity through – for example – solar panels. Because the generated electricity is for free, people may start buying energy intensive consumables, causing overall electricity and resource consumption to rise.

If efficiency rates outpace economic growth we speak of absolute decoupling. In that case economic growth is absolutely decoupled from resource consumption or environmental impact. That is: natural resource consumption or environmental impact decreases, whilst GDP continues to grow (Sandberg et al., 2019). That of course would solve a lot of problems, because we can continue to grow. However, absolute decoupling, particularly absolute resource decoupling, is considered a myth (Albert, 2020; Haberl et al., 2020; Hickel & Kallis, 2019; Ward et al., 2016). But is it?

Figures 1.2a, b and c provide information on relative change in relevant economic and environmental data for the 1970–2021 timeframe for three regions: the world, OECD countries and non-OECD countries. What we see in Figure 2a is that, globally, materials extraction (MF) almost perfectly follows the GDP growth rate. The same applies – although to a slightly lesser extent – for growth of global CO_2 emissions from energy. The economic growth, resource consumption and CO_2 emissions lines show dips in 2007/8 – the banking crisis and the subsequent global recession – and 2019/20 – a recession as a result of the covid pandemic, indicating that resource ($R^2 = 0.98$) and environmental impact ($R^2 = 0.99$) are economic growth driven. After the 2020 dip the CO_2 emissions growth rate is on the rise again.

In contrast to Figure 1.1, Figure 1.2 claims that relative resource decoupling is unlikely to happen. The reason for this probably lies in the different data sets underlying both figures. However, we can say that from a historical perspective relative decoupling is the best achievable proposition.

When splitting the world up into OECD countries (which is a proxy for rich Global North countries) and non-OECD countries (which is a proxy for relatively poor Global South countries), we see vast differences between these two regions and between each of these regions and the global situation. Most eye-catching are the differences in economic growth rates, which are much higher in non-OECD countries than in OECD countries. The same applies to resource consumption. For both regions growth in resource consumption is pretty much in line with economic growth, albeit the relationship is stronger for non-OECD countries ($R^2 = 0.88$ and 0.98 for OECD countries and non-OECD countries). What we see is that resource consumption is relatively decoupled from economic growth.

However, for CO_2 growth rates the situation differs substantially between the two regions. In non-OECD countries CO_2 emissions increase along with economic growth for the entire timeframe ($R^2 = 0.71$), whilst for OECD countries CO_2 emissions move up in tandem with economic growth until circa 2007, whilst in the 2008–2021 timeframe CO_2 and economic growth rates diverge ($R^2 = 0.6$ for the 1970–2021 time period). Ultimately, CO_2 emissions fall just below the 1990 mark, whilst GDP growth is substantially higher. For OECD countries CO_2 emissions growth and economic growth are absolutely decoupled, albeit very hesitantly, because CO_2 emissions are on the increase again, approaching the 1990 benchmark.

Although we have not seen any empirical evidence for absolute resource decoupling to exist, some challenge the claim that absolute decoupling is not feasible and believe that convergence of technological developments in,

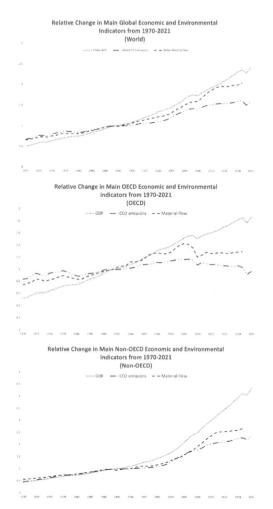

Source: http://www.resourcepanel.org/global-material-flows-database; https://databank.
worldbank.org/source/world-development-indicators; https://www.bp.com/en/global/
corporate/energy-economics/statistical-review-of-world-energy/downloads.html.
Note: Shown is the global material footprint (MF, equal to global raw material
extraction) and global CO_2 emissions from energy and GDP (constant 2015 USD). Indexed
to 1 in 1990.

Figure 1.2   *Relative change in GDP volume, CO_2 emissions and resource
extraction: (a) World, (b) OECD and (c) Non-OECD*

amongst others, the field of nanotechnology, biotechnology, information technology, artificial intelligence and 3D printing will provide solutions to make this happen (Albert, 2020). This hope is also upheld by the World Economic Forum (Schwab, 2017). It cannot be altogether denied that these technologies, and technologies we don't know about yet may indeed contribute to providing a solution to the absolute decoupling issue. However, as mentioned earlier, there is no empirical proof underpinning that claim today. We must therefore be wary of being too overly optimistic, because of the irreversible consequences it may have for future generations to satisfy their needs. What if current technologies cannot live up to expectations, and what if technologies we hoped for do not materialize?

However, it is technologically feasible to realize absolute carbon emission rate reductions as we have seen for OECD countries; it is highly unlikely that the 2015 Paris Agreement targets will be reached in time to ward off the negative long-term consequences of climate change (Hickel & Kallis, 2019). But we also need to realize that for technological solutions to be effective they need to be accompanied by reductions in total consumption and production (Alfredsson et al., 2018). Obviously, technological solutions alone are not the answer to tackling the global warming issue.

2.1.3   The energy transition

Now that we have seen that there is no empirical proof for absolute resource decoupling on a global, OECD and non-OECD level, and absolute impact decoupling is only hesitantly visible for OECD countries, one might wonder whether the transition towards renewable energies may be the answer to the CO_2 crisis and hence the global warming issue and its accompanying consequences as we discussed earlier. In that case GDP can continue to grow and we don't have to worry about ourselves and generations to come. However nice that may seem, the share of renewables in total energy consumption is – in 2021 – with 6.7 per cent globally, and 9.2 and 5.1 per cent for non-OECD and OECD countries respectively, still fairly low, although since 1990 consumption of renewables went up by almost a factor 23 (BP, n.d.). This implies that the energy transitions are mainly driven by fossil fuels, which sounds rather paradoxical: to combat climate change through renewable energy, we need to use fossil fuels, which contributes to climate change. This is because iron, aluminium and other materials need to be excavated, transported, molten and moulded, which requires energy (generated by fossil fuels). To keep global warming below the 1.5°C mark as agreed in the Paris Agreement, carbon emissions need to stay below the 460 Gt mark (Hausfather, 2022). To make the energy transition work on a global scale we need a carbon budget of 790 Gt (Alfredsson et al., 2018), which is about 1.5 times the maximum 1.5°C budget.

In other words: a full-blown energy transition contributes to global warming rather than combating it.

Besides, we also need to realize that fossil fuel reserves are finite. According to BP, reserve-to-production ratios of oil, gas and coal are respectively 53, 49 and 138 years (Statistical Review of World Energy, 2022). For copper, a critical metal in the transition towards a renewable energy society, the reserve-to-production ratio is no more than 40 years (Copper Alliance, 2018), which is less than two generations away! But it is not only the exhaustibility of our natural resources that counts, but also the impact the extraction and processing of these metals has on the wider environment. For example: the excavation of one tonne of iron ore comes with three tonnes of soil and rock, and for copper 99.5 per cent of extracted material is waste (Smit, 2022).

Building a 3.5 MW windmill requires 600 kilograms of rare earth metals (Morimoto et al., 2021), and the extraction of 1,000 tonnes of high-quality earth metals comes with 2,000 tonnes of radioactive and fluid chemical waste (Smit, 2022).

For economic growth to happen, preferably renewable energy is required, but as we have seen, the energy transition can't be realized to the max, because of the negative resource and environmental impact.

2.1.4   Boundaries

So far, I have mainly focused on economic growth and its consequences, and implicitly we have already come across at least two limits or boundaries: the amount of CO_2 in the atmosphere in relation to climate change and reserve-to-production-ratios in relation to resource consumption and availability. But there are more (critical) boundaries.

Back in 2009 Rockström et al. published a seminal paper in which they identified ten boundaries critical to maintaining the planetary biosphere: (1) climate change, (2) biodiversity loss, (3) ocean acidification, (4) change in land use, (5) nitrogen loading, (6) phosphorous loading, (7) global freshwater use, (8) atmospheric aerosol loading, (9) chemical pollution, and (10) stratospheric ozone depletion (Rockström et al., 2009). Three of these boundaries have been transgressed already, most notably the boundaries for biodiversity loss and nitrogen and climate change. Based on research reports by the IPCC, we now know that climate change has already crossed critical levels, and that it will be extremely difficult to keep global warming below 1.5°C (IPCC, 2021). The stratospheric ozone depletion process is under control, and for chemical pollution and atmospheric aerosol loading data are not robust enough yet. So, for climate change and biodiversity loss we know that these are somehow directly or indirectly connected to economic growth. For other boundaries, specifically freshwater use and change in land use we can sense a relationship with economic growth, whilst for other boundaries the connection may be less obvious or is yet to be established.

Meanwhile the planetary boundaries framework has been updated several times. Furthermore, these boundaries form the outer circle of Kate Raworth's Doughnut Economics framework (Raworth, 2017).

2.1.5 Debt creation

But there also other crises that are inherently connected to economic growth. One of these crises relates to a specific sector of the economy: commercial banks.

In the eyes of the general public, banks lend out money to clients (debtors) that was first attracted from clients holding demand deposits and savings accounts (creditors). The difference between the interest paid and interest earned, the interest margin, determines how profitable banks are. That at least is what people believe. However, moving money from creditors to debtors does not increase the amount of money in circulation and hence the money supply, and cannot accommodate economic growth for that matter. To accommodate economic growth, banks make use of so-called mutual debt agreements, which is a promise by the bank to make a sum of money available to a client whilst simultaneously the client promises to pay back the loan to the bank at some point in the future. For banks, this causes credit and debt on their balance sheet to increase. But what this actually means is that money is being created out of thin air, which is very lucrative for banks, because they do not have to attract any money; the interest margin equals interest earned.

Lending out money via mutual debt agreements is usually referred to as 'money creation', but it might as well be referred to as 'debt creation'. The higher economic growth, the more debt is being created, and it was exactly this growth-driven debt creation that caused the banking crisis and the subsequent social and economic crisis in 2007–2008. Since 2008, the world economy has expanded substantially, and so has the money supply and debt creation. What happened in 2007–2008 may happen again, the only question is when.

2.2 The Intragenerational Perspective of Sustainable Development

So far, I have explicitly focused on the intergenerational perspective of sustainable development. That is, I have tried to estimate the quantitative and/or qualitative impact current generations have on future generations. In this section I will concentrate on the intragenerational perspective of sustainable development by focusing specifically on inequality aspects amongst current generation members across a selection of world regions. Inequality can have many faces, but here I would like to accentuate differences in prosperity

Table 1.1   GDP and wealth per adult (Euro, ppp constant (2021))

Region	2021	2000–2021	2021	2000–2021
East Asia	23512	157.2%	145534	199.8%
Europe	40420	20.2%	200415	51.6%
Latin America	16491	0.3%	46490	35.1%
MENA	22014	16.0%	44039	51.7%
North America	63060	21.0%	337354	606%
Russia & Central Asia	20912	86.0%	56429	114.2%
South & South-East Asia	9987	107.4%	33309	203.0%
Sub-Saharan Africa	6148	25.4%	17679	65.3%
World	20263	43.3%	93582	84.4%

Source: WID – Wealth and Income Database (2019).

(income and wealth) and well-being. Although the two are associated, they are by no means identical.

Table 1.1 displays GDP and wealth per adult in a selection of world regions. In 2021, North Americans – on average – had the highest income per capita, whilst the income of residents of sub-Saharan African countries is lowest. On average, North Americans earn more than ten times as much as sub-Saharan Africans. Also, people living in South and South-East Asia and Latin America earn below average incomes. Some low-income regions are catching up on high-income countries, as is the case with East Asia, South and South-East Asia, and Russia and Central Asia. For other regions (e.g., Latin America) purchasing power has hardly risen over the last ten years. However, we should not forget that today some 750 million people are living in extreme poverty (i.e., on less than $1.90 per day) (Beaumont, 2021) and 11 people die from hunger and malnutrition every minute (Oxfam, 2021).

GDP and wealth per capita data are fairly similar. Here we also see that wealth levels are highest in North America and lowest in sub-Saharan Africa and the differences are even more extreme: North Americans are on average about 20 times wealthier than sub-Saharan Africans. Of all selected regions, wealth per capita is rising fastest in East Asia, but although wealth levels went up by more than 200 per cent in the last ten years, wealth per capita is still approximately one-third of that of the global average.

The conclusion should be that income and wealth differences amongst regions are substantial. But what about income and wealth differences *within* these regions? That is where Table 1.2 can provide us with some insights.

Table 1.2 shows us how income and wealth is distributed amongst the richest 1 and 10 per cent and the poorest 50 per cent of the population within the same regions that are mentioned in Table 1.1.

On a global level, the richest 1 per cent of the population claims almost 20 per cent of income earned, whilst the poorest 50 per cent earns circa 8 per cent of global income. But the situation is improving for the better: in ten years the income distribution improved to the benefit of the poor. Wealth is distributed even more unevenly: the poorest 50 per cent will have to do with a piece of just over 1.5 per cent of the global wealth cake, whilst the richest 1 per cent gets almost 40 per cent, although the wealth share of the poorest is rising.

Particularly in Latin America the situation is worse compared to the global situation. Here the poorest 50 per cent only receive about 8 per cent of national income and less than half a percentage point of national wealth. And what is even worse, their situation is deteriorating. The rich are getting richer and the poor are getting poorer. This also applies to North America and South & South-East Asia for both the income and wealth categories. In the Middle East and North Africa (MENA), the wealth distribution changes rapidly to the advantage of the poor, although the piece of the wealth cake remains low for them. But also in Europe, Russia, Central Asia and East Asia, wealth distribution developments are disadvantageous for the poorest 50 per cent.

In more egalitarian countries, people are generally happier and healthier; crime rates are lower, and people are more creative and more productive. In addition, educational attainment is higher (Dorling, 2017). If people are happier, they are also less likely to pursue higher incomes and buy more goods and services (that they may in the end not even need), which is likely to result in lower ecological pressures. Knowing this should urge governments and interest groups to strive for more egalitarian societies, because it pays off socially, ecologically and economically. In his seminal book *Less is More*, Jason Hickel mentions Denmark as a case in point. He states that:

> Consumer research shows that because Denmark is more equal than most other high-income countries, people buy fewer clothes – and keep them for longer – than their counterparts elsewhere. And firms spend less money on advertising, because people just aren't interested in unnecessary luxury purchases. (Hickel, 2020b, p. 185)

However attractive this may seem, building egalitarian societies requires an economic and societal transition, since the prevailing capitalist economic system is rooted in inequality (Brand et al., 2021). Or in other words: inequality is inherently connected to the capitalist system, implying that levels of inequality are not just caused by the capitalist system, but lie at the very basis of it. This is similar to what Piketty and Goldhammer assert in their

Table 1.2   *Income and wealth inequality across a selection of regions*

		Income inequality		Wealth inequality	
		2021	2000–2021	2021	2000–2021
East Asia	Top 10% share	0.449	-11.9%	0.6926	-3.4%
	Bottom 50% share	0.1355	20.2%	0.0523	-10.3%
	Top 1% share	0.1658	-6.5%	0.3179	-9.5%
Europe	Top 10% share	0.3619	-0.5%	0.608	2.2%
	Bottom 50% share	0.1849	10.9%	0.0319	-5.6%
	Top 1% share	0.1198	7.2%	0.2603	5.5%
Latin America	Top 10% share	0.586	-1.0%	0.77	1.4%
	Bottom 50% share	0.0786	7.1%	0.0045	-47.1%
	Top 1% share	0.2345	21.3%	0.4524	8.4%
MENA	Top 10% share	0.5516	-4.9%	0.751	9.2%
	Bottom 50% share	0.0986	-2.3%	0.0144	242.9%
	Top 1% share	0.2069	-13.6%	0.4295	-21.8%
North America	Top 10% share	0.4569	6.7%	0.7001	3.8%
	Bottom 50% share	0.139	-7.8%	0.0172	-12.7%
	Top 1% share	0.1899	9.7%	0.3446	8.8%
Russia & Central Asia	Top 10% share	0.492	-0.9%	0.7304	7.1%
	Bottom 50% share	0.143	10.5%	0.0302	-29.3%
	Top 1% share	0.2222	3.4%	0.4452	8.5%
South & South-East Asia	Top 10% share	0.5434	13.0%	0.6757	8.4%
	Bottom 50% share	0.1244	-14.0%	0.0451	-9.6%
	Top 1% share	0.204	5.4%	0.3425	18.6%
Sub-Saharan Africa	Top 10% share	0.5542	-3.7%	0.7312	-4.4%
	Bottom 50% share	0.0917	13.6%	0.0097	42.6%
	Top 1% share	0.2046	-2.1%	0.3797	-10.0%

		Income inequality		Wealth inequality	
		2021	2000–2021	2021	2000–2021
World	Top 10% share	0.5254	-8.8%	0.7709	-3.4%
	Bottom 50% share	0.0824	18.2%	0.0174	8.1%
	Top 1% share	0.1935	-4.2%	0.3961	-1.9%

Source: WID – Wealth and Income Database (2019).

book *Capital and Ideology*, where they argue that societies use ideology to legitimize inequality (Piketty & Goldhammer, 2020). Societies with a capitalist orientation therefore use the capitalist ideology to legitimize inequality. The reason for this is the asymmetry between dominant classes that control the investment process and accumulate capital on the one hand, and classes obliged to sell their labour power for income necessary for their subsistence on the other (Brand et al., 2021).

That the capitalist system is founded on asymmetrical power structures not only has implications for inequality *within* countries, but also helps to explain inequality *across* countries. Income per capita in Global North countries is higher compared to that of Global South countries in part because in the latter countries' resources (including labour) are extracted, and then are transformed into products in Global North countries. Subsequently, these goods are sold at high prices to people in Global South countries.

To boost the economy and to alleviate the poor, the rich need to become even richer. The idea behind this trickle-down theory is that the rich buy goods and services that are produced by poor people. Through their high and increasing purchasing power the rich share a part of their prosperity with the poor, causing the purchasing power of the poor to rise as well. This can easily be extended to the Global North-South divide. For people in Global South countries to prosper, prosperity in Global North countries needs to increase. However, the idea that growth in Global North countries is a prerequisite for Global South countries to prosper is a myth (Hickel, 2020b). Capital is accumulated in rich countries at the expense of people living in poor countries. To substantiate this claim, Olthaar and Schenderling estimate that 10 million people living in Global South countries work and live under dire circumstances to keep the consumption of 17 million Dutch citizens growing (Stichting Genoeg om te Leven, 2022).

In his book *What Should We Then Do?*, which was written between 1882 and 1886, the Russian author Leo Tolstoy spends an entire chapter on money as a means to enslaving people (Tolstoy, 1925).[2] In that chapter he takes the Fiji Islands as an example. In short, the story goes like this.

> In the mid-nineteenth century, residents from the Fiji Islands needed USD 45,000 to compensate the United States of America, for an act of violence that had been allegedly committed against US citizens. The Americans threatened to ruin the little kingdom if the Fijians refused to pay. The Fijians could not raise that sum of money, because goods and services were paid for with goods and services in return by neighboring states. Meanwhile the American government increased the sum of money to be paid to USD 90,000, because the Fijians were not able to pay the earlier mentioned amount in time. The Fiji king in an act of despair turned to tradesmen in Melbourne to borrow the required sum. The end of this tragical story was that the Fijians had to enslave themselves in order to pay back the sum of money. The once prosperous island state became the domain of tradesman who were only interested in making money. (Tolstoy, 1925, p. 365–366)

This story is a painful example of how the Global North enriched itself at the expense of people of the Global South. And although times have changed, the stories have not. In 2020 Apple and Google were named in a US lawsuit over Congolese child cobalt mining deaths (Kelly, 2020). Congolese children work in mines under dire circumstances to produce the cobalt that we in the Global North need for our smartphones, car batteries and other electrical devices. Children in the Global South are paying the price for our energy transition. Olthaar and Schenderling estimate that for the Netherlands alone some 10 million people live under dire circumstances to allow 17 million Dutch people to live the luxurious lives that they live (Olthaar & Schenderling, 2021).

Unfortunately, the situations described above are not new. On the contrary. We can safely say that the history of economic growth in the Global North is written in blood. Just think of the colonial past of many of the European countries and the atrocities committed by these countries or committed in their name. A notorious example is the conquest of the Banda Islands by the Dutch United East India Company (VOC) in 1621. To corner the nutmeg, mace and clove market, the Dutch butchered almost the entire population of the Banda Islands, which were at the time part of the Dutch East Indies and are now part of the Republic of Indonesia (Wikipedia, 2021a). The Spanish Conquistadores also displayed predatory behaviour in South America after Christopher Columbus 'discovered' the Americas. They wiped out or enslaved a substan-

---

2   This book was first translated from Russian to English by Aylmer Maude in 1934. Sieuwert Haverhoek translated this book to Dutch in 2020. The example of how money can become a means to enslaving people is taken from the Dutch translation.

tial part of the population of the Americas to be able to steal their gold, silver and other precious metals.

2.2.1   Well-being

It is true that resource and energy consumption need to fall, but that does not necessarily have to result in lower perceived well-being. What is more, well-being may very well increase instead (Hickel, 2020a). In contrast, if growth is perceived as something inherently good because it resonates with the idea that more is better, then the question is what 'good' actually means. As we have seen, economic growth has a devastating impact on planet Earth and the well-being of a substantial part of the global population. So, more is not necessarily better. Take income per capita for example. People earning a high income are not necessarily happier than people earning a low(er) income (Jackson, 2011). But also high levels of well-being can be achieved with low income, implying that economic growth will not necessarily increase life satisfaction among low-income populations (Miñarro et al., 2021). Furthermore, Easterlin found that on an aggregated national level in the USA, happiness scores did not increase over time despite rising GDP levels (Easterlin et al., 2010), implying that obviously happiness is decoupled from economic growth.

   Although income per capita in a country like the United States of America is 3.1 and 1.8, and wealth per capita is a factor 7 and 1.6 times higher than in Costa Rica and Spain, perceived well-being is almost equally high in all three countries. But also, life expectancy for Costa Ricans and Spanish people is – at 80.1 and 83.4 years – higher than for Americans (78.9 years) (Helliwell et al., 2021). Evidently, enjoying high prosperity levels does not necessarily come with high levels of well-being and higher life expectancies.

2.3   Conclusion

So far, I have discussed sustainable development, and taking the intergenerational and intragenerational perspectives of this concept as the starting point. In the eyes of the UN, the OECD and the EU, sustainable development is closely connected to green or sustainable growth. However, based on the above analysis I conclude that sustainable development and economic growth are incompatible concepts. Because economic growth, driven by overconsumption in Global North countries, is responsible for transgressing critical planetary boundaries and all due consequences. Although we do see signs of relative resource and impact decoupling, absolute resource decoupling is still far away, while absolute CO_2 decoupling can best be characterized as too little too late. For the intergenerational perspective, I mainly focused on the consequences of CO_2 emissions (i.e. climate change and resource use (i.e., biodiversity loss and resource depletion) . Even though not all critical planetary boundaries or limits were covered in this chapter, we can say that the results of economic growth are devastating: people are dying and life on our planet is under serious threat. The consequences for future generations are, referring to the definition of sustainable development mentioned earlier, that we have set a development in motion that meets the needs of the present, but hugely compromises the ability of future generations to meet their own needs.

The intragenerational perspective shows that income and wealth differences between and within regions are huge, particularly in Global South countries. This requires that we need to discuss the redistribution of wealth within and across regions. Not only do we in the Global North need to reverse economic growth, we also need to share our wealth with Global South countries. I consider that our moral obligation is towards these countries. We in the Global North have reached high levels of wealth and prosperity to a large extent at the expense of people living in the Global South.

On a global level, resource consumption has trespassed sustainable levels by far already. This means that we first need to bring back resource consumption to sustainable levels, and that Global South countries get a fair share of the resources they need to make sure that future Global South generations are able to meet their needs.

Since economic growth and inequality are expressions of the currently dominant capitalist system, sustainable development requires a transition towards a just and egalitarian economic system, implying that serving society and solving societal challenges should be the prime concern of economic actors. Talking about the capitalist system, economic growth unveils a major weak spot of our capitalist system: higher production volumes require that money (or debt) is being created by commercial banks, which pushes the economic system into a structural state of unbalance. Reversing economic growth is not only necessary to bring the economy back in balance with the living world, but also to rule out a major systemic flaw.

Having said this, I am convinced that degrowth is an authentic interpretation of sustainable development, which Hickel defined as a planned reduction of resource and energy consumption to bring the economy back into balance with the living world in a way that reduces inequality and improves human well-being (Hickel, 2020a, b). Will it be easy to transform the economic paradigm to a degrowth economy? Probably not, but in my view we have no other option. If we don't do anything at all, or if we don't take appropriate and accurate measures, the Limits to Growth business-as-usual scenario and the study by Herrington clearly indicate the consequences that we as a global community are facing. Only if we are able to reverse economic growth does the world still have a chance to ward off a societal collapse. The choice is ours!

3.   EXPRESSIONS OF MORAL RESPONSIBILITIES

In the previous section I argued that people living in the Global North have a moral responsibility towards saving and protecting the lives and sustaining the livelihoods of people in Global South countries. But this also includes reversing the harm done and bringing the economy back into balance with the living world. In other words: we, living in the Global North, have a moral responsibility to contribute to a degrowth economy by radically changing our (economic) behaviours. In this section I will provide some ideas and suggestions on how consumers, the business community and governments can express their moral responsibility.

3.1   Consumers

Consumers, or households, contribute more to society than is reflected by their purchasing power and buying behaviour. Examples of non-purchasing power-related contributions are mothers and fathers spending time on raising their children as responsible citizens, or children taking care of their ageing parents. But also, the work done by people who voluntarily work for a food bank, or the football coach who teaches their pupils about values such as self-discipline and perseverance.

However, buying and spending behaviour – more than societal contributions – may become problematic when it comes to obeying planetary boundaries. The higher consumers' purchasing power and, consequently, the higher their demand for goods and services, the more stuff needs to be produced, and the more resources and energy are needed, but also the more waste, pollution and greenhouse gas emissions are generated. Households can contribute to the transition towards a degrowth economy by refraining from (over)consumption through self-limitation (Brand et al., 2021), which entails that consumers sacrifice part of their individual autonomy for the betterment of society. Examples of self-limitation are: commuting by bike or public transport instead of commuting by car, or joining the tiny-house movement, or adopting sufficiency principles. Also moving towards consuming high-quality plant-based foods and abstaining or reducing consumption of animal-based foods, or changing to local diets, that is eating foods that are grown locally and sustainably, rather than pre-packaged foods shipped from other parts of the world (Wilkins & Murphy, 2021).

Although trespassing planetary boundaries may be beneficial to individual community members, it is disadvantageous to the community as a whole, and self-limitation may be (part of) the answer. But we also need to realize that self-limitation is not new, because before the market economy manifested itself in large parts of Europe, commons were the vehicles for generating wealth and income. And it was exactly these commons that were based on the principle of self-limitation (Brand et al., 2021).

Talking about commons – traditionally, the economy is divided into three separate sectors: households, business and government. Households are supposed to buy goods and services from the business sector and are not assumed to produce goods and services, since this is the domain of the business sector. The business sector, on the other hand, is not supposed to buy consumption goods, because this is the domain of the household sector. Governments, on the other hand, provide public goods and services, which aren't or can't be delivered via the business sector.

In fact, this situation is a caricature of what the economy really looks like. In reality, these sectors do collaborate in many respects. For example, in many countries the government and business sectors intensively collaborate in so-called innovation systems to boost corporate resilience and competitive strength. This is also the case in the USA where the private and government sectors are not always seen as best friends. The following quote from Mariana Mazzucato's book *The Entrepreneurial State* shows what reality looks like: 'From the Internet to nanotechnology, most of the fundamental technological advances of the past half century – both basic and research and downstream commercialization – were funded by government agencies, with private business moving into the game only once the returns were in clear sight' (Mazzucato, 2015). So, many of the innovations we know today would not have been possible without public-private partnerships.

But consumers and producers also collaborate, although their roles can be quite blurry at times. What to think of – for example – prosumers in the energy domain. A prosumer is someone who both consumes the goods he/she produces or produces the goods he/she consumes. The term is a combination of the words producer and consumer (Lang et al., 2020). Examples are:

- open-source software where multiple actors contribute to building software systems they themselves also use, like Wikipedia;
- growing one's own food, or together with neighbours, in which case people grow and harvest vegetables together; self-sufficient barter networks (Wikipedia, 2021b).

According to Nobel Memorial prize winner Elinor Ostrom, these types of self-governing initiatives, also referred to as commons, can be good alternatives to both business and government in sustainably stewarding and harvesting the earth's resources (Ostrom, 1999). Waddock's idea of cosmopolitan-localism comes very close to what Ostrom calls commons, but gives it an international twist. In Waddock's view cosmopolitan-localism 'takes a global perspective through globally linked local networks, whilst keeping participation and decision-making as place-based, decentralized and localized as feasible in a given socio-ecological context' (Waddock, 2020).

In these commons people actively work together to inclusively solve societal needs. Inclusively in this respect entails that whoever wants to and feels fit to do so is invited to join in – not only for moral but also for innovation reasons. Tackling the wicked problems of our times requires tapping into the wisdom of the crowd and democratizing the innovation process (Von Hippel & Euchner, 2015).

Dutch and Belgian researchers found a steep rise in the number of commons. This rise is 'related to a growing awareness amongst a layer of citizens that a social and ecological transition is necessary given the relative state and market failures, but also to the effects of the great economic and systemic crisis of 2008, which has seen an austerity-driven retreat from public authorities in terms of common infrastructures' (Commons Transition, 2017).

3.2   Business

For the business sector, taking moral responsibility goes beyond taking social responsibility. Traditionally, corporate social responsibility (CSR) is closely connected to institutional theory, and can be described as the economic, legal, ethical and discretionary expectations that society has of organizations at a given point in time (Carroll, 1979). In this context, responsibilities are tied to the expectations that society has. If business does not live up to these expectations, it may jeopardize its social fitness. An organization is considered 'socially fit' if its social values and norms are in line with those of the society to which it is part of (Dowling & Pfeffer, 1975). It is important to understand that traditionally CSR is not society oriented, but first and foremost is business centred (Dommerholt, 2009). Only by living up to societal expectations can business gain society's consent and licence to operate. That is, CSR is a business-society construct that is centred around the tension that exists between business and society, because the aims of business and society are not necessarily aligned.

In contrast, when taking moral responsibility, the business community aligns its aims with those of society, implying there is no divide between business and society.

Businesses can express their moral responsibility directly or indirectly. Expressions of direct moral responsibility are manifestations displaying how organizations internally contribute to reducing energy and resource consumption by modifying their production processes and by implementing new business models. Expressions of indirect moral responsibility refer to businesses urging and supporting actors external to the organization – most notably customers and consumers – to change their economic behaviour and lifestyles. Examples of both will now be discussed.

Urging consumers to change their lifestyle may result in lower demand for goods and services, or a shift in demand to less harmful, or better still, regenerative products and services. Or in terms of the Business for Sufficiency (BfS) framework developed by Niessen and Bocken, consumers can be enticed to Refuse (don't consume), Reduce (consume less) or Rethink (consume differently) consumption (Niessen & Bocken, 2021).

Businesses can urge consumers to do the 'right' thing by educating or engaging them (Bocken & Short, 2016). This is how Whole Foods Markets, a USA-based retail chain, tries do the 'right' thing:

> We have not a right answer once and for all, but our intent is always to educate and lead our customers to healthier eating habits, while simultaneously listening to their feedback and providing them with the products they want to buy. (Mackey et al., 2014)

To stay within the planetary boundaries, resource and energy consumption needs to decrease by 40–90 per cent (Hickel, 2018). To achieve this, the business community should focus on keeping products and materials in the loop as long as possible by extending the lifespan of products, through reuse, repair, refurbish, remanufacture and repurpose. The business sector can further take responsibility by avoiding planned obsolescence, which can be described as a policy of planning or designing a product with an artificially limited useful life or a purposely frail design, so that it becomes obsolete after a certain pre-determined period of time upon which it decrementally functions or suddenly ceases to function, or might be perceived as unfashionable (Wikipedia, 2022). The rationale behind such a strategy is to boost sales and profitability.

Products and materials can also be used smarter by increasing resource efficiency (i.e., optimizing) and through intensifying product use, for example, through product sharing. Furthermore, material resources can be replaced by biobased substitutes, albeit under the condition of strong sustainability. Although, as we saw in one of the previous sections, increasing resource efficiency is a sine qua non, the transition towards a degrowth economy requires resource use to be absolutely decoupled from economic growth. Therefore, increasing resource efficiency needs to be complemented by sufficiency-oriented strategies, which encourage consumers to make do with less (Bocken & Short, 2016).

Technological innovation is not only about increasing resource efficiency, but also about disruptive or leap-frog innovation (Bessant & Tidd, 2014). Whilst incremental innovation is mostly about doing things better, disruptive innovation is about doing things differently. A case in point is 3D printing.

A report by ING argues that 3D printing is in an upsurge, and although it is difficult to estimate its potential, some experts expect a share of 50 per cent in manufacturing over the next two decades, and that some 50 per cent of manufactured goods will be printed in the next 20–40 years. This could diminish international trade by as much as 40 per cent (Leering, 2018). All this will have a substantial impact on energy and resource consumption (e.g., less transportation movements resulting in lower consumption of fossil fuels, but also less shipping equipment and storage).

Most of the circular strategies mentioned above can be presented and prioritized on a circularity ladder (see Figure 1.3). The circular intensity of each of the stages of this ladder increases from the bottom up. The 'Recover' strategy – being the least circular strategy – ranks lowest, whilst the 'Refuse' strategy, which can be classified as a degrowth strategy, ranks highest on the ladder.

Circular economy	Strategies		
Increasing circularity	Smarter product use and manufacture	R0 Refuse	Make product redundant by abandoning its function, or by offering the same function with a radically different product
		R1 Rethink	Make product use more intensive (e.g. through sharing products, or by putting multi-functional products on the market)
		R2 Reduce	Increasing efficiency in product manufacture or use by consuming fewer natural resources and materials
Rule of thumb: higher level of circularity = fewer natural resources	Extend lifespan of product and its parts	R3 Re-use	Re-use by another consumer of discarded product which is still in good condition and fulfills its original function
		R 4 Repair	Repair and maintenance of defective product, so it can be used with its original function
		R5 Refurbish	Restore an old product and bring it up to date
		R6 Remanufacture	Use parts of discarded product in a new product with the same function
		R7 Repurpose	Use discarded product or its parts in a new product with a different function
	Useful application of materials	R8 Recycle	Process materials to obtain the same (high grade) or lower (low grade quality)
		R9 Recover	Incineration of materials with energy recovery

Source: Potting et al. (2017).

Figure 1.3   *Priorization of circular strategies*

To reduce energy reduction also requires local sourcing. By sourcing locally, resources do not have to be shipped across the globe, which can also be seen as an alternative refuse strategy, namely refusing to buy resources, materials and products that are not locally sourced.

Closing loops involves the collaboration of multiple business. Individual companies can't close materials and resource loops on their own. To make that

Table 1.3   The list of protected needs

Group 1: Focusing on tangibles, material things To be provided with the material necessities of life To realize their own conception of daily life To live in a livable environment
Group 2: Focusing upon the person To develop as a person To make their own life choices To perform activities valuable to them
Group 3: Focusing upon community To be part of a community To have a say in the shaping of society To be granted protection by society

Source: Di Giulio and Defila (2021).

happen involves the collaboration of multiple companies and other network partners in circular ecosystems. Working together like this contributes to reducing energy and resource consumption, because the waste streams (e.g., heat) of one ecosystem partner can be an input for the production process of another partner. Today, multiple initiatives exist aimed at closing material loops. A case in point is Auping, the Dutch bed and mattress producer. This is what they communicate on their website on their sustainability efforts and achievements:

> Of course, we also do all we can to give our planet more rest. For example, in the summer we store the heat released in the ground beneath our green factory. This means that nobody needs to go searching for a warm jumper in the winter. And drinking water is only used for drinking. For example, did you know that we use rainwater to flush the toilet and to wash our hands? We really do recycle almost everything: from your old mattress to the sawdust that falls on the floor when making your new bed. (Auping, n.d.)

But taking moral responsibility also includes reflection on prevailing business models. Not all that can be produced should be produced. Value propositions should first and foremost be aimed at satisfying needs rather than wants, whilst business model revenues and costs should go beyond mere financial aspects to also include social and environmental components. Ideally, business models not only contribute to (1) energy and resource reduction, thus contributing to obeying planetary boundaries (Rockström et al., 2009), but also to (2) reducing inequality and improving well-being, which very much resonates with the quality-of-life paradigm, operationalized by Di Giulio and Defila (2021) by – what they call – 'protected needs' (see Table 1.3).

And what about marketing? Generally speaking, marketing is aimed at the promotion and selling or buying of goods and services to boost business sales and economic growth. In so doing, marketing also creates demand for goods and services we don't need by incentivizing and cultivating dissatisfaction amongst consumers (Jackson, 2011). So, marketing not only contributes to economic growth but also to overconsumption, which in turns fuels economic growth and deepens symptoms such as global warming and biodiversity loss. Needless to say that marketing or the marketing concept as such does not contribute to sustainable development.

And sustainable marketing? Generally speaking, sustainable marketing can be seen as promoting sustainable and environmentally friendly products and services, although a universally accepted and agreed-upon standard for sustainable and environmentally friendly products does not yet exist. Often the adjective 'sustainable' is used for legitimizing corporate behaviours and to boost reputation and sales. However, sustainable marketing is still about marketing of goods and services, which in and of itself is at odds with sustainable development, making sustainable marketing an oxymoronic concept.

The same applies to sustainable marketing interpreted as the marketing of – let's say – regular goods and services in a sustainable manner. In this case the adjective sustainable refers to the marketing process as such: the process of promoting and selling goods and services. But it is still aimed at boosting sales and economic growth, albeit with an alleged sustainability lining.

In a degrowth setting, marketing could be part of a sufficiency-oriented strategy, primarily aimed at satisfying needs and not wants. Although marketing is not primarily aimed at boosting sales, this could be the outcome, but only if the concerning products socially and/or environmentally outperform or outsmart products produced by competitors. This implies that marketing should be aimed at informing audiences instead of manipulating them. Furthermore, marketing should be focused on promoting sufficiency rather than affluence. A case in point is the one-off advertisement in *The New York Times* by Patagonia, the outdoor clothing business, in which the company asked its customers to 'Not Buy' their jackets (Bocken & Short, 2016).

For the banking sector taking moral responsibility entails returning to their core business: attracting money from surplus households and lending it out to deficiency households, with the interest rate margin only reflecting the costs for the intermediary role banks play in the economy. Returning to their core business is another way of saying that banks will no longer finance economic growth through money (or debt) creation, which also wards off crises similar to the banking crisis we witnessed in 2007–2008.

Furthermore, taking moral responsibility also entails that banks wholeheartedly finance activities aimed at reducing energy and resource consumption on the one hand, and degrowth business models on the other.

3.3   Government

But how can we be sure that resource and energy reduction efforts by consumers and the business community in the end accurately and sufficiently contribute to reducing CO_2 emissions and resource consumption? How can we be sure that all collective efforts do not end in chaos?

The sum of the intensions of all economic actors may in the end result in undershooting or overshooting carbon emission and resource reduction aims essential to bringing the economy back into harmony with the living world. Here is where the moral responsibility of governments kicks in. The government needs to create a level playing field for all. The transition towards a degrowth economy can't be left solely to individual actors, and reducing carbon emission and resource use can also not be left to the invisible hand of the market. Or as Essex et al. put it: 'It is not, however, individual choices that will unlock the changes needed, but disruption to our current consumer economy and politics that frame the *daily practices* that constitute our ways of living' (Essex et al., 2022). This disruption should be initiated, incentivized and coordinated by governments.

The remaining carbon budget for a 50 per cent likelihood to limit global warming to 1.5, 1.7 and 2°C respectively, has reduced to 380 Gt CO_2, 730 Gt CO_2 and 1230 Gt CO_2 from the beginning of 2023. Based on 2022 emission levels these budgets are likely to be reached in subsequently 9, 18 and 30 years. However, the concentration of CO_2 in the atmosphere was set to reach 417.2 ppm in 2022, 51 per cent above pre-industrial levels (Friedlingstein et al., 2022), a tremendous increase with all due consequences. Also, industrial ecologists have proposed that a sustainable upper limit for global resource use might be around 50 billion tonnes per year. In 2017 the world is using over 90 billion tonnes already, which is way beyond the sustainable threshold level (Hickel et al., 2022).

It should not be too difficult to divide carbon and resource budgets fairly amongst world regions or countries. Some scientists already carried out this exercise, taking population size as the basis for their calculations (Hickel & Kallis, 2019; Hickel, 2020c). To effectively combat climate change and resource consumption, countries can't go beyond the fair carbon and resource shares or thresholds allocated to them. The function of these fair shares or thresholds is to cap resource use and CO_2 emissions.

As I clarified above, the fact that global resource use and (albeit to a lesser extent) carbon emissions have gone out of bounds and have reached critical levels is mainly due to the overconsumption of the affluent, especially in Global North countries. Therefore, governments in these countries should particularly focus on combating overconsumption. That is, governments should best concentrate on the demand side of product markets and not on the supply side as is currently the case. A case in point in this respect is the European Emission Trading System (EU ETS). This system entails that companies must buy CO_2 emission permits if they increase CO_2 emissions – for example – because of increasing demand for their products. The EU can manipulate the price of CO_2 permits. The higher the price, the more companies will be inclined to invest in CO_2 reduction innovations. However, the current system is far from perfect: only 45 per cent of all emissions is covered by the EU ETS (Schenderling, 2022).

One way of demand-induced carbon reduction is via a 'carbon card', which authorizes an individual to emit an annual quota (Piketty & Goldhammer, 2020). Implementing such a carbon card is fairly easy. Every citizen receives a fair carbon emission share in the form of a voucher. Every time a product or service is bought, the carbon card will be debited. In the Netherlands, Rabobank has already gained some experience with a carbon accounting system.[3]

With carbon vouchers there are two options. The first option is that entire vouchers, or carbon surpluses, that aren't needed, can be sold to people whose fair share is not enough to cover their carbon needs. The other is that vouchers and/or surpluses are not tradable. Both options have their downsides. As we have seen earlier, rich people are higher carbon emitters than poor people. If vouchers are tradable, it is likely that particularly poor people will sell these, or their carbon surpluses, to the rich. The consequence will be that, just like in the current situation, the most affluent will still be the highest emitters, and the rich may still be able to emit as much carbon as they like. If, on the other hand, vouchers can't be traded, the poor are left with carbon surpluses they don't need, whilst the rich are in need of surpluses they don't have access to. The result will be that carbon caps and therewith carbon thresholds can't be controlled effectively. But also, the business community is not really challenged to come up with innovative solutions to reduce CO_2 emissions.

As Piketty and Goldhammer claim: 'A better solution might be a true progressive tax on carbon emissions at the level of individual consumers. For example, the first five tons of individual emissions might be taxed little if at all, the next ten tons somewhat more, and so on up to some maximum level beyond which all emissions would be prohibited, with violations subject to fines (such as a confiscatory tax on income and/or wealth).' (Piketty & Goldhammer, 2020, p. 605).

A progressive tax option is likely to be more effective than carbon vouchers, as tax rates will be highest for the most affluent. Progressively taxing emis-

---

[3]   For more information see: https://www.rabobank.nl/over-ons/carbon-bank/carbon-insights.

sions incentivizes those who emit the most CO_2 to buy less carbon-intensive goods and services. In other words, it puts a price tag on high-carbon lifestyles. For resource use reduction, a similar system can be designed.

A system as described above forces consumers to consider the carbon content of their purchase. This in turn will incentivize the business community to invest in (disruptive) innovations aimed at reducing product-related carbon emissions and resource consumption. Competition amongst industry rivals will not (only) be on price, but also on carbon and resource efficiency. A progressive carbon tax can have undesirable income effects, especially for lower-income groups. Therefore, lower-income groups should be compensated by a lower tax on labour. A positive side effect of this is that labour will become cheaper and labour-intensive products and services (e.g., theatres, handmade furniture, restaurants, repair and refurbishment of goods, community services, personal development, etc.) will become cheaper and therefore more attractive to buy. Furthermore, governments need to create a level playing field for all businesses. That is, to prevent companies from foreign countries from gaining a competitive edge because of lower CO_2 and resource reduction standards, imported goods and services should be carbon taxed before entering the country.

To contribute to sustainable development requires governments to facilitate transitions towards more egalitarian societies, because – as I pointed out earlier – in egalitarian societies, like Denmark, people are generally happier and healthier, crime rates are lower, and people are more creative and more productive. Furthermore, educational attainment is higher as well (Dorling, 2017). These are strong arguments for governments to reduce inequality amongst their citizens by increasing income and wealth taxes and redistributing income to the less fortunate. Paying taxes is not only a matter of civilization, it also pays off socially.

What we have seen recently is that growth in top incomes has been driven mainly by two occupational categories: those in the financial sector, and non-financial executives. As Joseph Stiglitz states: 'evidence suggests that rents have contributed to a larger scale to strong increases in the incomes of both' (Stiglitz, 2016). Rent-seeking entails getting an income not as a reward for creating wealth, but by grabbing a larger share of the wealth that would have been produced anyway (Stiglitz, 2016). Creating an egalitarian society is at odds with rent-seeking. To achieve a more egalitarian society therefore calls for high(er) and (more) progressive income and wealth tax rates, but also that a maximum is set to transfer incomes such as inheritances passed from parents to children. Redistribution of income and wealth includes a universal basic income, as a reward for citizens who contribute to the betterment of society, but who are currently not being financially rewarded for their contributions.

To create a more egalitarian society we need more support for education, including pre-school; increasing the minimum wage; strengthening earned income tax credits; strengthening the voice of workers in the workplace, including through unions; and more effective enforcement of anti-discrimination laws (Stiglitz, 2016).

4.   CONCLUSION

In this section, I pointed out how different economic actors (consumers, businesses and governments), particularly in Global North countries, can take and express moral responsibility for contributing to the transition towards a degrowth economy. The list of examples I provided is by no means exhaustive, but I hope these examples will challenge and inspire readers to take action.

Furthermore, in my view, governments should play a pivotal role in making the transition towards a degrowth economy happen by incentivizing people to buy fewer carbon and resource intensive products and services. An effective way of achieving that goal is through designing a progressive carbon and resource tax system. This will not only reduce carbon emissions and resource use, but will also incentivize businesses to become more innovative, thus contributing to a nimbler and more resilient economy.

REFERENCES

A European Green Deal. (2019, 12 October). European Commission – European Commission. Retrieved 6 November 2021, from https://ec.europa.eu/info/strategy/priorities-2019-2024/european-green-deal_en.

Aguirre, B. E. (2002). 'Sustainable development' as collective surge. *Social Science Quarterly, 83*(1), 101–118. https://doi.org/10.1111/1540-6237.00073.

Albert, M. J. (2020). The dangers of decoupling: earth system crisis and the 'Fourth Industrial Revolution'. *Global Policy, 11*(2), 245–254. https://doi.org/10.1111/1758-5899.12791.

Alfredsson, E., Bengtsson, M., Brown, H. S., Isenhour, C., Lorek, S., Stevis, D. & Vergragt, P. (2018). Why achieving the Paris Agreement requires reduced overall consumption and production. *Sustainability: Science, Practice and Policy, 14*(1), 1–5. https://doi.org/10.1080/15487733.2018.1458815.

Auping. (n.d.). Auping. Retrieved 1 January 2023, from https://www.auping.com/en/about-auping/sustainability.

Banerjee, S. B. (2002). *Contesting Corporate Citizenship, Sustainability and Stakeholder Theory: Holy Trinity or Praxis of Evil?* https://www.academia.edu/5973231/ Contesting _Corporate _Citizenship _Sustainability _and _Stakeholder _Theory_Holy_Trinity_or_Praxis_of_Evil.

Bansal, P. (2002). The corporate challenges of sustainable development. *Academy of Management Perspectives, 16*(2), 122–131. https://doi.org/10.5465/ame.2002.7173572.

Beaumont, P. (2021, 3 February). Decades of progress on extreme poverty now in reverse due to Covid. *The Guardian*. Retrieved 17 December 2021, from https://www.theguardian.com/global-development/2021/feb/03/decades-of-progress-on-extreme-poverty-now-in-reverse-due-to-covid.

Belmonte-Ureña, L. J., Plaza-Úbeda, J. A., Vazquez-Brust, D. & Yakovleva, N. (2021). Circular economy, degrowth and green growth as pathways for research on sustainable development goals: A global analysis and future agenda. *Ecological Economics*, *185*, 107050. https://doi.org/10.1016/j.ecolecon.2021.107050.

Bessant, J. R. & Tidd, J. (2014). *Managing Innovation: Integrating Technological, Market and Organizational Change* (4th edition). Wiley.

Bocken, N. & Short, S. (2016). Towards a sufficiency-driven business model: Experiences and opportunities. *Environmental Innovation and Societal Transitions*, *18*, 41–61. https://doi.org/10.1016/j.eist.2015.07.010.

Bolger, M., Marin, D., Tofighi-Niaki, A. & Seelmann, L. (2021, 5 October). 'Green mining' is a myth: The case for cutting EU resource consumption. The European Environmental Bureau and Friends of the Earth Europe. Retrieved at 21 November 2021, from https://eeb.org/library/green-mining-is-a-myth/#:%7E:text=EU%20resource%20consumption-,'Green%20mining'%20is%20a%20myth%3A%20the%20case,for%20cutting%20EU%20resource%20consumption&text=The%20EU%20is%20already%20extracting,in%20metals%20and%20minerals%20mining.

BP. (n.d.). Retrieved December 17, 2022, from https://www.bp.com/.

Brand, U., Muraca, B., Pineault, R., Sahakian, M., Schaffartzik, A., Novy, A., Streissler, C., Haberl, H., Asara, V., Dietz, K., Lang, M., Kothari, A., Smith, T., Spash, C., Brad, A., Pichler, M., Plank, C., Velegrakis, G., Jahn, T., … Görg, C. (2021). From planetary to societal boundaries: An argument for collectively defined self-limitation. *Sustainability: Science, Practice and Policy*, *17*(1), 265–292. https://doi.org/10.1080/15487733.2021.1940754.

Carleton, T. A., Jina, A., Delgado, M. T., Greenstone, M., Houser, T., Hsiang, S. M., Hultgren, A., Kopp, R. E., McCusker, K. E., Nath, I. B., Rising, J., Rode, A., Seo, H. K., Viaene, A., Yuan, J. & Tianbo Zhang, A. (2020, 3 August). Valuing the global mortality consequences of climate change accounting for adaptation costs and benefits. NBER. Retrieved 8 November 2021, from https://www.nber.org/papers/w27599.

Carroll, A. B. (1979). A three-dimensional conceptual model of corporate performance. *Academy of Management Review*, *4*(4), 497–505. https://doi.org/10.5465/amr.1979.4498296.

Commons Transition. (2017, 4 December). A Commons Transition Plan for the city of Ghent. Retrieved 19 December 2021, from https://commonstransition.org/commons-transition-plan-city-ghent/.

Copper Alliance. (2018). The long-term availability of copper. Retrieved 17 December 2022, from http://copperallinace.org.

Di Giulio, A. & Defila, R. (2021). Building the bridge between Protected Needs and consumption corridors. *Sustainability: Science, Practice and Policy*, *17*(1), 118–135. https://doi.org/10.1080/15487733.2021.1907056.

Dobbs, R., Oppenheim, J., Thompson, F., Brinkman, M. & Zornes, M. (2011). *Resource Revolution: Meeting the World's Energy, Materials, Food, and Water Needs* (November). Retrieved from https://www.mckinsey.com/~/media/McKinsey/Business%20Functions/Sustainability/Our%20Insights/Resource%20revolution/MGI_Resource_revolution_full_report.ashx.

Dommerholt, E. (2009). *Corporate Sustainability Performance: Constructs, Measures and Investors' Responses* [PhD dissertation]. VU-University Amsterdam.

Dorling, D. (2017, 6 November). The equality effect: How greater equality makes us happier, less. *New Internationalist.* Retrieved 22 October 2021, from https://newint .org/features/2017/07/01/equality-effect.

Dowling, J. & Pfeffer, J. (1975). Organizational legitimacy: Social values and organizational behavior. *Pacific Sociological Review, 18*(1), 122–136.

Easterlin, R. A., McVey, L. A., Switek, M., Sawangfa, O. & Zweig, J. S. (2010). The happiness-income paradox revisited. *Proceedings of the National Academy of Sciences, 107*(52), 22463–22468. https://doi.org/10.1073/pnas.1015962107.

Ehrlich, P. (2014). Human impact: The ethics of I=PAT. *Ethics in Science and Environmental Politics, 14,* 11–18. Retrieved from https://www.int-res.com/articles/esep2014/14/e014p011.pdf.

Ehrlich, P. R. & Holdren, J. P. (1971). Impact of population growth; complacency concerning this component of man's predicament is unjustified and counterproductive. *Science, 171*(3977), 1212–1217. Retrieved from https:// science .sciencemag .org/ content/171/3977/1212.

Essex, J., Sims, P. & Storey, N. (2022). *Rethinking Energy Demand.* Green House Think Tank/Green European Foundation. Retrieved 6 November 2022, from https:// gef.eu/publication/rethinking-energy-demand/.

Friedlingstein, P., O'Sullivan, M., Jones, M. W., Andrew, R. M., Gregor, L., Hauck, J., Le Quéré, C., Luijkx, I. T., Olsen, A., Peters, G. P., Peters, W., Pongratz, J., Schwingshackl, C., Sitch, S., Canadell, J. G., Ciais, P., Jackson, R. B., Alin, S. R., Alkama, R., … Zheng, B. (2022). Global Carbon Budget 2022. *Earth System Science Data, 14*(11), 4811–4900. https://doi.org/10.5194/essd-14-4811-2022.

Geissdorfer, M., Savaget, P., Bocken, N. M. P. & Hultink, E. J. (2017). The circular economy – a new sustainability paradigm? *Journal of Cleaner Production, 143,* 757–768.

Haberl, H., Wiedenhofer, D., Virág, D., Kalt, G., Plank, B., Brockway, P., Fishman, T., Hausknost, D., Krausmann, F., Leon-Gruchalski, B., Mayer, A., Pichler, M., Schaffartzik, A., Sousa, T., Streeck, J. & Creutzig, F. (2020). A systematic review of the evidence on decoupling of GDP, resource use and GHG emissions, part II: Synthesizing the insights. *Environmental Research Letters, 15*(6), 065003. https:// doi.org/10.1088/1748-9326/ab842a.

Hausfather, Z. (2022, 11 April). Analysis: What the new IPCC report says about when world may pass 1.5C and 2C. *Carbon Brief.* https://www.carbonbrief.org/analysis -what-the-new-ipcc-report-says-about-when-world-may-pass-1-5c-and-2c/.

Helliwell, J. F., Layard, R., Sachs, J. D., De Neve, J. E., Aknin, L. B. & Wang, S. (2021). World Happiness Report 2021. Retrieved 28 December 2022, from https:// worldhappiness.report/ed/2021/.

Herrington, G. (2020). Update to limits to growth: Comparing the World3 model with empirical data. *Journal of Industrial Ecology, 25*(3), 614–626. https:// doi .org/ 10 .1111/jiec.13084

Hickel, J. (2018). Is it possible to achieve a good life for all within planetary boundaries? *Third World Quarterly, 40*(1), 18–35. https://doi.org/10.1080/01436597.2018 .1535895.

Hickel, J. (2020a). What does degrowth mean? A few points of clarification. *Globalizations,* September, 1–7. https://doi.org/10.1080/14747731.2020.1812222.

Hickel, J. (2020b). *Less is More* (1st edition). Penguin Random House.

Hickel, J. (2020c). Quantifying national responsibility for climate breakdown: An equality-based attribution approach for carbon dioxide emissions in excess of the planetary boundary. *The Lancet Planetary Health*, *4*(9), e399–e404. https://doi.org/10.1016/s2542-5196(20)30196-0.

Hickel, J. & Kallis, G. (2019). Is green growth possible? *New Political Economy*, *25*(4), 469–486. https://doi.org/10.1080/13563467.2019.1598964.

Hickel, J., O'Neill, D. W., Fanning, A. L. & Zoomkawala, H. (2022). National responsibility for ecological breakdown: A fair-shares assessment of resource use, 1970–2017. *The Lancet Planetary Health*, *6*(4), e342–e349. https://doi.org/10.1016/s2542-5196(22)00044-4.

IISD. (2019, 19 March). *Global Outlook Highlights Resource Extraction as Main Cause of Climate Change, Biodiversity Loss | News | SDG Knowledge Hub | IISD.* IISD/SDG Knowledge Hub. Retrieved 23 October 2021, from https:// sdg .iisd .org/news/global-outlook-highlights-resource-extraction-as-main-cause-of-climate-change-biodiversity-loss/.

International Energy Agency. (2018). *World Energy Outlook 2018 – Analysis*. IEA. Retrieved 19 December 2021, from https:// www .iea .org/ reports/ world -energy -outlook-2018.

IPCC. (2021, August). *Climate Change 2021 The Physical Science Basis*. https://www .ipcc.ch/report/ar6/wg1/.

Jackson, T. (2011). *Prosperity Without Growth* (2nd edition). Earthscan.

Kelly, A. (2020, 15 October). Apple and Google named in US lawsuit over Congolese child cobalt mining deaths. *The Guardian*. https:// www .theguardian .com/ global -development/2019/dec/ 16/apple-and-google-named-in-us-lawsuit-over-congolese -child-cobalt-mining-deaths.

Khazzoom, D. J. (1980). Economic implications for mandated efficiency in standards for household appliances. *The Energy Journal*, *1*(4), 21–40. doi:10.5547/issn0195-6574-ej-vol1-no4-2.

Lang, B., Dolan, R., Kemper, J. & Northey, G. (2020). Prosumers in times of crisis: Definition, archetypes and implications. *Journal of Service Management*, *32*(2), 176–189. https://doi.org/10.1108/josm-05-2020-0155.

Leering, R. (2018, 5 June). 3D printing: A threat to global trade. ING Think. https:// think.ing.com/reports/3d-printing-a-threat-to-global-trade.

Mackey, J., Sisodia, R. & George, B. (2014). *Conscious Capitalism, With a New Preface by the Authors: Liberating the Heroic Spirit of Business* (1st edition). Harvard Business Review Press.

Mazzucato, M. (2015). *The Entrepreneurial State: Debunking Public vs. Private Sector Myths* (Revised). PublicAffairs.

Meadows, D. H., Meadows, D. L., Randers, J. & Behrens III, W. W. (1972). *The Limits to Growth; A Report for the Club of Rome's Project on the Predicament of Mankind* (5th printing edition). Universe Books.

Miñarro, S., Reyes-García, V., Aswani, S., Selim, S., Barrington-Leigh, C. P. & Galbraith, E. D. (2021). Happy without money: Minimally monetized societies can exhibit high subjective well-being. *PLOS ONE*, *16*(1), e0244569. https://doi.org/10 .1371/journal.pone.0244569.

Morimoto, S., Kuroki, H., Narita, H. & Ishigaki, A. (2021). Scenario assessment of neodymium recycling in Japan based on substance flow analysis and future demand forecast. *Journal of Material Cycles and Waste Management*, *23*(6), 2120–2132. https://doi.org/10.1007/s10163-021-01277-6.

Niessen, L. & Bocken, N. M. (2021). How can businesses drive sufficiency? The business for sufficiency framework. *Sustainable Production and Consumption, 28,* 1090–1103. https://doi.org/10.1016/j.spc.2021.07.030.

OECD. (2018). *Global Material Resources Outlook to 2060 Economic Drivers and Environmental Consequences.* https://www.oecd.org/publications/global-material -resources-outlook-to-2060-9789264307452-en.htm.

Olthaar, M. & Schenderling, P. (2021). *Hoe handel ik eerlijk* (1st edition). Skandalon Uitgeverij B.V.

O'Neill, D. W., Fanning, A. L., Lamb, W. F. & Steinberger, J. K. (2018). A good life for all within planetary boundaries. *Nature Sustainability, 1*(2), 88–95. https://doi .org/10.1038/s41893-018-0021-4.

Ossewaarde, M. & Ossewaarde-Lowtoo, R. (2020). The EU's Green Deal: A third alternative to green growth and degrowth? *Sustainability, 12*(23), 9825. https://doi .org/10.3390/su12239825.

Ostrom, E. (1999). Coping with tragedies of the commons. *Annual Review of Political Science, 2*(1), 493–535. https://doi.org/10.1146/annurev.polisci.2.1.493.

Oxfam. (2021, 9 July). The hunger virus multiplies: Deadly recipe of conflict, COVID-19 and climate accelerate world hunger. Oxfam International. Retrieved 17 December 2021, from https://www.oxfam.org/en/research/hunger-virus-multiplies -deadly-recipe-conflict-covid-19-and-climate-accelerate-world.

Oxfam International. (2020, 23 September). Carbon emissions of richest 1 percent more than double the emissions of the poorest half of humanity. Retrieved 24 December 2021, from https://www.oxfam.org/en/press-releases/carbon-emissions-richest-1 -percent-more-double-emissions-poorest-half-humanity.

Piketty, T. & Goldhammer, A. (2020). *Capital and Ideology.* Belknap Press: An Imprint of Harvard University Press.

Potting, J., Hekkert, M. P., Worrell, E. & Hanemaaijer, A. (2017). *Circular Economy: Measuring Innovation in the Product Chain (Number 2544). https://dspace.library .uu.nl/handle/1874/358310.*

Raworth, K. (2017). *Doughnut Economics. Seven Ways to Think Like a 21st-Century Economist.* London: Penguin Random House.

Remarks at the University of Kansas, 18 March 1968/JFK Library. (1968). John F. Kennedy Presidential Library and Museum. Retrieved 28 November 2021, from https://www.jfklibrary.org/learn/about-jfk/the-kennedy-family/robert-f-kennedy/ robert-f-kennedy-speeches/remarks-at-the-university-of-kansas-march-18-1968.

Rockström, J., Steffen, W., Noone, K., Persson, S., Chapin, F. S. I., Lambin, E., Lenton, T. M., Scheffer, M., Folke, C., Schellnhuber, H. J., Nykvist, B., De Wit, C. A., Hughes, T., Van der Leeuw, S., Rodhe, H., Sörlin, S., Snyder, P. K., Costanza, R., Svedin, U., … Foley, J. (2009). Planetary boundaries: Exploring the safe operating space for humanity. *Ecology and Society, 14*(2). https://doi.org/10.5751/es-03180 -140232.

Sandberg, M., Klockars, K. & Wilén, K. (2019). Green growth or degrowth? Assessing the normative justifications for environmental sustainability and economic growth through critical social theory. *Journal of Cleaner Production, 206,* 133–141. https:// doi.org/10.1016/j.jclepro.2018.09.175.

Schenderling, P. (2022). *Er is leven na de groei: Hoe we onze toekomst realistisch veiligstellen* (1st edition). Bot Uitgevers.

Schwab, K. (2017). *The Fourth Industrial Revolution.* Crown.

Smit, M. (2022). Naar een duurzame landbouw in 2040: Een ongemakkelijke weg. Nearchus.

Statistical Review of World Energy. (2022). BP. Retrieved 17 December 2022, from https:// www .bp .com/ en/ global/ corporate/ energy -economics/ statistical -review -of -world-energy.html.

Steg, L., Vlek, C. H., Feenstra, D., Gerbens, W., Karsten, L., Kok, R., Lindenberg, S., Maignan, I., Moll, H., Nonhebel, S., Schoot-Uiterkamp, T., Sijtsma, F. and van Witteloostuijn, A. (2001). *Towards a Comprehensive Model of Sustainable Corporate Performance. Three Dimensional Modelling and Practical Measurement* (Interim report). Groningen, Departments of Economics, Environmental Sciences, Management Science, Psychology and Sociology, University of Groningen.

Stichting Genoeg om te Leven. (2022, 28 September). *10 miljoen mensen doen slaafse arbeid voor Nederlandse consumptie.* Genoeg Om Te Leven. https:// www .genoegomteleven.nl/onderzoek-moderne-dagloners/.

Stiglitz, J. E. (2016). Inequality and economic growth. In Jacobs, M. & Mazzucato, M. (eds), *Rethinking Capitalism* (1st edition). Wiley.

Tolstoy, L. (1925). *What Then Must We Do?* Translated by S. Haverhoek. Sieuwert. Haverhoek@gmail.com.

Turner, G. & Alexander, C. (2017, 25 May). Limits to growth was right. New research shows we're nearing collapse. *The Guardian.* https:// www .theguardian .com/commentisfree/2014/sep/02/limits-to-growth-was-right-new-research-shows -were-nearing-collapse.

United Nations DESA/Population Division. (n.d.). World Population Prospects 2018 [Dataset]. Retrieved 10 January 2021, from https:// population .un .org/ wup/ Download/.

US Department of Agriculture. (2021, 1 August). *USDA ERS – International Macroeconomic Data Set.* International Macroeconomic Dataset. Retrieved 20 October 2021, from https:// www .ers .usda .gov/ data -products/ international -macroeconomic-data-set/.

Vigran, D. (2021, 13 August). Faster, more intense, with more devastating impacts: New IPCC report lays out the scientific basis of the climate emergency. CityTalk. Retrieved 27 November 2021, from https:// talkofthecities .iclei .org/ faster -more -intense -with -more -devastating -impacts -new -ipcc -report -lays -out -the -scientific -basis-of-the-climate-emergency/?gclid=Cj0KCQiAy4eNBhCaARIsAFDVtI0aZO IflTejF3hJHgpj05czth-56ufZlINwrlo5HHoewGsIJfZJjNYaAlI-EALw_wcB.

Von Hippel, E. & Euchner, T. (2015). User innovation. *Research-Technology Management, 56*(3), 15–20. DOI:10.5437/08956308X603003.

Waddock, S. (2020). Reframing and transforming economics around life. *Sustainability, 12*(18), 7553. https://doi.org/10.3390/su12187553.

Ward, J. D., Sutton, P. C., Werner, A. D., Costanza, R., Mohr, S. H. & Simmons, C. T. (2016). Is decoupling GDP growth from environmental impact possible? *PLOS ONE, 11*(10), e0164733. https://doi.org/10.1371/journal.pone.0164733.

WCED: World Commission on Environment and Development. (1987). *Our Common Future.* Oxford: Oxford University Press.

WHO. (2018, 2 May). 9 out of 10 people worldwide breathe polluted air, but more countries are taking action. World Health Organization. Retrieved 17 December 2021, from https://www.who.int/news/item/02-05-2018-9-out-of-10-people-worldwide -breathe-polluted-air-but-more-countries-are-taking-action.

WID – Wealth and Income Database. (2019, 5 January). *Data.* Retrieved 23 October 2021, from https://wid.world/data/.

Wiedmann, T., Lenzen, M., Keyßer, L. T. & Steinberger, J. K. (2020). Scientists' warning on affluence. *Nature Communications*, *11*(1), 1–10. https:// doi .org/ 10 .1038/s41467-020-16941-y.

Wikipedia. (2021a, 23 August). *Verovering door VOC van de Banda-eilanden*. Wikipedia. Retrieved 30 October 2021, from https:// nl .wikipedia .org/ wiki/ Verovering_door_VOC_van_de_Banda-eilanden.

Wikipedia. (2021b, 19 November). *Prosumer*. Retrieved 19 December 2021, from https://en.wikipedia.org/wiki/Prosumer.

Wikipedia. (2022). *Planned Obsolescence*. Retrieved 30 December 2022, from https:// en.wikipedia.org/wiki/Planned_obsolescence.

Wilkins, J. & Murphy, B. (2021). *Investing in Degrowth: Funding the Transition to a New Economy*. Heliocene. Retrieved 30 December 2022, from https://heliocene .org/reports/investing-in-degrowth/.

World Bank Open Data. (n.d.). Retrieved 18 December 2022, from https:// data .worldbank.org/.

World Wildlife Fund. (n.d.). *Effects of Climate Change | Threats | WWF*. Retrieved 24 December 2021, from https:// www .worldwildlife .org/ threats/ effects -of -climate -change #: %7E: text = More %20frequent %20and %20intense %20drought ,on %20people's %20livelihoods %20and %20communities . & text = As %20climate %20change %20worsens %2C %20dangerous ,becoming %20more %20frequent %20or%20severe.

2. Let's get digital: understanding different discourses on digitalization

Berber Pas and Jasper van den Berkmortel

1. INTRODUCTION

The development of *digital technology* – electronic tools, systems, devices and computing resources (e.g., AI, machine learning, quantum computing) which generate, store, and analyse vast amounts of 'big data' – emerges fast and simultaneously. Similarly fast is the development of different terms related to this trend, such as 'digitization', digitalization', 'digital transformation', 'datafication', 'dataveillance', 'dataism', et cetera. Some of these terms stem from a positivist perspective and address how digital technology is expected to enhance particular objectives. Take, for example, the term 'digital economy', referring to how countries, governments and organizations aim to take advantage of digital technologies (ICT) and (big) data to meet their public and private objectives (OECD, 2020). Other terms, however, are more frequently used by those taking a critical perspective. The term 'datafication', for example, highlights a new paradigm in which the increasingly normalized transformation of social action into online quantified data (datafication) allows for real-time tracking and predictive analysis (Van Dijck, 2014) and a continuous surveillance through the use of (meta)data ('dataveillance') (Raley, 2013). Although it is sometimes vague what all these terms and concepts precisely refer to, what it does indicate is how the societal consequences of the use of digital technology increasingly attracts attention from researchers and practitioners in all fields, including that of organization and management literature (Batistič & van der Laken, 2019). In a mere 28 years, this specific field of research on the use of (big) data and digital technology has grown to include over 4,500 management- or business-related publications in the Web of Science's core collection. Of those 4,500 publications, more than 1,100 have been published since 2019 (van den Berkmortel, 2021). What all these definitions also signal is the relevance of the semantic reality of digital technology – meaning that it does not necessarily refer so much to the tangible material objects and practices, but as something we talk and write about (*discursively*) in order to anticipate, envision and give meaning to the present and future in which all these material artifacts come into being (Stevens et al., 2018).

Instead of providing a limited overview of examples on how digital technology will (or will not) change, improve or (unintendedly) harm our working and private lives, we prefer to address the *different discourses on digital technology* in this chapter instead. Why is it important to acknowledge these discursive differences? First, because the examples of how digital technology affects our society, our organizational practices and private lives one presents highly depend on underlying assumptions of the discourse one uses. If we want to understand and eventually theoretically explain the range of implications of digital technology we need to understand the underlying assumptions of scientists and practitioners (Stevens et al., 2018; Beer, 2016; Lakoff, 1978). Second, because how people talk about and make sense of digital technology heavily impacts how digital technology is actually produced and reproduced. Many terms and concepts related to digital technology are future oriented – they often describe or define how digital technology could affect our lives, they do not (yet) refer to actual practices. Nevertheless, these terms are needed and thus used by scientists and policy makers as it allows them to formulate goals and roles, and attract interest. As such, these future orientations regarding how digital technology can affect our economy and society at large play a crucial role in mobilizing resources on the macro (institutional) level, to form networks for collaboration and innovation between organizations (meso-level) and steer the work of the individual professional (micro-level).

The chapter will be structured in the following way. First, based on existing frameworks to categorize different sociological and organizational perspectives (e.g., Burrell & Morgan, 1979; Deetz, 1996; Schultze & Stabell, 2004), a framework is provided to categorize different digital technology, discourses along the lines of two dimensions; the *ontological/epistemological* and the *social order*. After explaining the two dimensions, four different digital technology discourses will be distinguished and elaborated upon: the '*normative (neo-functionalist) discourse*', the '*(social)constructivist/interpretivist discourse*', the '*critical discourse*' and the '*dialogic discourse*'. Sequentially, each discourse will be discussed in terms of the two dimensions its characteristics and the concerns (for individuals, organizations and/or society at large) those using the particular discourse have. Each discourse will also be illustrated with an example of a *practical case*. In the discussion, we will address the challenges and concerns with digital technology and digitalization for society, organizations and individuals. In the final paragraph of this chapter, we will provide some suggestions for future research to which all academic discourses can contribute, albeit with different takes on what the most pressing research questions that need to be addressed should be.

The aim here is not to bring different perspectives together, as it would deny deeply rooted distinct assumptions which have a purpose. Contrarily, addressing different academic dialogues prevents a particular paradigm to become dominant and restrictive, which is potentially harmful to the development of insights on possibilities and consequences (Schultze & Stabell, 2004). The provided overview of discourses is also not an attempt to normatively describe how a digital technology should be managed or implemented for it to miraculously lead to some kind of value. What we do hope this four-paradigm grid will provide is some clarification and understanding regarding different standpoints between practitioners dealing with organizational changes related to digital technology. For academic purposes, the proposed framework can be very useful for making sense of contradictory information (Deetz, 1996), synthesize past research (Zupic & Čater, 2015), delineate subfields and provide insights for future research (Batistič & van der Laken, 2019).

2.   THEORETICAL BACKGROUND: TWO DIMENSIONS, FOUR DISCOURSES

When aiming to categorize a rapidly growing amount of literature on a topic, a basic distinction is needed based on researchers underlying ontological and epistemological assumptions, as well as their assumptions regarding the nature of society. The work of Burrell and Morgan (1979) who propose a framework for sociological paradigms and organizational analysis has often been the base for such endeavours. Schultze and Stabell (2004), for example, used their framework in their pursuit of making sense of different discourses regarding knowledge management. Although using different concepts and terms, all authors provide two dimensions behind general assumptions regarding organizational phenomena, which are useful for making sense of how digital technology is discursively used in organizations and society: an *ontological-epistemology dimension* and a *social order dimension*. Before distinguishing four different discourses on digital technology the underlying dimensions need to be explained first.

2.1   Ontology-epistemology Dimension: Dualism Versus Duality

The first dimension as described by Schultze and Stabell (2004) is the epistemological dimension. In this dimension they distinguish two extremes: dualism and duality. The distinction between a duality-based worldview and a dualism-based worldview comes from Giddens (1976), who discussed duality and dualism as part of his Structuration Theory. In his work, he suggests that dualism-based authors focus on dichotomies that need not be there. Instead, he argues that often contradictions are not exclusive, but mutually constitutive. Orlikowski (1992) coined the term 'duality of technology', with which she describes the rejection of what she sees as false dichotomies between human actions and structural properties. But overall, the two underlying theoretical framings that can be distinguished in current literature on the use of digital technology can be captured in the questions '*what* is digital technology?' and '*when* is digital technology? These questions form the basis for distinguishing between research and practice that applies an ontological-epistemology of *dualism* (the 'what' questions) from that which applies an ontological-epistemology of *duality* (the 'when' question) (Schultze & Stabell, 2004, p. 553). A dualism perspective refers to *either/or thinking* (Orlikowski, 1992). With a dualism perspective, the physical and social reality are regarded as objective, 'out there' independent of our perception, existing independently of humans. Taking a dualism perspective, the physical and social reality can only exist through human action, or at least interaction between human and non-human (Orlikowski & Baroudi, 1991). The either/or thinking associated with dualism constructs the world in terms of binaries or mutually exclusive opposites – something is either this or that, it can never be both at the same time. Digital technology, according to a dualism perspective, is thus to be understood as an objective, independent object, possibly used by (subjective) humans. In contrast, the concept of *duality* resists the construction of (false) dichotomies such as subjective-objective, macro-micro, self-other binaries and categories (Schultze & Stabell, 2004; Bowker & Star, 1999; Orlikowski & Baroudi, 1991). Duality implies *both/and thinking* which 'implies a dialectic yet integrative strategy … and is associated with pragmatism and theories of practice. Theories characterized by duality are associated with emergence and cyclical causality rather than uni-directional' (Schultze & Stabell, 2004, p. 553). Applying such a 'socio-material' understanding of digital technology, means that digital technology can only continuously become digital technology when used by human subjects. Moreover, digital technology also affects how human action is enacted – digital technology and human action can thus not be understood as separate entities, but should be regarded as socio-material assemblages (Introna, 2013). Theories based in a duality perspective would appreciate paradoxes and contradictions as they would enable to explain how different forces at the same time affect the phenomenon, whereas when based in a dualism perspective this would require further investigation until it can be decided into which (binary) category a phenomenon would fit – hence, it would rely on the interpretation of the researcher eventually. Furthermore, theories embedded in a dualism perspective would frame (the increased use of) digital technology as a phenomenon frozen in time, and as having a separate identity from, for example, organizational change – another phenomenon. A duality perspective would emphasize how digital technology is continuously shaped and being shaped by situated practice – what is digital technology is

Table 2.1   Dualism versus duality

	Dualism	Duality
Theoretical frame	Either/or Taxonomies, contingency models	Both/and Stucturational models, theories of practice, pragmatism
Fundamental research question	What is the phenomenon?	When is the phenomenon?
Framing of research phenomenon	Object is frozen in time; phenomena have a separate identity	Object is continuously shaping and being shaped by situated practice; phenomena are mutually constitutive
Assumptions about causality	Uni-directional Deterministic	Cyclical, circulating Emergent
Assumption about the world	Finite Completely knowable	Infinite within parameters (i.e., constantly changing yet staying the same) Not completely knowable
Ability to handle paradox/contradictions	Contradictions do not exist; they are merely a sign that taxonomies and contingency models are not sufficiently granular	Embraces contradiction and paradox; considers opposing forces operating simultaneously

Source: Reprinted from Schultze and Stabell (2004, p. 554).

specific for that momentum in time, in that place. Also regarding 'causality', perspectives differ: a dualism point of view would explain the use of digital technology as depending on a set of (independent) variables, either or not effectively contributing to a particular goal. As such, the use of digital technology can be something that can be completely knowable. From a duality perspective, however, the focus will be on the cyclical, emergent nature of how digital technology comes about and falls out. It acknowledges the infinite number of parameters that affect how digital technology is produced and reproduced practices, and how it emerges will never be completely knowable.

A complete overview of all the characteristics of the epistemological dimension can be found in Table 2.1.

2.2   Social Order Dimension: Consensus Versus Dissensus

The second dimension as explained by Schultze and Stabell is the social order dimension. The social order dimension is based on Burrell and Morgan's framework, who made the distinction between a *sociology ruled by radical change* (dissensus) and a *sociology ruled by regulation* (consensus) (Burrell & Morgan, 1979).

Authors who lean towards the consensus end of the spectrum tend to take the current social state of the world as '[a] given and unproblematic' (Schultze & Stabell, 2004, p. 555). In the consensus perspective the world has a natural (or hegemonic) order. There is no denial of power, but power is not problematized, nor seen as the driving force behind interaction. Researchers and practitioners who (unconsciously) adopt the sociology of regulation usually accept existing structures, such as the division of labour, as given and unproblematic (Schultze & Stabell, 2004). Here, researcher and practitioner approaches would be in line with the dominant social order, meaning the dominant ways of structuring knowledge, social relations and identities (Schultze & Leidner, 2002). An example of this perspective in relation to digital technology would be a study or project that aims to seek a particular equilibrium, a desired state of a digital technology being used in an organization and would see achieving this state as natural and even necessary. Stakeholders' interests would overlap and the leadership of the project would be taken by the dominant party, with *trust* being the underlying assumption, because all stakeholders having a common interest in what the use of digital technology is about and what it should provide, for all.

On the *dissensus* end of the spectrum, authors consider the world as being in a constant state of conflict, with forces of coercion and change continuously challenging the established social order. Because in the dissensus perspective everything is political, there is no such thing as a natural order. Even if there was order somewhere, it would constantly be challenged and changed through various mechanisms. Within the dissensus view, it is often the case that there are groups struggling for power, and power is seen as an explanation for interaction. Applied to digital technology, a dissensus perspective would be characterized by perceiving the use of digital technology as a playing ground for power struggles, where tensions – for example, related to possession of access to data or computing power – would be the natural state. Additionally, from a dissensus point of view, digital technology assumes that digital technology is multiple, conflicting (e.g., with other identities) and fragmented. A complete overview of all of the characteristics of the social order dimension can be found in Table 2.2.

Table 2.2   Consensus versus dissensus

	Consensus	Dissensus
Assumptions about social relations	Trust Common interest	Suspicion Conflict of interest
Assumptions about social world	Hegemonic order as natural state	Conflict over order as natural state
Assumptions about the social role of knowledge	Science/knowledge is neutral; present order is naturalized	Science/knowledge is political; present order is historized and politicized

Source: Reprinted from Schultze and Stabell (2004, p. 555).

3.   FOUR DISCURSIVE PERSPECTIVES ON THE USE OF DIGITAL TECHNOLOGY

3.1   The Normative Discourse: Digital Technology as Asset and Means

The normative discourse on the use of digital technology in and between organizations reflects that of modernity with its assumptions of progressive enlightenment as well as increasing rationalization, management and control (Schultze & Leidner, 2002). Here, terms such as *'digital transformation'* are often used, referring to 'a process that aims to improve an entity by triggering significant changes to its properties through combinations of information, computing, communication, and connectivity technologies' (Vial, 2019, p. 118). Digital technology is then regarded as the collection and interpretation of massive, high-volume data sets, combined with fast computing power that monitors a variety of digital streams – e.g., sensors, digital marketplace interactions and social information exchange, as well as process tracing data or meta data retrieved from (work) processes (Davenport, 2014; Kitchin, 2014). What is added to the definition of digital transformation is that digital technology is 'to improve an entity by triggering significant changes'. What exactly 'improve' or 'significant' entails is not defined. Nevertheless, the phenomenon of digital transformation is regarded as a positive, inevitable development, as is the beneficial effect of big data for organizations (Stevens et al., 2018). The underlying epistemological assumptions are based in a *dualism* and *consensus* worldview. In the normative discourse, for example, researchers and practitioners implicitly or explicitly consider digital tecnology as a 'thing' to be governed by humans. For example, the data that is gathered by organizations exists independently of these organizations (as separate objects) and is considered to be a representation of the truth. Authors in the normative discourse often use words like 'data mining' as an activity one can perform to obtain the 'raw material' that data represent. For example, Liao and Tasi (2019) discuss using big data as a method to redesign retail store layouts. They write: 'The availability of massive amounts of data provides unprecedented opportunities for organizations' (p. 1784). Liao and Tasi implicitly assume that big data is out there to be used by whomever wants to use it. As with many authors using a normative discourse, the availability of data is taken for granted – almost as if it was an object waiting to be used; nor is it problematized or even discussed how data was retrieved or produced. Other terms in this vein of discourse are 'capturing' and 'harvesting' data, where data is perceived as fuel for digital technology, in which big data is analysed based on techniques such as pattern recognition, data mining and machine learning (Stevens et al., 2018). The idea is that it will illuminate managers and decision makers in organizations to make best use of data and often focus on predefined or innovative ways for how to do so, for example, by providing new analytical techniques. Brynjolffson and McAfee (2012) write that: 'the big data of this revolution is far more powerful than the analytics that were used in the past. We can measure and therefore manage more precisely than ever before. We can make better predictions and smarter decisions' (p. 62). This quote illustrates yet another characteristic of the normative discourse: its projection of a better future due to the use of digital technology. The emphasis is always discursively laid upon the end result, namely 'a solution' which provides benefit for all stakeholders. The 'lessons learned' during the process are expected to trigger new, often more focused business questions, and subsequent data mining processes will benefit from the experiences of previous ones. Eventually, the idea is that some form of advantage will be achieved through some form of digital transformation. Nascimento, Oliveira and Tam (2018), for example, illustrate by arguing that:

> Wearable technology and especially smartwatch technology, are exciting new technologies to be investigated because they allow for the continuous and reliable collection of data (Rawassizadeh et al,, 2015) and the augmentation of human abilities and capabilities. (Starner, 2001; p. 157)

This fragment is also an example of a consensus worldview on what digital technology can bring, in which big data is 'harvested' through digital, wearable technology, all associated with positive adjectives such as 'exciting', 'reliable' and 'augmentation'. Such – often not empirically proven – use of wording and (often) sweeping statements is typical to be used by scholars and practitioners using a normative discourse. Not only organizational competitive advantage is attributable to digital transformation, but so too is overall economic growth (McAfee & Brynjolfsson, 2016) and other public goods, such as improved, more efficient, effective and safer and therefore less costly provision of health care (e.g., Noffsinger & Chin, 2000). In a similar vein, digital transformation is often portrayed as a crucial facilitator in inducing a much-needed transition towards fair and sustainable energy futures (Blue, Shove & Forman, 2020). These grand promises and positivistic rhetoric are typical for a normative discourse on digital technology. The focus is not so much on the accuracy or evidence-based outcomes of scientific studies, but mostly on what digital technology – through vague processes such as digital transformation, as if logically and automatically – can do for humanity.

This is not to say that normative-based publications are always blind to some of the risks associated with digital technology, and associated risks such as decreased privacy or so called 'black-box decisions' due to the reliance on algorithms in decision support. They seem to be aware of the existence of other discourses in that respect. For example, Hajli et al. (2020) write: 'Privacy concerns can engender a breach of trust or even cause financial harm to people whose data are harvested in their encounters with organizations seeking a competitive advantage in the market' (p. 1). But instead of problematizing the power imbalance between those whose data are harvested and those who harvest that data, privacy concerns are presented as a common interest. For example, stakeholders' possibly opposing goals, namely customers' privacy and the company's aim to maximize profit, are married in the rhetoric that the retention of customers (or attracting new ones) in a digital age can only happen through safeguarding their privacy (Hajli et al., 2020). Such an argument circumvents obvious contradictory goals, as safeguarding privacy will ultimately lead to less (potential) client information, and, hence, the possibility to analyse and predict customer behavior (Zuboff, 2019). Or consider the story that *The New York Times* magazine did on Target and its success in identifying women who are pregnant in order to take advantage of the opportunity to change purchasing habits (Dean, 2014). Dean refers to a relatively well-known story about Target, which identified pregnant customers in order to send them coupons for baby-related products (Hill, 2012). Dean calls their efforts a success. What he left out is the part where this led to a father discovering his teenage daughter's pregnancy (Hill, 2012).

3.1.1   Example from practice

Digital technology, according to a normative discourse in practice, is much focused on obtaining or getting access to data, to then – with an instrumentalist approach – reap as much benefit from it, ideally according to a somewhat orderly, chronological stepwise procedure. The most famous example of this is IBM's CRISP-DM method – the cross-industry standardized process for data mining (as depicted in Figure 2.1).

Although the sequence of the phases in the CRISP-DM method is claimed not to be strict and moving back and forth between different phases is usually required, it does provide somewhat of a stepwise procedure for how to manage

Source: Retrieved from https://www.datascience-pm.com/crisp-dm-2/ (4 April 2023).

Figure 2.1   *CRISP-DM cycle*

and control data mining activities. As shown in Figure 2.1, a data mining process continues after a solution has been deployed.

CRISP-DM is a method supported by software for data mining developed by IBM, in collaboration with others. SPSS Modeler, for example, can be purchased and downloaded, offering a gateway into a stepwise guidance by the IBM website, all aiming to support their clients with (big) data analysis and data mining techniques that can help them improve their business outcomes. The CRISP-DM process is not only a somewhat chronological, linear approach to data mining, but so too regarding the organizational change processes that go along with that, as can be distilled from the text retrieved from IBM's website (see Box 2.1).

BOX 2.1   CRISP-DM: BUSINESS UNDERSTANDING OVERVIEW

Even before working in IBM® SPSS® Modeler, you should take the time to explore what your organization expects to gain from data mining. Try to involve as many key people as possible in these discussions and document the results. The final step of this CRISP-DM phase discusses how to produce a project plan using the information gathered here.

Although this research may seem dispensable, it's not. Getting to know the business reasons for your data mining effort helps to ensure that everyone is on the same page before expending valuable resources.

Source: Website text retrieved from https://www.ibm.com/docs/en/spss-modeler/18.2.0?topic= understanding-business-overview (2 August 2022).

3.2   The Interpretivist/constructivist Discourse: Digital Technology as Socio-material Practice

The constructivist discourse is defined by its duality and consensus-based worldview. This implies a basic understanding of data as a both/and relationship between material (data and technology) and humans. Authors relying on a constructivist discourse see big data and related digital technology as having 'agency', as it both shapes society and is being shaped by society simultaneously. Contrary to a normative discourse, authors using a constructivist discourse take what is defined as data less as a representative object 'out there', but they acknowledge the role of human interpretation and action in it, and thus, for example, regard 'data collection' as an iterative process, sensitive to the fact that someone decided to collect data and the reasons behind this collection, often referred to as the 'situatedness' of data collection. Constructivist authors are sensitive to the inherent limitations that come with collecting data, such as systemic biases. Big data as a part of digital technology is seen as social phenomenon, as a practice, meaning that it is not solely the act of collecting and analysing data, but includes related practices such as analytical skill training, societal expectations, regulation, et cetera. This also places more weight on what is actually being done with digital technology, and how that is used to attribute meaning. Concepts that are more frequently used in this discourse are *digitalization*, referring to the ways in which social life is organized through and around digital technologies (Leonardi & Treem, 2020). The emphasis is very much on increasing our understanding of how organizational and societal practices are enacted (differently) through digital technology.

One of the examples of an author writing on the duality perspective is Wielki (2015). He considers big data a phenomenon and not a thing: 'Despite Big Data being quite a recent phenomenon, there are numerous examples of organizations effectively utilizing the possibilities connected with it' (p. 195). Wielki highlights how big data – as an integral part of digital technology – influences society and vice versa, but also admits that it involves 'challenges' to actually benefit from it. Typical for the interpretative discourse is to 'zoom out' and try to understand the phenomenon of digital technology as an interplay between human intentions (agency) and material affordances or constraints (material agency). A particular strand of researchers that adhere to this approach, often referred to as 'sociomateriality', particularly focus on how material forms and spaces through which humans act and interact have explanatory value in how organizational practices are formed (e.g., Orlikowski, 2007). Leonardi (2011), for example, shows how human and material agencies interact and are imbricated. Such imbrications of human and material agencies create infrastructure in the form of routines and technologies that people use to carry out their work. In particular situations, people either perceive digital technology to constrain their ability to achieve their goal, while sometimes digital technology affords the possibility of achieving particular new goals, or existing goals, faster. Depending on such perceptions of affordance or constraint, it is either the routines that will be adjusted (when the technology is perceived to offer affordance) or the technology that is adjusted when the technology is perceived to offer constraints) (Leonardi, 2011). Other researchers, such as Barad (2007) or Introna (2013), more aligned with Orlikowski's take on matters, see technology and human as entangled material-discursive assemblages, in which what is done with and by digital technology and humans becomes enacted in particular contexts, continuously.

Within the constructivist discourse, power relations and managerial control over labour are not seen as the main driver for behaviour in organizations, nor is the use of digital technology regarded as a way to obtain more power of management over workers; nor as a way to normalize what is regarded as 'knowledge'. Digital technology, according to this view, can be seen as something that can change the world for everyone, but not necessarily to exert control over people. In that sense, the constructivist discourse belongs to a consensus-based worldview. Researchers and practitioners would like to further investigate how this is actually working out in practice, most of the time driven by curiosity and by making things work, and less so based on conflated ideas about how competitive or digital, or even public, advantages could be achieved in doing so. In a recent article on the development of AI for hiring practices, Van den Broek, Huysman and Sergeeva (2022) focused on how developers managed the tension between the AI system that needs to produce knowledge independent of domain experts (HR professionals specialized in hiring) and the need to remain relevant to the domain the AI system serves. Although AI hiring systems are developed with the claim that algorithms will produce insights superior to those of experts by discovering the objective 'truth' derived from data, their study showed that developers of the AI hiring system and experts arrived at a new hybrid practice that relied on a combination of AI and domain expertise. It thus did not replace the HR experts but became an integration of ML systems and HR experts' knowledge, resulting from a process of mutual learning in which engagement with the technology triggered HR experts to reflect on how they produce knowledge (e.g., selection of candidates).

BOX 2.2   EXAMPLE FROM PRACTICE: THE CASE OF THE 'LATEX GLOVE'

When in an emergency situation, for example, a patient in an ambulance being transported to an emergency room for treatment, patient data need to be exchanged quickly, accurately and effectively to ensure patient safety. Although digital information exchange systems are in place allowing ambulance workers to share information upfront with the hospital's emergency room, in many cases patient information is still exchanged by manually written-down notes on paper, or – as some emergency situations revealed – on the ambulance worker's latex glove that is then thrown at the patient's stretcher. Over the past 30 years, digitization of patient data has facilitated the exchange of health information between health care providers in the Netherlands. These developments are driven by the overall expectations that digital exchange of information between health care providers improves the quality, efficiency and safety of health care (Dobrow et al., 2019; OECD, 2022; Sprenger, 2020). Besides technical requirements, the exchange of (patient) data requires the health organizations to collaborate on how to exchange information in a way that is understandable and, more importantly, usable to all involved parties. This is also known as interoperability between organizations (European Commission & Directorate-General for Informatics, 2017). To become interoperable, health care organizations not only need to agree on which ICT applications to use, but also to standardize their information and the way they exchange it. However, this process of alignment concerns many stakeholders working in different contexts – albeit somewhat similar – characterized by different languages, work practices and current Health Information Systems. Getting patient data exchanged digitally has turned out to be complex and demanding for those involved (Everson, 2017; Sprenger, 2020). Moreover, even if alignment is organized and information standards are in place to exchange patient data between health providers, studies on health information exchange (HIE) practices between organizations showed that even after implementation of an HIE infrastructure (digital technology), the usage per patient was only 2.3% because of time constrains and (the lack of) perceived usability of the exchanged information (Vest et al., 2011). Recently, the Dutch Minister of Health, Welfare and Sport (HWS) presented a new bill to legally enforce the use of information standards when exchanging patient data, called the 'Electronic data exchange in healthcare' bill (in Dutch: Wet Elektronische Gegevensuitwisseling in de Zorg (Wegiz)) (Ministry of Health, Welfare and Sport, 2021). The law is designed to enforce and gradually expand the amount of mandatory information standards when the field is deemed mature enough for legal enforcement by certifying IT vendors to use the standards. However, the field is far from 'mature enough' to enforce such regulation, and little is known as to why health care providers still exchange patient data outside of HIE systems. Similarly, it is unknown why – after many financial injections – in many regions the collaborative projects to set up improved patient data exchange do not pass the point of 'pilot phase'.

What this practical case shows is that solely developing the digital technology to enable HIE practices as described above does not 'automatically' mean that this technology will be adopted, nor result in the promised improvement of efficiency, accuracy, timeliness and – eventually – lower the costs of health care in general.

Source: Retrieved from PhD research proposal Stijn Bruls, MA, August 2022.

3.3   Critical Discourse: Digital Technology to Obtain (Retain) Power

The critical discourse *discourse* is defined by having both a dualism-based and a dissensus worldview. This means that digital technology can be regarded as an 'object'. However, what characterizes the critical discourse's *discourse* view on digital technology (or big data solely) is its focus on who benefits. More specifically: the focus lies on how big data and digital technology are used by – mostly large – tech corporations to suppress or even extort others, for the sole reason of increased market share and profit maximalization. The normative rationale of 'what benefits the firm, benefits society and the individual' is rejected in the critical discourse *discourse* (Schultze & Stabell, 2004). Besides addressing how classical power struggles between capitalists and managers on the one side and employees and self-employed (nowadays often including online platform 'gig') workers on the other side are fought out in a digital age, critical discourse *discourse* literature is more likely to address concerns regarding privacy and the lack of legislation to protect consumers from unwanted ethical consequences of companies' use of digital technology.

The critical discourse *discourse* on digital technology is marginal compared to the normative discourse – both in the number of articles that can be found in academic journals and in the number of newspaper and social media articles written on it. Here, the term 'dataveillance' (Van Dijck, 2014) is often used, signalling the role of those who have access to big data who carefully analyse, interpret and then intervene in its producer's life, mostly for the benefit of those already in power. One researcher who recently introduced a typical critical discourse *discourse* concept 'surveillance capitalism' is Shoshana Zuboff (2019). She addresses the disruptiveness of digital innovations based on big data harvesting and big data analytics as it changes power relations. She defines surveillance capitalism as: '1. A new economic order that claims human experience as free raw material for hidden commercial practices of extraction, prediction, and sales', but also as '2. A parasitic economic logic in which the production of goods and services is subordinated to a new global architecture of behavioral modification. Surveillance capitalism relies on hidden operations intentionally designed to bypass "users" awareness' (Zuboff, 2019, p. 39). These operations begin with the harvesting of the online behaviour data of people drawn from online browsing, searching and social media behaviour, referred to by Zuboff (2019) as 'behavioral surplus'. These operations now, but in the future even more, encompass every movement, conversation, facial expression, sound, text and image that is, or can be, accessible to the always-on ubiquitous internet-enabled digital extraction architecture that she calls the Big Other (although she mostly points to Big Tech companies, particularly Google, that form this Big Other). Based on this data, predictions on our future behaviours are calculated by algorithms. These predictions are then offered on the market, turning these into 'behavioral future markets'. Surveillance capitalists have grown immensely wealthy from these trading operations, which in turn have led to further imbalanced markets and thus economies and societies (Zuboff, 2019).

The critical discourse *discourse* is often used in tandem with a dialogic discourse, as the ways in which Big Tech companies, for example, obtain power with access to digital expertise and technology is accomplished partly by surveillance mechanisms also argued in the dialectic discourse, on which more in the next section. Already a while back, Smith and Tabak in 2009 discussed how employers monitor their employees' e-mail and refer to it as a form of 'privacy violation' (p. 37). They continue by stating: 'In spite of this legal vacuum, courts have consistently supported the rights of employers to monitor employee e-mails' (p. 34). In this fragment, the monitoring of employee e-mails (i.e., collecting their data) is seen as an activity that someone can perform to obtain the data that is expected to be in those e-mails. Here, employees' e-mail data (either the content of those e-mails and/or the meta-data on e-mail exchanges, time spent in e-mail application, et cetera) is perceived as being an accurate representation of what employees do with regard to their e-mail. This illustrates the dualism perspective, where the context and human interpretation of such data is pushed to the background. Smith and Tabak (2009), for example, explain that such e-mail monitoring may lead to short-term productivity gains (as was expected to be the goal of managers); decision makers need to take into account longer-term effects of turnover and performance declines resulting from increased negative work attitudes as well as individual forms of resistance.

As can be derived from the work from Smith and Tabak already more than 15 years ago, critical researchers discussing digital transformation often address the further problematized labour relations between capitalists and workers. This addresses how digital technology has transformed where people work, when and how. Moore, Upchurch and Whittaker (2018) in their book *Humans and Machines at Work* explain how digital transformation, overall, is detrimental for employees, despite how organizations – using a normative discourse – introduce these technologies to their workers. 'Accelerometers, Bluetooth, triangulation algorithms and infrared sensors allow managers to monitor workers far beyond traditional hours logged by swipe cards in the current era. Call-centre data reporting has long been used to view workers' emotional responses to customers but the types of monitoring and tracking this book outlines, take things a step further.' These new technologies reflect 'significant changes in management patterns and workplaces'. (p. 9). What this short synopsis of the current digital technological trends applied in the workplace highlights is mostly how – from a critical perspective – digital transformation is based in capitalist, neoliberalist convictions regarding how business models can create profit, however, at the expense of those not in power: employees and workers whose toilet breaks are clocked and timed, and working conditions not protected against violence and distress.

BOX 2.3   AMAZON WAREHOUSE AND THEIR 'HUMAN ROBOTS'

Many online (newspaper) articles from a critical vein are concerned with how big tech companies such as Apple, Microsoft, Alphabet (Google), Amazon and Meta Platforms (Facebook) gain too much power, and world leaders are nearly unanimous in their belief that new regulatory mechanisms are needed to contain the tech giants (Swabey and Harraca, 29 July

2022, retrieved from: https://techmonitor.ai/policy/big-tech/power-of-tech
-companies). These companies have economic power due to their digital
technological expertise, but also – based on that – 'platform power'. Big
tech companies almost all have a platform business model, meaning that
they connect suppliers to consumers, whether it is connecting advertisers to
social network or search engine users, app developers to device owners, or
vendors to online shoppers. Platform business models benefit from network
effects – the more customers you acquire, the more appealing you are to
suppliers (Swabey & Harraca, 29 July 2022). However, this 'platform power' comes with a price, often paid by low-paid employees working to make
these 'matches' on a platform become tangible exchanges of products and
services. In 2020, Amazon was scrutinized by its (former) employees and
labor unions which approached the media to condemn the unsafe and gruel-
ling working conditions at Amazon's warehouses (*The Guardian*, 5 February
2020, retrieved from: https://www.theguardian.com/technology/2020/
feb/05/amazon-workers-protest-unsafe-grueling-conditions-warehouse).
Besides the unsafe conditions at conveyor belts, digital technology in the
form of wearable trace technology allowed Amazon to track its employees'
performance, and set strict targets for the number of packages packed per
hour. As one former worker stated in *The Guardian*'s article: 'I was a picker
and we were expected to always pick 400 units within the hour in seven
seconds of each item we picked. I couldn't handle it. I'm a human being,
not a robot.'

3.3.1   Example from practice: the case of the power of Big Tech at the expense of workers

In line with dualism, 'this OR that' thinking, critical discourse *discourse*
perceives power gained from control over access to (big) data and digital
technology, and related knowledge (as resource) as something an actor either
has, or not. Complementary to long-existing human-to-human surveillance
modalities, some organizations, particularly 'gig economy platforms' such as
Deliveroo and Uber, are adopting an emerging form of 'algorithmic surveillance', where monitoring, assessment and managerial tasks are conducted by
algorithms (Newlands, 2021). Individual users thus become established by
social media, instead of them being perceived as complex, flesh-and-blood
individuals, and business and management practices further build upon these
unsettling underlying phenomena. Pastuh and Geppert (2020) illustrate how
Uber is based on 'circuits of power', in which 'algorithmic control' has
replaced middle management, dictating when drivers (legally self-employed
subcontractors but strongly resembling employees) are to ride to which places,

meanwhile putting assessing the quality of their services at the mercy of online customer reviews. However, such underlying surveillance mechanisms in which platform user data is used to continuously adjust what is offered and presented to customers online also resonates with the concerns of the dialectic discourse, as we will discuss below.

3.4   Dialogic Discourse: Digital Technology as a Means for Discipline

Finally, the dialogic discourse sits on the duality side of the ontological/epistemological dimension and – in this framework – the dissensus end of the social order dimension. For example, regarding (big) data, researchers would highlight the situatedness of data collection, as is illustrated in the following quote from Jones (2019).

> There are no 'isolated pieces of simple facts' unless someone has created them using his or her knowledge … [R]ather than being the raw material of information, data are created from information and this information is itself shaped by a body of knowledge held by a particular thought community … 'data are always already "cooked" and never entirely "raw"'. (p. 7)

As the reference to 'a particular thought community' shows, what is considered data, information or knowledge is for dialogic researchers continuously created, broken down and recreated by the temporary dominant thought community. This dominant thought community has a disciplinary nature: it prescribes what is considered to be information and knowledge embedded in and derived from material-discursive practices that is often normalized; meaning: not contested, until contested. It therefore denies the existence of digital technology, of which data is an integral part, as an object or clear-cut process, yet embraces contradictions and apparent paradoxes embedded within digital technology, and the use of it. In a sense, digitalization is regarded as an ongoing organizational (or institutional) dialectic change process. Such a process perceives a change process as one in which there is a thesis (digital transformation is X) and an anti-thesis (digital transformation is not X) which between actors results in conflict. After a while this conflict is temporarily settled (periods in which what is considered 'digital technology' or 'digitalization' is not disputed and taken for granted) until particular marginalized groups by such normalized knowledge claims contest the underlying norms and values, which then triggers a new thesis – anti-thesis situation, resulting yet again in conflict (Van de Ven & Poole, 1995). As do constructivists, so do authors in the dialogic discourse assign agency to (big) data and digital technology, and human and material artefacts cannot be understood apart from each other. In that sense, the dialogic perspectives often share a socio-material, discursive and practice-oriented approach. However, contrary to a constructivist discourse, dialectic discourse takes power struggles over how knowledge regarding digital technology is produced and reproduced into account, stressing how the use of digital technology is continuously being normalized and simultaneously contested and particularly how digital technology as a means for disciplining plays in this. For example, consider the discussion on the value of big data as discussed by Leicht-Deobald et al. (2019). In their publication about algorithm-based HR decision making (making decisions with 'algorithms designed to support and govern HR decisions' (Leicht-Deobald et al., 2019, p. 378)) they write:

> the recent technological changes around big data are accompanied by an 'ideology of dataism,' emphasizing a belief in the 'objective quantification and potential tracking of all kinds of human behaviour'. (p. 384)

In this fragment, the authors distance themselves from the idea that big data provides nothing but value. 'Dataism' is indeed an example of a typical dialogic discourse concept. Dataism can loosely be explained as the unconditional belief that data has the capability to show the one and only truth (Van Dijck, 2014). Instead, they antagonistically contest this normalized, dominant idea and refer to it as 'ideology of dataism'.

Furthermore, the dialogic perspective moves beyond who does/does not have access to data and digital technology (as does the critical perspective), but – based on Foucault's explanation of the 'technologies of the self' (Foucault, 1987) – it emphasizes how the use of digital technology allows for a form of surveillance, resulting in people becoming *subjectified*. That is, individuals are presented with an image of themselves, for example, based on feedback from a digital, wearable device (e.g., Strava), which allows them to create and recreate a particular identity ('I am a runner') which then becomes the basis of their self-knowledge. The latter then provides the basis for individuals to modify or change their behaviour ('I need to run more laps per week in order to become a better runner') (Townley, 1996). Through the process of digitalization individuals become prompted for self-reflection, avowal and confession (Schultze & Stabell, 2004). As innocent as this might seem, digital technology reinforces how people – especially young adults – act on themselves to achieve transformations that align them with notions of what it means to be 'normal', 'good' or 'beautiful' to such an extent that it has unhealthy consequences (e.g., Fardouly & Vartanian, 2016). The emphasis here is on how through the use of big data and digital technology, particular – often hidden – mechanisms of self-*disciplining* are (re)produced. But also in an organizational context, researchers in this discourse are concerned how the constant data-driven work and associated accountability practices, combined with digital surveillance techniques, discipline the way in which people work. A recent study by Pachidi et al. (2021) showed how a regime-of-knowing in a sales organization radically changed despite initial resistance towards big data analytics as a base for understanding client behaviour. Through digitalization, the sales organization's regime of knowing moved from one focused on a deep understanding of customers via personal contact and strong relationships to one based on model predictions from the processing of large data sets.

The example given in Box 2.4 stems from a Master's student's thesis on the topic 'data-driven strategizing', which was conducted at the 'Energy Systems business area' of an international consultancy firm that we will here call 'The Transition Company' (TTC, pseudonym).

BOX 2.4 EXAMPLE FROM PRACTICE: AN ENERGY CONSULTANCY FIRM USING CUSTOMER BEHAVIOURAL SURPLUS

TTC aims to support its customers to transition faster to a decarbonized and more sustainable energy future by assuring that energy systems work safely and effectively. At the heart of the business strategy lies a customer-centric approach, meaning that Energy Systems strives to optimize customer satisfaction by continually delivering superior customer experience in a proactive and responsive manner. The Marketing, Communications and Public Affairs (MCP) function is responsible for contributing to this superior customer experience and does so in part by generating leads and proactively sensing and responding to customer needs. To this end, a new data-driven performance management system was implemented, through which (big) customer and marketing data could be collected, analysed and presented to proactively enable more informed customer-centric strategizing. This case study illustrated how big data is pivotal in strategizing nowadays, and how TTC and its employees actually integrated big data into strategizing practices. As the study of Pachidi et al. (2021) above already indicated, the MCP department of TTC had similar struggles between management and employees in terms of what was considered to be reliable, truthful representations of customers' interests regarding their products and services. What the study revealed, however, was not only how a new regime of knowing was created, which partly or potentially replaced traditional knowledge on customers based on long-standing relationships and personal contact, but also how data analytics on customers' online behaviour became useful as evaluation and accountability instruments. For example, particular PR events were evaluated based on online reviews and comments in social media, which speeded up the evaluation process and strategic decision making on which events to continue with and which to abolish. Additionally, outcomes of data analytics were connected to individual performance indicators, which then triggered employees to flag many activities as possible leads in order for them to boost their performances in the management information system. The researcher, together with the department head and subordinate managers, concluded that data-driven strategizing is not simply a matter of only relying on the online available customer behavioural surplus data and adapting all strategizing practices to it. Instead, it is a continuous interplay of evaluating the possibilities and risks (e.g., privacy breaches) of relying on customer data, in which counter-effects such as employees' instrumental behaviour or loss of contextual information on customers had to be brought back into strategic decision-making processes.

Source: From '(big) Data in, decisions out? How big data affects strategizing practices', Master's thesis, Tim Dekker, July 2022

What this example shows is that customer data and surveillance mechanisms, redefining what is considered valuable and truthful knowledge, can be used for capitalist purposes, but also offer ways to support a more general, public purpose, which is to help organizations to become more sustainable regarding their energy usage. For those producing a dialectic discourse, however, the concern will be mostly focused on through which mechanisms knowledge claims are constructed and how transparent the underlying mechanisms are, allowing these knowledge claims to be disputed; and to what extent digital technologies create (self-)disciplining mechanisms, which can be detrimental for the needed transparency.

4.   DISCUSSION

Figure 2.2 summarizes the four discourses on digital technology, as can be distilled from academic literature and discourse used by practitioners.

As already mentioned in the introduction, in distinguishing discourses on digital technology by their underlying ontological/epistemological assumptions and views on how social order is produced, we reveal how contradictions between the core arguments in common talk and critique on digital technology often stem from fundamental contradictions in how the world is understood and explained. Secondly, yet stemming from the first argument, laying bare such underlying contradictions could help both researchers and practitioners to understand counter-arguments other than those commonly used in the discourse they rely on themselves. What is seen as a possible solution from a normative perspective could be a further deepening of current power imbalances

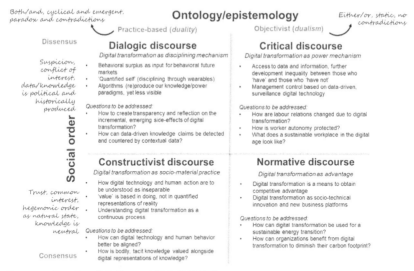

Source: Based on Schultze and Stabell (2004).

Figure 2.2   Overview of four discourses on digital technology

according to a colleague adhering to a critical perspective. Understanding the root rationale behind these perspectives could support necessary discussions between those in favour and those against the increased use of digital technology, in the workplace and in society at large. Such discussions are much needed, as none of the discourses should become the dominant perspective as they all bring valuable points to the fore. Simply perceiving arguments belonging to another discourse as 'resistance' to digital transformation does not allow for the development of a sustainable way in which digital technology is (re)enacted.

This brings us to some concluding reflections. What would a sustainable way of relating with digital technology then be? Although the answer to this question is of course dependent on which perspective and discourse you take, we would like to reflect here based on personal experience and inspired by all discourses on digital technology. For us, a sustainable use of digital technology incorporates two crucial elements: *social responsibility* and *energy reduction/ climate preservation*. With social responsibility regarding the development and use of digital technology, we aim to address both ethical and moral values. Moral and ethical values such as privacy, autonomy, equality are inherently related to many of the Sustainable Development Goals (SDGs). In line with the constructivist and dialectic perspective, we perceive digitalization as how digital technology is embedded in our (organizational and private) doing. In so doing, these technologies can emergently alter existing values regarding workers' autonomy, and meaningfulness of work, and privacy, but also regarding our public values such as security, justice and freedom (see iHub – Radboud's interdisciplinary research hub on digitalization and society – for more on these topics at: iHub – Home (ru.nl)). Sustainable digital transformation – to give future developments regarding digital technology a name – in terms of social responsibility,, for example do not only focus on whether robots will further automate and replace (both low- and high-skilled) work, but also on how workers retain autonomy over what they perceive as the right thing to do (for which they feel responsible), despite data-driven, networked digital surveillance and accountability mechanisms that currently gain traction in organizations (Pas et al., 2023). In a similar vein, sustainable digital transformation incorporates concerns and solutions for how unwanted side-effects of digital technology, such as filter bubbles and fake news, reshape the political field (Bozdag & Van den Hoven, 2015) or allow for a 'Googlization of health' (the phenomenon of big tech companies entering the domain of health care based on their retrieved data) (Sharon, 2016). Social responsibility regarding the use of digital technology includes critical reflections on the widespread reliance on underpaid workers used to train AI models (Crawford, 2021) and the detrimental effects on our economy and society due to the rise of a platform-based 'gig economy' (Fleming, Rhodes & Yu, 2019). This evidently includes the need for more regulatory control and policy frameworks. This is not to reject or ignore all the examples that evidently contributed to SDG goals – the use of digital technology has and will continue to provide solutions and treatments in health care, in our energy consumption, and improved education. However, what is needed is an eye for the unforeseen, unanticipated side-effects that could worsen precisely what digital technology was designed to solve. If, for example, only particular groups of children in elementary school have access to the benefits of AI in school, it will only increase inequality.

The second element of our definition of a sustainable digital transformation requires a specific but much-needed reversing of the environmental costs of AI, which is often the underlying technology on which promises of digital transformation are based (Crawford, 2021). What remains hidden from our common knowledge about the use of digital technology is the exceptionally high energy consumption of the current large computational models, energy used to store data (which is often never to be used again) and the carbon footprint of building and operating modern tensor processing hardware (Crawford, 2021; Strubell, Ganesh & McCallum, 2019). Despite FAIR (Findable, Accessible, Interoperable, Reuseable) principles regarding data becoming a well-known phenomenon, in practice, making data 'fair' is not as easy as it seems (RDA FAIR Data Maturity Model Working Group, 2020). Unfortunately, many of the instances in which digital technology did not manage to substantiate its promises are attributed to the resistance of human agents assigned to work with digital technology (e.g., Heath & Porter, 2019). Although it is only human nature to perhaps resist change at first, in many situations it is not resistance but the complexity of real life that make it impossible to 'reap the benefits for digital technology'.

5. CONCLUSION

What can managers, advisors, consultants and government institutions take from this, other than recognizing the different discourses in our framework that they too often use or encounter themselves when discussing the next 'digital transformation' project or implementation of digital technology in their organization? Based on our own experiences stemming from research but also as a leader of digital transformation-related programmes on our campus, one of the biggest hurdles to progress in the sustainable use of digital technology is the dominance and taken-for-granted-ness of the neofunctionalist discourse, combined with digital technology illiterateness. The complexity and rapid development of digital technology leave many executive boards clueless in terms of which development to invest in, how to assign resources and where to find the people who know what digital technology can do for their organization. Digital technology creates FOMO – the fear of missing an opportunity, followed by huge investments of which the return on investment (ROI) is hard to define. This is the playing field of ICT consultants, software developers and those in possession of data storage and computing facilities. Sustainable use of digital technology starts with acknowledging our inadequate knowledge of what digital technology is and what it does – intended and unintended. This is followed by an effort and willingness to (facilitate to) learn and understand the terms used, as all discourses have different terms and connotations, and without having to agree, knowing that what is actually meant is a basic need in all developments. Consultants should not sell organizations the most fancy digital technology if that organization is not ready or suited to implement these technologies, but instead help to start from where it is at. Paradoxically, the organizations that use the most sweeping rhetoric regarding what digital technology will bring them in terms of efficiency, effectiveness, productivity, value creation, et cetera, become deadlocked the quickest as each attempt to implement will crumble once it meets the complexity of reality. Each failed attempt reduces people's expectations regarding what the next attempt will achieve, and hence, the positivistic, non-realistic discourse on digital technology will indeed create its own resistance. To put it in line with the title of this book, to (re)create a sustainable future economy, digital technology as a means should be handled with great care so as not to create more problems than it aims to solve. We hope that this chapter offers the first step in how to do this, by addressing the pivotal role of discourses we use when we talk about digital technology as a means to create our future economy.

REFERENCES

Barad, K. (2007). *Meeting the universe halfway: Quantum physics and the entanglement of matter and meaning.* Duke University Press.

Batistič, S. & van der Laken, P. (2019). History, evolution and future of big data and analytics: A bibliometric analysis of its relationship to performance in organizations. *British Journal of Management, 30*(2), 229–251.

Beer, D. (2016). How should we do the history of Big Data? *Big Data & Society, 3*(1), 1–10.

Berkmortel, J. van den. (2021). *Talking about Big Data: Making sense of big confusion.* Master thesis Business Administration, Organizational Design & Development.

Blue, S., Shove, E. & Forman, P. (2020). Conceptualising flexibility: Challenging representations of time and society in the energy sector. *Time & Society, 29*(4), 923–944.

Bowker, G. & Star, S. L. (1999). Sorting things out. *Classification and its Consequences,* 4.

Bozdag, E. & Van den Hoven, J. (2015). Breaking the filter bubble: Democracy and design. *Ethics and Information Technology, 17*(4), 249–265.

Brynjolfsson, E. & McAfee, A. (2012). *Race against the machine: How the digital revolution is accelerating innovation, driving productivity, and irreversibly transforming employment and the economy.* Digital Frontier Press.

Burrell, G. & Morgan, G. (1979). *Sociological paradigms and organisational analysis.* Heinemann.

Crawford, K. (2021). *The atlas of AI: Power, politics, and the planetary costs of artificial intelligence.* Yale University Press.

Davenport, T. (2014). *Big data at work: Dispelling the myths, uncovering the opportunities.* Harvard Business Review Press.

Dean, A. (2014). *Big data, data mining and machine learning.* John Wiley & Sons, Inc.

Deetz, S. (1996). Crossroads – describing differences in approaches to organization science: Rethinking Burrell and Morgan and their legacy. *Organization Science, 7*(2), 191–207.

Dobrow, S. R., Weisman, H., Heller, D. & Tosti-Kharas, J. (2019, July). Calling attention to 20 years of research: A comprehensive meta-analysis of calling. In *Academy of Management Proceedings, 2019*(1), 12789. Academy of Management.

European Commission & Directorate-General for Informatics. (2017). Annual Activity Report 2017. Brussels, Belgium.

Everson, K. C. (2017). Value-added modeling and educational accountability: Are we answering the real questions? *Review of Educational Research, 87*(1), 35–70.

Fardouly, J. & Vartanian, L. R. (2016). Social media and body image concerns: Current research and future directions. *Current Opinion in Psychology, 9*, 1–5.

Fleming, P., Rhodes, C. & Yu, K. H. (2019). On why Uber has not taken over the world. *Economy and Society, 48*(4), 488–509.

Foucault, M. (1987). The ethic of care for the self as a practice of freedom: an interview with Michel Foucault on January 20, 1984. Raúl Fornet-Batancourt, Helmut Becker, Alfredo Gomez Müller and J. D. Gauthier. In *Philosophy & Social Criticism, 12*(2–3), 112–131.

Giddens, A. (1976). *New rules of sociological method*. Hutchinson. 2nd edition, 1993, Cambridge: Polity.

Hajli, N., Shirazi, F., Tajvidi, M. & Huda, N. (2020). Towards an understanding of privacy management architecture in big data: An experimental research. *British Journal of Management, 00*, 1–18.

Heath, M. & Porter, T. (2019). Sensemaking through a storytelling lens: Physician perspectives of health information exchange. *Qualitative Research in Organizations and Management: An International Journal, 14*(4), 428–443.

Hill, K. (2012, 16 February). *How Target figured out a teen girl was pregnant before her father did*. Retrieved from Forbes.com: https://www.forbes.com/sites/kashmirhill/2012/02/16/how-target-figured-out-a-teen-girl-was-pregnant-before-her-father-did/.

Hoekman, J. H. (2020). Privacyontwerp strategieën (Het Blauwe Boekje). Retrieved from: https://www.cs.ru.nl/~jhh/publications/pds-boekje.pdf.

Introna, L. D. (2013). Epilogue: Performativity and the becoming of sociomaterial assemblages. In F.-X. Vaujany,. & N. Mitev (eds), *Materiality and space: Organizations, artefacts and practices* (pp. 330–342). Springer.

Jones, M. (2019). What we talk about when we talk about (big) data. *Journal of Strategic Information Systems*, 3–16.

Kitchin, R. (2014). *The data revolution: Big data, open data, data infrastructures and their consequences*. Sage.

Lakoff, G. (1978). Some remarks on AI and linguistics. *Cognitive Science, 2*(3), 267–275.

Leicht-Deobald, U., Busch, T., Schank, C., Weibel, A., Schafheitle, S., Wildhaber, I. & Kasper, G. (2019). The challenges of algorithm-based HR decision-making for personal integrity. *Journal of Business Ethics*, (160), 377–392. doi:10.1007/s10551–019–04204-w.

Leonardi, P. M. (2011). When flexible routines meet flexible technologies: Affordance, constraint and the imbrication of human and material agencies. *MIS Quarterly, 35*(1), 147–167.

Leonardi, P. M. & Treem, J. W. (2020). Behavioral visibility: A new paradigm for organization studies in the age of digitization, digitalization, and datafication. *Organization Studies, 41*(12), 1601–1625.

Liao, S. H. & Tasi, Y. S. (2019). Big data analysis on the business process and management for the store layout and bundling sales. *Business Process Management Journal, 25*(7), 1783–1801.

McAfee, A. & Brynjolfsson, E. (2016). Human work in the robotic future: Policy for the age of automation. *Foreign Affairs, 95*(4), 139–150.

Ministry of Health, Welfare and Sport. (2021), Programma Wet Elektronische Gegevensuitwisseling in de Zorg. The Hague, the Netherlands.

Moore, P., Upchurch, M. & Whittaker, X. (2018). *Humans and machines at work: Monitoring, surveillance and automation in contemporary capitalism*. Palgrave Macmillan.

Nascimento, B., Oliveira, T. & Tam, C. (2018). Wearable technology: What explains continuance intention in smartwatches? *Journal of Retailing and Consumer Services, 43*, 157–169.

Newlands, G. (2021). Algorithmic surveillance in the gig economy: The organization of work through Lefebvrian conceived space. *Organization Studies, 42*(5), 719–737.

Noffsinger, R. & Chin, S. (2000). Improving the delivery of care and reducing health-care costs with the digitization of information. *Journal of Healthcare Information Management*: JHIM, *14*(2), 23–30.

OECD. (2020). OECD Digital Economy Outlook 2020. OECD Publishing, Paris. Retrieved from: https://doi.org/10.1787/bb167041-en.

OECD. (2022). *Economic outlook 2022*. Château del a Muette, France.

Orlikowski, W. J. (1992). The duality of technology: Rethinking the concept of technology in organizations. *Organization Science*, *3*(3), 398–427.

Orlikowski, W. J. (2007). Sociomaterial practices: Exploring technology at work. *Organization Studies*, *28*(9), 1435–1448.

Orlikowski, W. J. & Baroudi, J. J. (1991). Studying information technology in organizations: Research approaches and assumptions. *Information Systems Research*, *2*(1), 1–28.

Pachidi, S., Berends, H., Faraj, S. & Huysman, M. (2021). Make way for the algorithms: Symbolic actions and change in a regime of knowing. *Organization Science*, *32*(1), 18–41.

Pas, B. R., Introna, L. D., Wolters, R. & Vosselman, E. (2023). Professional responsibility in the borderlands: Facing irreconcilable accountability regimes in veterinary work. *Human Relations*, *76*(12), 1904–1939. https:// doi .org/ 10 .1177/ 00187267221120161.

Pastuh, D. & Geppert, M. (2020). A 'circuits of power'-based perspective on algorithmic management and labour in the gig economy. *Industrielle Beziehungen. Zeitschrift für Arbeit, Organisation und Management*, *27*(2), 11–12.

Raley, R. (2013). *Dataveillance and countervailance*. In L. Gitelman (ed.), *'Raw data' is an oxymoron* (pp. 121–146). The MIT Press.

RDA FAIR Data Maturity Model Working Group. (2020). FAIR Data Maturity Model: specification and guidelines. Research Data Alliance.

Schultze, U. & Leidner, D. E. (2002). Studying knowledge management in information systems research: Discourses and theoretical assumptions. *MIS Quarterly*, 213–242.

Schultze, U. & Stabell, C. (2004). Knowing what you don't know? Discourses and contradictions in knowledge management research. *Journal of Management Studies*, *41*(4), 549–573.

Sharon, T. (2016). The Googlization of health research: From disruptive innovation to disruptive ethics. *Personalized Medicine*, *13*(6), 563–574.

Smith, W. P. & Tabak, F. (2009). Monitoring employee e-mails: Is there any room for privacy? *Academy of Management Perspectives*, *23*(4), 33–48. doi:10.5465/ AMP.2009.45590139.

Sprenger, M. (2020). *Social-emotional learning and the brain: Strategies to help your students thrive*. ASCD.

Stevens, M., Wehrens, R. & De Bont, A. (2018). Conceptualizations of Big Data and their epistemological claims in healthcare: A discourse analysis. *Big Data & Society*, *5*(2), 2053951718816727.

Strubell, E., Ganesh, A. & McCallum, A. (2019). Energy and policy considerations for deep learning in NLP. arXiv preprint arXiv:1906.02243.

Townley, B. (1996). Accounting in detail: Accounting for individual performance. *Critical Perspectives on Accounting*, *7*(5), 565–584.

Van de Ven, A. H. & Poole, M. S. (1995). Explaining development and change in organizations. *Academy of Management Review*, *20*(3), 510–540.

Van Den Broek, E., Huysman, M. & Sergeeva, A. (2022). Fairness in flux: The role of algorithms in reconfiguring moral values. In *Academy of Management Proceedings, 2022*. Academy of Management.

Van Dijck, J. (2014). Datafication, dataism and dataveillance: Big Data between scientific paradigm and ideology. *Surveillance & Society 12*(2), 197–208.

Vest, J. R., Zhao, H., Jaspserson, J., Gamm, L. D. & Ohsfeldt, R. L. (2011). Factors motivating and affecting health information exchange usage. *Journal of the American Medical Informatics Association, 18*(2), 143–149.

Vial, S. (2019). *Being and the screen: How the digital changes perception.* Published in one volume with *A short treatise on design.* The MIT Press.

Wielki, J. (2015). The social and ethical challenges connected with the Big Data phenomenon. *Polish Journal of Management Studies, 11*(2), 192–202.

Zuboff, S. (2019). *The age of surveillance capitalism: The fight for a human future at the new frontier of power: Barack Obama's books of 2019.* Profile Books.

Zupic, I. & Čater, T. (2015). Bibliometric methods in management and organization. *Organizational Research Methods, 18*(3), 429–472.

3. The circular economy: a conceptual exploration of value creation through value preservation

Niels Faber and Jan Jonker

1. INTRODUCTION

Headlines and excitement refer to the circular economy and the notion is gaining momentum at various levels of society. The urgency to fundamentally change the ways of production and consumption of physical goods and the ever-increasing pressure this puts on natural resources forms the pinnacle of the desire to realise a transition to circularity.

The seminal concept of the circular economy was introduced by Stahel (1982; Stahel and Reday, 1977) as an intermediate stepping stone towards a performance economy. The term itself was launched in a report written and commissioned by the European Committee. The concept remained underdeveloped for two decades. Meanwhile the servitisation concept was introduced (Vandermerwe and Rada, 1988) and elaborated in the more encompassing product-service system concept (Tukker, 2004; Tukker and Tishner, 2006a, 2006b). Both conceptual developments occurred against the backdrop of growing attention for environmental issues (e.g., IPCC reports, Sustainability Institute, Resilience Institute Stockholm) demonstrating their impacts on society at large. On the one hand issues such as global warming were identified and rose on the societal and political agendas. On the other hand, it spurred the empirically substantiated theory of the 'limits to growth' (Meadows et al., 1972) increasingly revealing the limitations of our natural resources to support the paradigm of our linear growth economies. All these developments together cumulated in the 'rediscovery' of the circular economy concept, which was popularised in the 2010s by the Ellen MacArthur Foundation (2013, 2014). In particular, the Ellen MacArthur Foundation was able to bring the circular economy to the realm of business practice on an international scale. In a relatively short period, it established a foundation for applied research transcending national agendas. As a result, a network of collaborating multinational enterprises operating across various domains and addressing a plethora of aspects of the circular economy was quickly put in place. The by-product of this development was that the topic was put on agendas of the world business council for sustainable development (WBCSD), the World Economic Forum (WEF), and others. And, last but not least, the topic of the circular economy reappears on the agenda of the European Union (e.g., European Union, 2015).

Not surprisingly, following the rising political interest, national institutes of applied research start to develop programmes in a variety of domains and in various ways. The institutes SITRA from Finland and VITO from Belgium promote and conceptually develop the concept of the circular economy further. They push the envelope towards fundamentally rethinking the positions of economic agents, the business models they apply, and the institutional frameworks that enable a circular economy. Besides, national organisations for applied sciences such as TNO (Netherlands) develop the notion of the circular economy much more into a practice for specific domains, such as chemicals, construction, and energy (TNO, 2023). These developments are propagated and framed by national policy agendas on transition towards the circular economy, for example, the Dutch National Transition agendas (Ministerie van Infrastructuur en Waterstaat, 2023), the Nordic Playbook (Nordic Innovation, 2023), et cetera. These developments converge into the development of the European framework programmes in the early 2000s and its successor Horizon 2020, leading to the current policy frameworks of the Green Deal in its turn followed by the elaboration in the Fit for Fifty-Five programme, and most probably in the near future accelerated in the Sustainable Products Initiative (European Commission, 2019, 2020a, 2020b, 2020c, 2021c, 2022). Since Stahel's initial introduction of the concept of a circular economy, the contours of a solid structure have been sketched in which the concept is empirically founded, and has found its ways into business practices, policies, political agendas, and societal interest. Five decades of labour have provided us with a promising concept, yet we are still just at the beginning of fully grasping the implications of its transitional and transformational consequences. In the following sections of this contribution, we elaborate the concept of a circular economy.

2.   BACKGROUND OF THE CIRCULAR ECONOMY

2.1   Historical Developments[1]

Thinking about limitations to economic activity and the circularity of physical resource flows finds its origins in the seminal work *The economics of the coming spaceship earth* by Kenneth Boulding (1966). The principal idea is that the earth forms a confined space, imperatively bounding humans and their pursuit of fulfilling needs and desires. While physical bounds are generally recognised by individuals, Boulding (1966) particularly addresses the inability of economic thought to do the same. He states that '[e]conomists in particular, for the most part, have failed to come to grips with the ultimate consequences of the transition from the open to the closed earth' (Boulding, 1966, p. 1). The open earth refers to the ability of humans to always push the frontier when a situation becomes too complicated, e.g., when resources run out and the land can no longer nourish them. This open earth perspective has dominated societies' perception of the planet for millennia. The change to thinking about the habitat as a closed system is therefore not an easy task, and requires not just some adjustments. Instead, '[t]he closed earth of the future requires economic principles which are somewhat different from those of the open earth of the past' (Boulding, 1966, p. 4).

This insight has spurred the thinking about human activity and the impact it has on the planet, along two lines of reasoning. One line has focused on earth's natural and biological systems, looking for the boundaries within which human (economic) activities may become manifest (see, for instance, the works of the Stockholm Resilience Centre). The arrangement of the economic system itself is hardly contested, while analyses show that in essence this is where most of the problems emerge. In contrast, the second line of reasoning has more closely looked at the design of the economic system, exploring new configurations that are more aligned with the natural, biological, and social systems it relies on to function. This line looks into the principles and ideologies underpinning economic thought and practices, and has aimed to develop alternative positions. While each line has its own proponents, they have from the outset been strongly intertwined and consequently have affected each other on multiple occasions.

More urgent calls for economic change were published in the decades following. Meadows et al. (1972) warned against the inevitable exhaustion of essential resources for the economy. Meanwhile, Stahel (1982; Stahel and

---

[1]   This part is based on an earlier work which was co-authored by Jonker, Stegeman, and Faber (2017).

Reday, 1977) developed the idea of an alternative economy that builds on circular use of materials. Daly laid the foundations of incorporating ecological principles into economic thought and founded the movement of ecological economics (Daly, Cobb, and Cobb, 1990). Following the publication of the Brundtland Report (WCED, 1987), Karl Henrik Robèrt founded The Natural Step organisation in 1989 (The Natural Step, 2021). This organisation fosters the development of integrated thinking about a sustainable society, focusing on developing system conditions for sustainable human activities. A similar approach originates from the Stockholm Resilience Centre, setting a course towards discovery of the boundaries for '[a] safe operating space for humanity' (Rockström et al., 2009). Almost ten years later, Raworth (2017) added to the concept of the safe operating space for humanity the social dimension, formulating this as 'both an ecologically safe and socially just space for humanity' (2017, p. 45), leading to the concept of the doughnut economy. The latter specifies in addition to environmental ceilings (the maximum burdens that may be placed on the various planetary support systems (Rockström et al., 2009)), social foundation. These social foundations indicate a minimal level of social support systems that need to be in place to ensure societies may function. Her work has led to a framework that encapsulates the performance of an economy by the extent to which the needs of people are met without the overshoot of the natural, ecological carrying capacities. The model thus reframes economic problems, raising the demand to set new goals.

During the same period, other actors coming from a variety of professional backgrounds, including business and academia, have developed their own interpretations of the problems at hand and ways forward. We mention two from a long and rich list of possibilities. The first is the Austrian philosopher Christian Felber, who pleads for a radical transformation of the economic system in which companies should take the lead. His proposal is that the economic system should favour ethical companies that strive to contribute to the common good, instead of profit maximisation (Felber, 2011). His concept of the Economy of the Common Good is one in the midst of a great many alternative philosophical and practical reconceptualisations of how to construct the economy. The second is the Belgian author and entrepreneur Gunter Pauli, who has coined the Blue Economy concept (Pauli, 2010). At the surface this economy aims to create 100 million jobs based on 100 innovations in ten years. The fundament underneath this growth strategy is to explore and adopt natural systems, in other words to look at the ways the biological systems around us have already solved problems of sustainability. This copying of biological solutions is also known as biomimicry. Biomimicry is the design and art of imitating ideas and solutions from nature into human applications, with the aim to improve and above all sustainify (Benyus, 2002 [1997]). In its essence, these biomimicry solutions are fundamentally circular. Since Benyus'

ground-breaking publication, a group of strong believers is continuously propagating the concept. A vivid example is the book by Gorissen (2022), *Building
the future of innovation on millions of years of natural intelligence*. However,
it seems unable to escape its niche status and has not reached mainstream
status yet.

Looking back, we observe a very rich and promising past while at the same
time it took quite a while for a clear concept of the circular economy to emerge.
And even today, over four decades after the introduction of the concept by
Stahel (1982; Stahel and Reday, 1977), it has not reached general consensus
across academic disciplines and practitioners, let alone the political opinion
which varies between administrations. Against this backdrop, we make the
following three observations.

1. Historically, we witness a rich, but also very diverse, theoretical, conceptual, and practical background across disciplines, sectors, and nations
   regarding the circular economy.
2. It is only recently that the concept of the circular economy implying the
   reconfiguration of the economic system based on value preservation
   becomes a common denominator.
3. Despite an explosion of efforts in recent years, the tools to design and
   implement a part of the economy that fits the ambition of circularity are
   still lacking, even though the European Union has started a pan-European
   campaign to stimulate circularity.
4. Perceived as a confusing debate, companies have thus far not been able to
   make the translation to implementing it strategically and operationally.
5. The debate fails to address that the notion of the circular economy unfolds
   in a reality that is systemically linear. Despite all their efforts, organisations striving for circularity are accounted for their business operations
   and financial performance, and not rewarded for their efforts in this
   direction.

So far, the circular economy has not lived up to its promise. This while
the concept fundamentally addresses the issue of sustainable development,
propagating in the debate an economic overhaul. What we see is piecemeal
applications leading to incremental improvement, while keeping the linear
economic fabric intact as much as possible. At present, the actual responsibility for making the transition happen lies with business and related institutions.
No wonder the present situation is often framed by the saying 'the turkey who
came to dinner'. Moving forward requires overall guidance to realise the economic and societal transition. Recent political developments in the EU hold the
promise to provide exactly that.

2.2 Developments in the Institutional, Legislative and Political Theatre

The EU aims to be climate neutral by 2050, an economy with net-zero greenhouse gas emissions (European Commission, 2023a). This ambition aligns with the Paris Agreement objective of 2015 and aims to keep global temperature rise below 1.5 degrees centigrade compared to the pre-industrial era (ref: Paris Agreement). Underlying this ambition is the quest to reduce carbon dioxide emissions by 2030 with 55% below 1990 emission levels. The Paris Agreement has been the tipping point in the debate, since for the first time a majority of countries and business organisations have signed the legally binding international treaty. In this section we provide a reconstruction of how this ambition towards climate change is linked to the roadmap towards circular economy. The circular economy has become instrumental to climate objectives. What we observe is that in little more than half a decade the ambition to create a circular economy has become instrumental to the climate neutrality ambition while being a target in its own right.

The work on developing a circular economy in the European Union started with the first Circular Economy Action plan (European Commission, 2020). This plan operates on three objectives simultaneously. First, it intends to aid all its members in stimulating the transition to a circular economy. In doing so, the second objective is to strengthen the European capabilities to compete at a global scale. And linking to the ambition to become a sustainable continent, the third objective has been to realise sustainable economic growth and provide new jobs. From this first plan onwards, the organisational focus has been to cover the entire lifecycle, starting at the design stage through the phases of production and consumption, ending with uniform waste management, prescribed in directives.

Following upon the First Circular Action Plan, the Paris Agreement (United Nations, 2015) or COP21 came into play. In addition to remarks made above, this agreement is 'a landmark in the multilateral climate change process because, for the first time, a binding agreement brings all nations into a common cause to undertake ambitious efforts to combat climate change and adapt to its effects' (UN Climate Change, 2018). The optimism immediately after the signing of the treaty has been great, yet over the past years the operational execution of the promises made with passion has not been fulfilled by far. The legally binding character of the treaty seems to have eroded to a letter of intent.

To translate the ambitions of COP21, the Climate Disclosure Project (CDP), together with the United Nations Global Compact, the World Resources Institute (WRI), and the World Wildlife Fund for Nature (WWF), proposed the Science Based Targets Initiative (SBTi) (Science Based Targets, 2023). This initiative supports the use of metrics and best practices on emission reductions in line with COP21 and underpinning scientific climate targets as identified by the Intergovernmental Panel on Climate Change (IPCC).

Four years after COP21, the European Commission (2019) launched the Green Deal. The Green Deal programme fits a long-standing EU practice in which sustainability research is sponsored. The overarching denominator is the EU Funding LIFE programme, which has funded over 5,500 projects since 1992 (European Commission, 2020). At present the LIFE programme's scope is 2021–2027. Elaborating the LIFE programme, the Green Deal is an encompassing roadmap for long-term actions, for which an impressive budget has been allocated, aiming to boost efficient use of resources within the borders of the European Union. Ultimately, the objective is to realise a circular economy that contributes to fighting climate change, enhances biodiversity, and eradicates pollution. Besides providing necessary funds, it also lays down the groundwork for a just and inclusive transition to this new economic concept. Since its launch, a number of follow-up plans have been published, of which the first is the New Circular Economy Action Plan (CEAP) (European Commission, 2020b).

The CEAP provides a first step in making the Green Deal ambitions more practical. It has three main targets. First, it describes how circularity translates into product design. Second, what the consequences are for processes of production, (return) logistics, and waste collection. Third, to see waste as a resource to be kept in the EU economy for as long as possible. In parallel to these industry-focused targets, the Green Deal promotes sustainable consumption amongst EU citizens, which led to the Green Consumption Pledge in 2021 (European Commission, 2021b). This pledge invites people, communities, and organisations to climate actions leading to a greener Europe. The underlying idea is that industrial efforts may only contribute to the ultimate objectives of the Green Deal when supported by aligned patterns of consumption.

Supporting the development of the CEAP and Green Deal, we observe four parallel developments that enable making both more operational. The first development concerns the Eco-design Directive (European Parliament, 2009). This long-standing directive provides a framework for mandatory ecological requirements for energy-using and related products. Over 40 product groups fall within the scope of this directive. Together, they are responsible for around 40% of all greenhouse gas emissions in the EU (Wikipedia, 2023). The foundations of the Eco-design Directive (European Parliament, 2009) underlie the new EU eco-design regulations that are mandatory from 1 September 2021. The directive now covers all energy-related products sold in the domestic, commercial, and industrial sectors. It extends the old framework, now also including performance criteria for manufacturers to meet before they can legally bring their product to the EU market. A direct link exists between the new Eco-design Directive and the CEAP, since both aim that products are made fit for a climate-neutral, resource-efficient, and circular economy. The second development is the 'Fit for 55' package. As part of the Green Deal, it offers a set of metrics for a 'fitness test' for sustainability, and taxation policies for shaping and accelerating the reduction of greenhouse gas emissions in 2030 compared to 1990. Additionally, it tightens the EU Emission Trading System (European Commission, 2021b). Third, the European Climate Law (European Parliament, 2021) provides a legally binding framework to reduce greenhouse gas emissions. This law provides the necessary footholds within the confines of the European Union to enforce climate neutrality to all its economic activities.

A fourth development concerns the Extended Producer Responsibility (EPR). EPR only covers the post-consumer stage of a product's lifecycle. The essence is that a producer is ultimately deemed liable for the process of collecting and treating end-of-life products. The consequence is that producers need to design products in such a way that their dismantling leads to better reusability and harvesting of commodities and spare parts. The assumption is made that both consumer and producer share the costs of returning end-of-life products (Academy of European Law, 2022). Next in line, Product Ownership (PO) regulations are in preparation that extend EPR to cover the entire product lifecycle from design, through use, dismantling, and finally end-of-life treatment, culminating in the Sustainable Product Initiative (SPI).

The groundwork for the SPI is an amalgamation of the Eco-design Directive, the Fit for 55 package, European Climate Law, and EPR. The SPI – launched in 2022 – is seen as a crucial instrument to change the European approach towards production, use, resource management, and ownership policies. As such the SPI can be seen as a game-changer and a switch of paradigm since the underlying transaction model moves from one that is based on change of ownership towards one that is based on servitisation and access to functionalities (Vandermerwe and Rada, 1988). The SPI extends the narrow scope of the Eco-design Directive and sets sustainability criteria based on harmonised indicators and lifecycle assessments such as environmental footprints, to the broadest range of products (European Commission, 2022).

The SPI only flourishes when grounded in a uniform methodology of measuring the impacts of products during their entire lifecycle, which is provided under the heading of the Product Environmental Footprint (PEF) methodology (European Commission, 2021a) combined with the Organisational Environmental Footprint (OEF; Pelletier et al., 2010). This combination of PEF and OEF methodologies provides a standardised overall framework for measuring a product's impact with regard to its use and the way it is produced (European Commission, 2021a).

In fact, this marks the birth of a circular economy lifecycle assessment or CE-LCA. After more than ten years of preparatory work the PEF was launched in 2021. In a similar vein, work has been carried out on the development of a Digital Product Passport (DPP). This passport provides information on the origins, composition, repair possibilities ('right to repair'; European Commission, 2023b), and disassembly and recycling options. The aim is to include all quintessential material and environmental data of the entire lifecycle of a product, its maintenance, and its use of (virgin) materials, including emissions in the future. Ultimately, the DPP is thought to be the cornerstone to move to a circular economy. It will help consumers to make informed, sustainable choices, and will provide authorities with the necessary tools to verify compliance to legal obligations. Estimates, although contradictory, indicate that the DPP will be available uniformly across all product groups from 2030 onwards.

Looking across the landslide of activities in the past seven years, building on previous directives, an encompassing construction has emerged. In light of the need to address global challenges, it may be seen as a positive development that the EU sets a compulsory, legal framework that stimulates the development towards a circular economy. No country on its own has the power nor the reach to establish the necessary coherent sets of rules, regulations, and methodologies to create a 'level playing field' for countries and organisations alike on this scale. At the same time, we observe that it has taken quite some time to come to this point, and it will take considerable time to put all desires laid down in policies, frameworks, et cetera into operation across all industries and sectors. Three issues are important in this regard. First, the scope is limited, for the circular economy is only a small part of the entire economy, at least at this time. This raises the question of how the remaining parts of the economy in which we consume and stock the majority of resources should be sustainified or circularised. Second, the ambition to circularise part(s) of the economy is not an aim in itself, but intends to make an impact that is expressed in a reduced use of virgin materials, and consequently a lower emission of carbon dioxide. The question then is what impact is desired and to what stage in the lifecycle of products we attribute and measure this. Is it about production, actual use, the use in various lifecycles, preservation of the quality of commodities, et cetera?

This measurement issue gives ample room for new varieties of greenwashing. Third, and lastly, developing methodologies and embedding these in policy frameworks and directives raises the question of how actual practices, across countries, institutions, and cultures, are enforced. This issue of law enforcement comes in a vast array of variations and connotations across countries, also in the European context.

As usual, the devil lies in the details. The question is how much we allow ourselves to stray from the course that has now been paved given unexpected and far-reaching disruptions including the COVID-19 pandemic and current developments in Ukraine.

2.3   Disruptive Dynamics

Taking a bird's-eye view of the above-described historical and political developments leads to the identification of a series of 'slow' dynamics, each having a fundamental impact that appears over time. We observe five distinct yet intertwined disruptive dynamics (see Table 3.1).

The disruptive dynamics as described in Table 3.1 call for rethinking and redesigning the ways we have arranged our economic and social systems. The idea that societal well-being thrives on the basis of throw-away products that dominate the growth of the gross national product is at stake at its foundations. This calls for a rethinking and redefinition of the engrained concepts around production and consumption. Responsibilities in the current institutional arrangements are chiefly devolved to the positioning of ownership. By default, it is the consumer who holds ownership of products and materials. In the process of the transfer of ownership from producer to consumer, responsibility regarding products and materials is transferred to the latter. Choices made by the producer are not within reach of the consumer. Relatively recent developments, such as extended producer responsibility (EPR), are a first attempt to address this systemic flaw. Future-oriented plans to push the EPR further back into the value chain, moving towards integral Producer Ownership, thus extend the responsibility across the lifecycle of products and materials.

Given the above-described historical, political, and transitional developments, it is not surprising that the circular economy concept, although still conceptually and practically underdeveloped, receives increasing attention from business, politics, and society at large. Moreover, it implies a fundamental discussion on how to restructure and redesign the current, linear economy in such a way that it becomes 'radically' sustainable while at the same time further developing and integrating the concept of the circular economy (CE). This calls for a new paradigm in which the prevailing linear perspective and the notion of value preservation converge. We see a black hole in the CE debate, namely that it assumes the full abandonment of the linear economy, ignoring the fact that we have invested in developing smart and efficient methods, techniques, procedures, et cetera, to produce products and services for the past 150–200 years. In the current CE debate, there is virtually no discussion on harvesting this rich heritage in shaping the circular economy. We would even state that abandoning current linear production methods is impossible and undesirable. No perspective is currently being offered on how these entangled lines of thought blend together. In the following paragraphs we address these wicked issues.

Table 3.1   Disruptive dynamics

Disruptive dynamic	Description
From waste-policy to production-policy	All across Europe we observe a revision of the status of waste. This implies that we start looking at waste as a resource. The missing link is to connect this resource-thinking to appropriate logistics and thus a production-policy. In this respect, we observe an array of initiatives including urban mining, (local) material exchange platforms, and value extraction from incineration.
From mining to eco-based substitution	The present linear economy is based on the transformation of excavated minerals and ores into products. This industrial approach is questioned by a growing need and desire for material substitution. The underlying notion is to build on regenerative characteristics, leading to eco-based substitutes.
From value-recovery to value-cascading	Current thinking is dominated by the notion of the waste hierarchy (Lansink, 1979), leading to a focus starting with waste-avoidance, through value-recovery, recycling, and ultimately incineration. Essence is to extract whatever value present in waste. A value-cascading perspective starts from the premise that residual material flows are resources and may be upcycled and thus embed value.
From central to local production and consumption	The industrial paradigm automatically leads to volume and concentration of production facilities (following on the notion of economies of scale). This leads to a plethora of externalities that are more and more critically revised. Consequently, local production and consumption of goods and services are explored as a sustainable alternative.
From ownership to accessibility (functional, …)	This movement is based on questioning the omnipresent idea of ownership. To organise our lives, access to functionalities such as washing, mobility, et cetera, trumps the ownership of the goods that provide these. This insight is growing and as a consequence moves incentives to maintain and preserve goods that render such functions from consumer to producer. This leads to the popularised idea of Product as a Service.

3. THE PARADIGM OF THE CIRCULAR ECONOMY: VALUE CREATION REVISITED

The above arguments lead to the inevitable conclusion that our economic fabric needs to be revisited. Over the past centuries we have built our economic ideas on unsustainable principles, meaning that they do not start from the premises of value preservation. The current and ongoing make-up of the system is based on transformation of materials, obsolescence design, and limited use all fuelled by the ultimate desire for ongoing economic growth and consumption. In the light of these observations, it is appropriate to investigate the paradigmatic foundations of the CE. What we need is a conceptualisation that builds on the premise of value preservation from the start.

This implies a conceptualisation in which obsolescence as the driving force of the economy is replaced by the premise of preserving the value of products (functionalities), components, and materials throughout a potentially unlimited number of lifecycles. Essentially, we need to look at the notion of value creation, how this has developed over time, and what the requirements are when it comes to rethinking and redesigning an economy different from the linear. This process starts in the design phase, and has its consequences throughout the extended lifecycle. The implication is that circularity, or a circular way of organising, is not an add-on in the process of making, using, and refurbishing products, et cetera, but a design principle straight from the start. Furthermore, it is relevant to link value preservation with the principles of lifetime extension and servitisation. Inherently, designing and manufacturing products with the aim to preserve value create a basis to use them for a longer period of time. For instance, compare washing machines of low and high quality. Both offer the same functionality. However, the former offers around 600 washes, the latter around 2,500 against a price that is fourfold, while the machines are made of the same materials. Simultaneously, the functionality of the washing machine may be offered as a service. Both lifetime extension and servitisation may be applied to the same object simultaneously, yet they are inherently different. Lifetime extension does not lead to servitisation, nor the other way around.

Yet, before we discuss the improbability of use of materials for an unlimited period of time, it might be good to clarify the foundational principles of the CE. We identify the following:

- **Ambition of value preservation.** The core of the circular economy is the systemic organisation of value retention in loops of materials (both raw and processed), components, and products.
- **Lifecycle extension.** Loops are the basis for lifecycle extension. This leads to different designs, smarter maintenance (right to repair), and the use of new (substituted) and refurbished materials.

- **Organising in cycles.** Organising can be done in several ways: (1) within an organisation, (2) in value chains, (3) in a loop (bearing in mind that loops themselves can be shaped in a variety of ways), or (4) in a system of loops (ecology). For the circular economy to be effective, it requires to be organised at all these levels.
- **Loop in phases.** Loops can be deconstructed in six phases that comprise the entire lifecycle of a loop: (1) design, (2) production, (3) operate, (4) maintain, (5) reuse, and (6) recover. These phases do not follow an obligatory order but may be interlinked. For example, recovery may link to production.
- **Value creation.** Organising value retention leads to various moments of value creation. There are three dominant forms: (1) transforming, (2) recycling, and (3) circularising. We depart from a multiple value perspective on value creation. This means that there is always a relationship with social and ecological values. In other words, the circular economy is embedded in sustainable development thinking, materialising in the United Nations Sustainable Development Goals (SDGs).
- **Business models.** Value creation and retention take shape through various logics made operational in business models. We foresee a necessary change with regard to the thinking underpinning these business models. After all, the present breed of business models has its foundations in the current, linear economic paradigm.
- **Revenue models.** While often confused with business models, revenue models provide a logic around the tangible and intangible outcomes of a business model. Commonly, only the financial outcomes are taken into account. The principle of multiple value creation calls for a wider perspective on how to measure multiple values.
- **Transaction models.** Part of the revenue model is the transaction model describing the mechanism that is in place to realise the actual value creation based on the intentional outcome. Once more, we observe a rich variety of transaction models that may be combined with the revenue and business models.
- **Impact.** The ambition of the circular economy is to organise value creation with less (or preferably no) negative impact in the making, use, and discarding of products, parts, and even used commodities. This characteristic is a shared feature of sustainability and circularity. The position of having no (negative) impact is problematic in itself, since every product suffers from wear and tear during its lifecycle. Moreover, many products only function due to the actual consumption of commodities such as energy, food, water, et cetera.

The mentioned foundational principles lead to a set of requirements that need to be met in order to make the circular economy function. First, it requires organising the institutional embeddedness of these principles. For instance, an accommodating system for taxation (from labour to virgin material use) and accounting (residual value estimation to value preservation accounting). Second, organising the governance of the circular economy, in particular guidelines, policies, rules, and laws. This involves the repositioning of the issues of residual material streams and waste, both providing them with legal frameworks appropriate to establish their use in a circular way. In the current economic and institutional arrangements, they are integrally considered waste, which consequently means that they are unsuitable to be used as resources. As a result, only virgin materials are acceptable as resources. Any new framework will have to give way to the use of residual and waste streams as a resource for circular activities. Third, but certainly not last, reframing of a set of basic values is needed in relation to materials, products, and even happiness; new is no longer by definition good, nor better than old. Thus, it is not only the way we produce goods and services, but also the way we think about goods and services. This touches on the mental dimension of the circular economy. In fact, this is the flip side of the previously mentioned governance dimension. Essentially, the governance dimension has institutionalised the sentiment that new is always better. The transition to a circular economy implies that both the sentiment, and the translation to institutional arrangements, need to merge. These changes have a fundamental character, and will only manifest themselves over a period of many decades. We consider this to lie at the core of transition, which by definition unfolds slowly over a longer period of time. By transition we mean a fundamental, systematic rearrangement of production systems embedded in institutional and organisational configurations. Still, if the mentioned requirements are not met gradually, efforts to shape a circular economy around value preservation will run ashore.

4. VALUE CREATION AND BUSINESS MODELS FOR CE

The transition towards a circular economy raises first and foremost the need to reflect on the organisational dimension of such an economy. It goes without saying that at present we act in a fundamentally linear economy, as it has been crafted since the Enlightenment, shaped during the Industrial Revolution(s), and perfected after the Second World War during the 1950s. Fundamental economic concepts such as growth (Friedman and Friedman, 1980), obsolescence (London, 1932; Stevens, 1960), depreciation, scarcity, unlimited resources (Boulding, 1966), and externalisation (Coase, 1960) have been introduced and embedded in the fabric of the economy and society during these centuries.

This has had principal consequences for the underlying mental frameworks, organisational concepts and arrangements, and resource availability, leading to an institutional framework that laid the architecture for our legal rights to act (Vivarelli, 1991; Laloux and Wilber, 2014; Mintzberg, 2015; Hickel, 2020).

Over this lengthy period of time, a concept has emerged in which the organisation is postulated as the central entity. This implies that the entire institutional framework, including legal, financial, insurance, responsibility, et cetera, is linked to a physically non-existing economic actor. In other words, people (and planet) hold no responsibility. Instead, it is the legal structures that bear responsibility. Also, we have moved towards a way of organising around specialisation, resulting in an increasing fragmentation of tasks, distributed over a growing number of organisations. As a result, we find a complex and vast inter-organisational construct, giving rise to the use of additional organisational concepts such as sectors and functional domains to keep it understandable and controllable. However, with the increasing specialisation we have lost a perspective on integral lifecycles, which lies at the core of the circular economy. The use of new hierarchical concepts such as sectors and functional domains provides no resolution. While building this functionally specialised, organisation-centric economy we have simultaneously redefined the notion of value, monetising every economic (trans)action. Consequently, what cannot be monetised has no value. In the organisation-centric economy, business models, as the concept that provides the underlying logic for organising value creation (Jonker and Faber, 2021), have from the start focused solely on financial performance. In other words, value creation has been framed as purely financial. This has had far-reaching consequences for the work on business models in general (Osterwalder, Pigneur, and Clark, 2010). We have witnessed a large variety of business models, yet their foundations in line with our discussion above have not been subject to debate and criticism. While the debate on sustainability itself is longstanding over five decades, bringing this into the realm of business models has only taken shape recently (Bocken et al., 2014). The same goes for circular business models (Lacy and Rutqvist, 2015). Connecting sustainability and circularity to value creation and thus to accommodating business models brings to the fore the need to question the organisation-centricity as the leading organisational principle of an economy. It thus questions the previously mentioned underlying principles of the present linear economy (see section 3).

No wonder we have been struggling for quite a while with classifying the variety of circular business models. Table 3.2 provides an overview of classifications since 2014 (Bakker et al., 2015), the first year in which one was published. Since then, over 20 additional classifications have been proposed, the most recent in this overview originating from Gillabel et al. (2021).

Additionally, explicit attention was paid to recent publications commissioned by the European Commission.

We observe two main causes for our struggle here. First a void is noticed between the original Stahel (1982; Stahel and Reday, 1977) conceptualisation of a performance and circular economy, with an emphasis on the latter, and how this materialises in the organisational ramifications. With due respect for his seminal work, the consequences for organising, the way of operating, and evidently the business model have until recently not been addressed, let alone their environmental impact or economic consequences. While the debate started with the word *economics* at its core, the translation to a variety of logics for value creation and as such addressing the core of organisational activities has only gradually taken shape as illustrated in Table 3.2. Second, once the efforts of classification started, there appeared to be no systematic or method-ological framework to guide the various attempts conceptualising third-party empirical resources originating from research, practice, and policy. Moreover, authors who work on a classification come from totally different academic and practical backgrounds. We see people with a design, waste, economic, ecolog-ical, and policy background engaging in those classifying activities. Not sur-prisingly, most of what they have tried to do is seminal work. Last but not least, they are not always aware of the works of others working on the same subject. This leads to a wide and varied array of self-invented methodological classifi-cations with different scopes, hampering the systematic build-up of a coherent body of knowledge across the field. Consequently, the result addresses the same issues time and again and unavoidably has a repetitive character.

The whole process of analysing revealed that many classifications have similar objectives, albeit with different wording or slightly different accents and intentions. Despite indicated shortcomings, the collection of these publica-tions has been analysed, compared, and condensed. By the latter we mean that taking a closer look at some of the obtained materials, some were elaborations that merely skimmed the surface. These have been excluded from further consideration. Last but not least, the classification that gradually emerged was presented to various respondents. All in all, this process of collecting and classifying resulted in a classification of three groups and seven basic types of CBMs. Figure 3.1 depicts the seven CBM types and the three groups to which they belong.

The three groups we have distinguished are based on a growing degree of responsibility for the lifecycle management of products, spare parts, and mate-rials attributed to the producer. This leads to the central assumption that they show an increase in the extent to which they contribute to circularity.

1. The first group of CBMs consists of resource models and design models. The first basic type focuses on the recovery and reuse of (processed) raw

Table 3.2   *Overview of publications with existing CBM typologies about the period 2014–2021 used to arrive at the classification*

No.	Year	Author(s)	Title	Institute or publisher	Country
1	2014	Bakker, C. et al.	*Products that last*	BIS Publishers	Netherlands
2	2014	Bocken, N. et al.	A literature and practice review to develop sustainable business model archetypes	Elsevier	Netherlands
3	2014	Lacy, P., Keeble, J., and McNamara, R.	Circular Advantage	Accenture	England
4	2015	Lacy, P., and Rutqvist, J.	*Waste to wealth*	Palgrave Macmillan	England
5	2015	Morlet, A. et al.	Delivering the circular economy	Ellen MacArthur Foundation	England
6	2016	Guldmann, E.	*Best practice examples of circular business models*	The Danish Environmental Protection Agency	Denmark
7	2016	Kraaijenhagen, C., Van Oppen, C., and Bocken, N.	*Circular business*	Circular Collaboration	Netherlands
8	2017	Ewen, D. et al.	*Route circular*	Royal Van Gorcum Publishers and Printers	Netherlands
9	2018	Hofmann, F., Jokinen, T., and Marwede, M.	*Circular business models*	Fraunhofer IZM	Germany
10	2018	Larsson, M.	*Circular business models*	Palgrave Macmillan	Sweden England
11	2019	Haugland, M., Arponen, J., and Töndevold, A. B.	*The circular economy playbook*	Nordic Innovation/ Sitra/Accenture	Norway Finland Sweden
12	2019	OECD	*Business models for the circular economy*	OECD Publishing	France

No.	Year	Author(s)	Title	Institute or publisher	Country
13	2019	Van Muiswinkel, J. et al.	Circulaire verdienmodellen	KPMG Advisory N.V./ Copper8/ Kennedy van der Laan	Netherlands
14	2020	Circular Economy Initiative Germany	*Circular business models*	Acatech/ SYSTEMIQ	Germany England
15	2020	Haffmans, S. et al.	*Products that flow*	BIS Publishers	Netherlands
16	2020	Mosangini, G., and Tunçer, B.	*Circular economy business strategies*	The Switchers	Spain
17	2020	Pieroni, M. P. P. et al.	*Circular economy business modelling*	Technical University of Denmark	Denmark
18	2020	Smith-Gillespie, A.	*Defining the concept of circular economy business model*	Carbon Trust	England
19	2020	Takacs, F., Stechow, R., and Frankenberger, K.	*Circular ecosystems*	Institute of Management & Strategy	Switzerland
20	2021	De Mey, N., and Shahbazi, K.	The circular economy	Board of Innovation	Belgium
21	2021	Gillabel, J. et al.	*Business models in a circular economy*	European Topic Centre on Waste and Materials in a Green Economy	Belgium

materials and components. The second basic type looks at the design of a product, et cetera, so that both the production and the use of products are designed with minimum use of virgin materials. As many materials as possible are substitutable, and there is the least possible negative impact in terms of polluting emissions, depletion, or social and ecological destruction.

2. The second group of CBMs includes lifetime extension models, platform (sharing) models and product-as-a-service models. These three basic types have in common that they focus on the characteristics – longer, smarter, better – and use. This group ideally assumes designs that provide

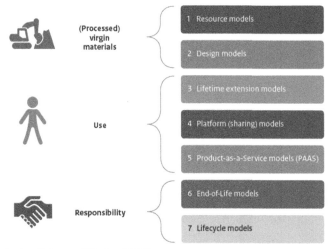

Source: Jonker, Faber, and Haaker (2022).

Figure 3.1   Classification of circular business models

extended product lifetimes. However, a longer lifetime not only requires smart designs, but also (or especially) timely (preventive) maintenance, fast assembly and disassembly, and data and digitalisation. For platform (sharing) models, the starting point is that we rarely use the full capacity of many products. Therefore, there is always a greater or lesser degree of 'idle capacity'. With the help of social and digital networks, this residual capacity can be better utilised. The product-as-a-service models are about access to and provision of a service. Sales or ownership are not central to transactions, but providing services such as heat, mobility, or a chemical function is.

3.   The third group of CBMs, end-of-life models and lifecycle models, shows a growing degree of responsibility. End-of-life models involve the retrieval of (processed) raw materials, components and products in the end-of-life phase. Lifecycle models are about producer responsibility for the entire lifecycle of a product, component, or even (processed) raw material. These two CBMs make the highest contribution to circularity.

When elaborating these three groups using our analysis of previous classifications, seven different basic types of CBMs become visible. They demonstrate existing and future CBMs. Below, this classification is listed and briefly explained.

1. Resource models: the essence of these models is the recovery of products, components, and (processed) raw materials at the end of the lifecycle (discard phase).
2. Design models: the essence of design models is to design products to fit within the logic of circularity. This includes: design for repair and maintenance, design for recovery and recycling, and design for lifetime extension.
3. Lifetime extension models: the essence of these models is to extend the lifetime of products, components, and (processed) raw materials.
4. Platform (sharing) models: the essence of platform (sharing) models is to increase the use of the existing functional capacity of assets (products) that are already in circulation.
5. Product-as-a-service models: these models focus on providing access to the function of a product to a user. The user no longer automatically becomes the owner of the product.
6. End-of-life models: the essence of these models is that producers and importers retain responsibility for the collection and safe and appropriate processing of products they have made or imported at the end of the lifecycle.
7. Lifecycle models: the essence of these models is that producers retain ownership of the products they make throughout the entire lifecycle.

4.1 Going Back in Time and Moving Forward

Three reflections are appropriate here. Previously we have introduced concepts such as value creation and retention as primordial to the circular economy. Underlying here are the notions of dematerialisation and servitisation (Vandermerwe and Rada, 1988; Tukker, 2004; Tukker and Tischner, 2006a, 2006b), implying that the sales of products are no longer the means of value creation. This implies that value is not created from the transfer of ownership of a good. Instead, goods are made part of services. These services are offered, and customers pay for the service by a certain unit (e.g., by the hour, by kWh, by km et cetera). Servitisation is certainly not a new phenomenon, since few people have their own plane, train, or power plant. In this respect, the ground-breaking work of Tukker and Tischner (2006a, 2006b) has not received the attention it deserves. Their work provides a solid typology of services linked to material assets. Even though this work was published more than a decade and a half ago, it still stands as a landmark publication in the field of servitisation and is an extension of the seminal work on the circular and performance economy concepts by Walter Stahel (1982; Stahel and Reday, 1977). Only recently, the potential of dematerialisation has gained more attention, thus making a direct link to one of the pillars of the circular economy: 'access to functionality replaces' (Ellen MacArthur Foundation, 2013–2014). What Figure 3.2 shows is how Tukker's (2004) original work on servitisation remains to provide a basis to our classification of circular business models

Typology of circular business models (CBM)

Ambition is to organise value retention in cycles focused on (a) zero impact in design and usage, (b) extended functional and material use, (c) effective and efficient recovery components and materials.

Value creation primarily based on product value	Commodity value	Material value	Components value	Product value	Service value	Value creation primarily based on functional value
	Transactions based on material transformation (with transfer of ownership)				Transactions based on functional usage (without transfer of ownership)	
Pure raw material	Focus on use and recovery of commodities and components	Focus on access, performance and product as a service			Focus on lifecycle responsibility (make, maintain, and recover)	Pure service
	CBM (1) Resource models CBM (2) Design models	CBM (3) Lifetime extension models CBM (4) Platform(sharing)-models CBM (5) Product-as-a-Service models (PAAS)			CBM (6) End of Life models CBM (7) Lifecycle models	

Source: Inspired by Tukker (2004).

Figure 3.2   *Typology of circular business models in product-service system framework*

in three groups and seven basic types. In hindsight we have elaborated his original dichotomy of product versus service, in terms of dematerialisation as the basis of value creation in the circular economy. Additionally, we have added the notion of transactions at the core of circular business models. In our approach we move from a mode of 'transfer of ownership' to a mode of 'accessibility' and 'functional use'. Consequently, we arrive at our distinction in three groups of business models, focusing on (1) use and reuse of commodities and components, (2) access, performance, and Product-as-a-Service (PAAS), and (3) life-use responsibility.

Next to the move towards servitisation, we witness a shift in the transactional model implicitly underpinning the nature of business models. From a traditional and established point of view, transactions lead to the transfer of ownership, which automatically leads to the transfer and fixation of liability, responsibility, and assurance. It is this system perspective that comes into question due to compounding concepts such as extended producer responsibility (EPR), producer ownership (PO), and the EU Sustainable Product Initiative (SPI) . We see this as a transition, sparked by changes in policies and directives, in which the lifecycle responsibility of materials, parts, and products ultimately lies with the producer. The producer remains liable to track the whereabouts and conditions of any product that is produced, and assure its return for mandatory and growing percentage of reuse, refurbishment, and only if unavoidable recycling. This emerging policy framework has a fundamental impact on the nature of the classical value chain (Porter, 1985), since the above-described principles of liability, responsibility, and assurance are no longer transferred to the next actor in the value chain but remain with the original producer. This implies, for example, that a car may be sold, but the traction battery within the car remains with the battery producer. The car now becomes a carrier of (hybrid) services from various producers. During the lifecycle the producer of the traction battery is responsible for tracking and maintaining its quality and ensuring timely recovery. This change in transaction models has far-reaching implications for business models, since it is no longer 'just' a matter of servitisation. Instead, we move towards an over-encompassing system around lifecycle responsibility.

Third, such a system unavoidably requires an integral perspective on how materials move through the lifecycle of parts and products, from the earliest moment onwards of a product's design. This integral perspective implies the registration of all materials used, and how they are embedded in use. Furthermore, this necessitates tracking and tracing the actual status quo of these materials, their wear and tear, and ultimately determines and the timely prediction of the moment it needs to be repaired, refurbished, or replaced. Such a systematic approach relies on the introduction of a material passport for all products produced. The material passport is a file that contains all materials included in a product or part. It consists of providing and defining the characteristics of the materials, and how they are used. Material passports can be passive or active. The first concerns a static description of the set of materials embedded in a product, and readable through, e.g., a QR code. The second allows online tracking and tracing of the wear-and-tear during the actual use of a product. The active version allows for novel concepts of servitisation, leading to the timely prediction of failure of parts, thus allowing for pre-emptive maintenance. It goes without saying that such a system may only be realised under the condition that all parts are datafied and digitised from the beginning at molecular levels. This gives way to an additional generation of business models. More importantly, this way of thinking finally addresses the heart and the marrow of the circular economy. If this is the way forward, we are heading for several decades of redesign, renovation, and reconstruction of how we design, produce, and use products, parts, and materials, before the full meaning of a circular economy takes shape.

5.   LINKS TO OTHER ECONOMIC TRENDS

We see the following strong ties: (1) to the functional economy, (2) to the bio-based economy, and (3) to the Internet of Things and Internet of Services (IoT/IoS). In addition to the IoT/IoS we introduce the notion of the Internet of Materials (IoM) , which is strongly linked to our previous elaboration on the need for digitisation and datafication linked to material passports (see previous section). Additionally, we suggest the collaborative economy, having a weak tie with the circular economy, especially when it comes to the development of collaborative or collective business models.

5.1   Link to the Functional Economy

The circular and functional economy are seemingly overlapping economic trends at first glance. Yet when taking a closer look, we distinguish different foci. The circular economy first and foremost focuses on the systemic organisation of value preservation. The ambition of this approach is a better use of natural resources in materials, components, and products, leading to lifetime extension for all three. This results in business models in which the value of materials, components, and products is recurrently used in transactions. The functional economy is an economic system focusing on access to services at the leading value creation paradigm. It focuses on a more efficient but not necessarily longer use of materials, components, and products. This often results in business models based on the concept of servitisation, leading to the offering of, e.g., access, performance, and assurance. The transfer of ownership is no longer the essence of transactions, but instead the services a product renders.

5.2   Link to the Bio-based Economy

The bio-based economy is an economic system in which value is created using biological, renewable resources. While it sometimes seems that the concept of the bio-based economy is a novelty, we have been using bio-based resources (e.g., trees, grass, hemp, water, manure, et cetera) ever since mankind started to organise into groups, tribes, and communities. Especially through the works of the Ellen McArthur Foundation (2013–2014), and more in particular its depiction of the economic system in its famous 'butterfly' figure, balancing inert and bio-based materials has been brought to the fore in the circular economy discourse. This figure implicitly incorporates an ambition to gradually replace the use of inert bio-based resources. The downside of this laudable ambition is that it takes resources such as land, water, transport, nutrients, et cetera, to create those bio-based resources. Ultimately, this again raises the question of the sustainability balance. Will we utilise available arable land for, e.g., construction materials, or will this land be used for food production in a world where famine still is an ongoing concern for many people and nations?

5.3   Link to Internet of Things, Internet of Services and Internet of Materials (IoT/IoS/IoM)

Historically, the linear economy is based on organising a rationally functional value chain. This system was developed based on the principles of mass production for the manufacturing of cars, tin cans, and televisions. Automation of these practices has led to the fulcrum of linear economic possibilities, creating products with no other ambition than the shortest possible lifespan and promoting the throw-away mentality as the norm. This has been a dominant practice until today. Simultaneously at the end of the 1980s, public access to a rudimentary form of the Internet took shape. In the years thereafter, various developments laid the foundations for the creation of amongst others the World Wide Web (www), electronic mail (e-mail), and instant messaging (IM). These developments in turn provided the necessary functional basis for connecting appliances thus creating 'smart' products. This preluded what is now known as the Internet of Things (IoT). In its turn, interconnecting appliances has led to a layer of agents, often operating in a semi-autonomous way (IoS). As a result, refrigerators may order milk, and cars may diagnose the damage inflicted in a crash. IoT and IoS are strongly linked to servitisation-based business models. The next step, following on from the omnipresence of the digital realm, is the digitisation of commodities. Consequently, we presently witness a movement in which all elements used in products, buildings, cars, et cetera, are registered in digital material passports (MPs). The latter development strongly supports the core notion of value preservation, since it offers real-time insights into the stocks and flows of present and future materials, and their qualities within the confines of emerging circular economies.

5.4   Link to the Collaborative Economy

The essence of the collaborative or collective economy is to enable value creation from a collective perspective. Key to this is revitalising the notion of the Commons (Ostrom et al., 1999). The Commons entails the sharing and use of collective assets, granting access to all parties involved, in a balanced way. The rules of this game of collective engagement are (1) consensus amongst the parties about the underlying principles, (2) use and value preservation are considered to be two sides of the same coin, and (3) governance mechanisms are in effect to attribute fair use. This configuration of principles leads to (business) models for collective value creation, not necessarily derived from a conventional (monetised, economic) perspective. In organising assets and transactions from the perspective of the Commons, functional capacities – not simply in a material but also in a natural sense – are organised in a much more balanced manner. Worthy of note is that the original meaning of sustainability as postulated by von Carlowitz (1732) is similar to the concept of the Commons. Likewise, the Commons provides a suitable context for the realisation of a circular economy, through its foundational principle of value preservation.

6.   CASES

The cases we present here exemplify how circular business models are currently taking shape in practice. This is by no means the end of the game. Figure 3.3 (source: Jonker, Faber, and Haaker, 2022) is based on an inventory of approximately 240 cases analysed across Europe in 2021. These cases were taken from open access sources. This secondary material has not been verified at the source. Nor do we know if this collection is representative for the entire population of cases of circular business models. Figure 3.3 provides an overview of the registered cases, arranged according to the classification provided in section 3.4.

What we witness is that many initiatives predominantly focus on lifetime extension models followed by material models. Together they represent over 50% of this sample of circular business models. This is not surprising since the circular economy emerges out of a dominant linear economy. The focus for half a century has been on the reduction of waste streams and the recycling of residual materials. This thinking started with the depiction of the three operations – reuse, reduce, recycle – in the well-known three-arrow logo Gary Anderson designed in 1970. Fifty years down the line, this thinking is still dominant. Only in the past decade has conceptualising the circular economy started, despite Stahel's seminal work (Stahel, 1982; Stahel and Reday, 1977), stimulated by negative developments such as resource scarcity, ecological depletion, and climate change leading to all sorts of natural catastrophes. These themes, under the umbrella of sustainable development, have been the talk of the town, fuelled by an increasing and long-standing number of global authoritative publications. Most recently the urgency to move to a sustainable society has been dramatically underlined by the IPCC (2022). Currently, political destabilisation has been added to this list of pressures, finally accelerating global awareness and the need to change. After many years of discussion, disasters and urgent calls, we are at the point that circularity and sustainability are merging in one wicked, encompassing challenge. Despite this painful observation, and at the expense of many environmental and social damages, we are finally in the process of connecting the dots, while time for natural recovery in many domains is not on our side (Rockström et al., 2009; Persson et al., 2022).

While design models take centre stage in the discourse on the circular economy, it is striking that these are not more prominently present in practice. Furthermore, we take the platform- and servitisation models as one related group of business models, since both focus on a more efficient use of available, functional capacity. Taken together, they represent the third major form of circular business models. Finally, business models that run ahead of the European directives regarding extended producer responsibility (EPR) and sustainable product initiative (SPI) are not surprisingly a minority, since these directives are presently in the process of taking shape in national legislation and institutional directives. The translation of EU frameworks and directives to national levels has a lead time of roughly seven to eight years. Consequently, we expect that the effects on circular business models will become visible by the end of this decade. Notwithstanding, the first directives came into effect in 2023 and 2024, with regard to particular product families such as batteries, e-waste, and textiles.

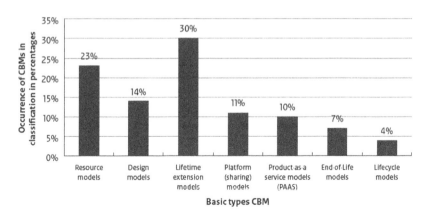

Figure 3.3   *Occurrence of CBMs in classification based on existing cases in percentages*

Below, we briefly present three actual Dutch cases of circular business models; namely Westerzwam (mushrooms), Gispen (furniture), and Pooling Partners (pallets), recently renamed as the Faber Group. These cases range in size from very local to multinational, and from upcycling waste (coffee grounds) to extending the lifecycle of load carriers.

The circular business model of Westerzwam primarily creates value through the use of locally collected coffee grounds as the growth bed for oyster mushrooms. Coffee grounds are collected in a CO2 neutral manner, using bikes, from local restaurants, by people at a distance from the labour market. These oyster mushrooms are resold to the restaurants involved, and are used to create vegetarian dishes. In addition, Westerzwam provides supporting services, enabling their customers to grow their own mushrooms at home.

Gispen's core focus is the fabrication of office furniture. Its primary strategy is 'product life extension'; furniture is offered as a full service. During the use phase, Gispen applies maintenance to this 'external' stock of furniture. When a piece of furniture can no longer be repaired or refurbished they deploy recycling of materials as a secondary strategy.

The Faber Group provides pallets made from sustainable timber. Faber brings these pallets to the market as a pooling service for their customers. Instead of selling as much as possible they maintain ownership of the pallets. The pooling service is based on the track-and-trace of stocks and flows of pallets in use. The track-and-trace allows for timely maintenance, leading to a lifespan of pallets of approximately ten years. Ideally, at the end of their lifecycle, pallets are shredded and used as compost, as a basis for plywood, or for incineration.

Based on the provided overview of cases, we observe that it is still early days when it comes to conceptualising circular business models. We allow ourselves the observation that the discourse is stuck at a focus on materials and commodities on the one hand and lifetime extension (including servitisation) on the other. When taking a bird's-eye perspective on this, we try to develop a circular solution towards value creation within a strongly dominant linear institutional setting. This implies that entrepreneurs and managers alike have to 'translate' their circular efforts into linear accountability. It goes without saying that at the end of the day this leads to institutional disappointment and individual frustration, since the criteria for judging success or failure lie in paradigms that fundamentally stand apart.

7.   BALANCING SUSTAINABILITY AND CIRCULARITY

We observe that in recent years sustainability has collided with the larger debate on climate change, while the latter, due to landmark reports by the IPCC and the COP conferences, has gained significant attention. This debate concentrates on the effects of a plethora of greenhouse gas emissions on global temperature rise, the changes this brings to the climate, and ultimately the consequences this has on the global economic system. This leads to a fundamental debate on the transition of current patterns of production and consumption. This transition is not discussed from a single perspective but unfolds into a wide array of interlinked sub-debates. To us, circularity on the one hand and sustainability on the other are two of these debates. While commonly debated as separate subjects, we plead for (1) a perspective in which both are addressed simultaneously and (2) the search to define in a particular context and with regards to a specific object the optimum balance between the two. Considering this perspective, the debate should focus more on the commonalities between sustainability and circularity. Instead, we amplify their differences, putting to the fore the fundamental paradox that we can easily strive for sustainability, without organising in a circular manner, and vice versa. Since we separate the two debates, inescapably this leads to situations in which the search for an optimum between the two is obscured. Instead, we try to optimise for only one, e.g., we sustainify tyres, bricks, and houses, disregarding their potential for circularity. Conversely, we develop material passports, which help to design for circularity, while the factual sustainability impact is not taken into account. Last but not least, the link to the climate debate from within the circularity perspective is lost entirely.

In the schema of Figure 3.4, we portray the two developments of sustainability and circularity as a progressive process. On the one hand, the process of sustainability is shaped around several R-strategies, leading to what we have called the 'law decreasing impact on sustainability'. On the other hand, we have designed the process of circularity, also underpinned by several R-strategies, leading to the 'law of increasing value retention'. The schema converges towards a theoretical optimum in the middle. Depending on context and object this optimum needs to be determined again and again. This observation implies that the quest for sustainability does not enhance circularity; nor does the contrary apply, namely that more circularity leads to more sustainability.

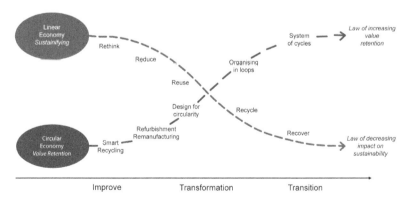

Figure 3.4   *X-curve change, transformation and transition*

7.1   Practical Implications

While the call to implement a circular economy becomes louder and louder, the practical obstacles from an institutional (legal, fiscal, administrative, et cetera) perspective are hardly addressed, and only enter into policy as a trivial matter, and its ramifications are largely ignored. In comparison to the way we engage in climate issues, this is all the more striking. Fundamental issues to realising a level playing field for circular actors, and lifting the many barriers they encounter, are not resolved. The EU initiatives such as EPR and SPI are promising, yet their actual implementation will take various years to unfold, and in the process of shaping these policies factual outcomes remain uncertain.

Fundamental discussions that arise from moving towards a circular economy are, amongst others: (1) CO_2-neutral production including transportation, manufacturing, packaging, reuse, and recycling; (2) closing loops of, for instance, materials, in particular encapsulated in consumer products and construction works; (3) the 'cri de coeur' for renewable energies fuelled by uncertainties emerging from geopolitical instabilities such as war, protectionism, or ideological propagation. These and many other discussions lead to a wicked discussion (Rittel and Webber, 1973) across a wide and varied array of stakeholders who disagree on specific fundamental issues.

Against this backdrop it comes as no surprise that companies 'hold their horses' to invest deeply in transforming their existing business towards circularity or in developing new ventures. A recent example is the development of the hydrogen market, in which everybody seems to be waiting on the others to make the first move. Consequently, nothing happens. It appears to be the ultimate bystander effect. With regard to the actions that are taken, the question arises as to whether these lead to the processes supposedly shaping the desired transition towards a circular economy. The recognition that ultimately striving for a circular economy implies collective multi-level processes of change still needs to be acknowledged. Here lies an urgent joint task for practitioners and policy makers alike.

7.2   Theoretical Implications

The circular economy proclaims to be an economy in which value preservation is the core issue. When observing the existing theoretical body of knowledge on the economy of value preservation, we notice that an encompassing theory addressing the conceptual (and empirical) implications and its relations is still missing. As a consequence, the terminology used in the circular economy discourse remains superficial. To escape this situation of lock-in, investing in the development of a theory of value in the context of the circular economy is urgently needed, in prominence of the urgency of the discourses on circularity and sustainability. The building blocks of a conceptualising discourse revolve around the development of a coherent and interrelated framework including notions such as value creation, value destruction, value loss, and value retention. Consequently, how sustainability and circularity link requires further enhancement in this discourse. We observe that at this moment the discourses on sustainability and circularity – historically emerging from empirically and mentally disjunct backgrounds – are still evolving and acting in separate silos. To strengthen our previous call on the collaboration between practitioners and policy makers, academia may contribute by constituting a collective, long-term research agenda around (1) the development of a theory on value and value preservation offering an alternative route for the market economy, (2) providing insights in a coherent set of building blocks that enable actors to frame the economy ahead and their position within, and consequently (3) a collective discourse on the change and transition this alternative route implies.

7.3   Political Implications

The task that lies ahead is a fundamental reconstruction of the linear, welfare-based economic system and institutional framework that has come into being since the Second World War. Signs of the limits to this economic system are evident, given the overwhelming scientific evidence (see, for instance, the recent report by the IPCC (2022)). Still, the current institutional framework we have developed finds its basis in linear economic thinking, and its underpinning ideologies are manifested in a broad array of policies, rules, and legislation. No wonder political parties and factions (both progressive and conservative), their ideological schools of thought, and institutes such as the Organisation for Economic Co-operation and Development (OECD), the European Investment Bank (EIB), the International Monetary Fund (IMF) and others have time and again demonstrated their inability to think outside a market economy doctrine. In addition to the previously identified theoretical 'poverty', we also observe a lack of alternative ideologies that step away from the devastating principle of unlimited and compounding economic growth to offer an alternative path ahead. While the principle of unbounded growth was the core of the criticism of the Club of Rome, igniting the sustainability debate in the 1970s (Meadows et al., 1972, 1992), this did not result in a changing course. Instead, for over 50 years now, we have addressed the issues raised by the Club of Rome with nothing but piecemeal technological innovations. Necessary social and institutional changes have not been part of the package. What has been lurking for over 50 years is to shape a multi-level debate (including economic, political, and societal) on the leading socio-economic ideology that will bring us into the 21st century.

7.4   Mental Implications

Underlying these observations, last but not least we feel compelled to address the mental implications of shaping such a socio-economic ideology as the backbone for transition. Looking back, it is the 1954 policy of obsolescence by Stevens (Adamson, 2003; suggested already by London, 1932), leading to the leitmotif: 'happiness based on consumption'. This has formed the basis for the mentality that new always trumps old, that repairing is old-fashioned, that buying new is cheaper, thus culminating in a throw-away-society. If we engage in the transition as described above, two challenges need to be addressed. First, owning is not better than access to goods and services, including maintenance and refurbishment. Second, new no longer will be valued as better than old. These challenges are quite fundamental. They are set against the backdrop of over 70 years of meticulously crafting the practice of obsolescence, embedding this deeply in product design. But, more importantly, obsolescence has become the broadly accepted practice in society at large. At both ends of the economy, consumers and producers keep each other in a locked-in situation. It is good to realise that while the window of opportunity to make a transition towards a more circular economy is rapidly diminishing, there are no shortcuts to reduce the time needed to realise this kind of paradigm shift.

7.5   Research Agenda

The circular economy landscape debate is immature at best. For certain, there is a hallelujah crowd, considering the CE as the silver bullet to address all current societal and ecological problems. There is even a faction in this 'crowd', who postulate the CE as the means to sustain and boost the existing economic growth paradigm. Taking a closer look at current CE practices, a vast number of small, emerging projects can be observed, mainly driven by a plethora of start-ups, unable to reach the stage of scale-up.

Examples are entrepreneurial activities such as creating value from making candy from seaweed, edible insects in lollipops, tarmac with recycled tyres as supplement, fashion from recycled textiles, ink made from coffee grounds, and so forth. While these examples herald explorations of possibilities of the circular economy and definitely deserve sympathy, many of these start-ups are stuck at low volumes and can be qualified as 'cuddlable' at best. They are often inspired and driven by developing piecemeal solutions to technical challenges; a comprehensive perspective to organising solutions to the larger societal challenges such as mobility, energy, reduction of the use of critical materials, et cetera is missing.

While the above examples demonstrate novel entrepreneurial activities, they also raise the question of what kind of entrepreneurs are needed to shape the transition towards a circular economy. Research indicates time and again that business schools deliver a uniform breed of managers and entrepreneurs, operating from linear economic convictions. We plead to revise the foundations of business schools, including Harvard Business School, INSEAD, or Montreux Business School. More particularly, the economic foundations need to be extended to include social inclusivity, environmental impact, and biodiversity at the core of value theory. An immediate consequence is the internalisation of externalities. Furthermore, if value preservation becomes the leading principle, the well-established concept of obsolescence, be it in design, use, or accounting (i.e., depreciation), needs to become obsolete by itself. This has as a consequence the fabric of entrepreneurial behaviour changing fundamentally, from generating revenues to taking responsibility for creating a broader range of values simultaneously, throughout the lifespan of products, commodities, and services. Needless to say, this radical change of thinking has severe consequences for the entrepreneurial mindset. Rewriting the MBA programmes at business schools in this spirit will be a challenging and rewarding endeavour.

To stimulate this development, there is a growing number of critical thinkers who aim to dig into the foundations of the CE as suggested by Stahel in the late 1970s, promoting concepts such as degrowth (Hickel, 2020), sufficiency (Bocken and Short, 2016), the economics of enough (Coyle, 2011), capitalism as if the world matters (Porrit, 2007), the doughnut economy (Raworth, 2017), the purpose economy (Hurst, 2014), the revitalisation of the concept of Commons (Ostrom, 2010), and the capability approach (Sen, 1985; Nussbaum, 2013). The common denominator in all of these developments is an appeal to rethink the foundations of industrial economics as developed and perfected since the 1850s.

What is needed to escape from this are ways to determine what initiatives may provide a solid foundation to build a circular economy at large and consequently ways to upscale these initiatives. This seems sheerly impossible, since the neoclassical economic paradigm holds us captive. This paradigm is based on unlimited growth of production and consequently unlimited resources, not taking into account (negative) externalities (Coase, 1960) and environmental boundaries (Rockström et al., 2009). In order to escape, we need an overarching, international transition framework that provides guidance and stipulates obligations to actors and institutions alike. Such a framework demands collaboration across countries to create a level playing field. Institutions such as the European Union may be the beacon to guide such a transition over a period of decades. A tricky paradox here is that the European Union sees the circular economy as a rejuvenation of the growth paradigm. The economic future as articulated in the Green Deal package including the Circular Economy Action Plan (CEAP) and its first steps to becoming operational as described in the

Responsible Product Initiative (RPI) are at a crossroads between a promise and a trap.

Against this backdrop of promises and traps, we propose a research agenda that unfolds along five main themes.

1. The need for philosophical and fundamental underpinnings of the circular economy, focusing on the nature of value creation and transactions. What is the meaning of value creation and preservation and how do these become manifest in transactions that are driven by a circular economic perspective?
2. The fundamentals of the concept of ownership versus the concept of access to functionalities and their use. This leads to two research questions. The first addresses the psycho-sociological foundations of ownership. What does ownership mean to people and how does this affect the ways they fulfil their needs? The second is of an organisational and governance matter, addressing the conditions under which access and use to functionalities is offered.
3. Risk and impact assessment of stocks and flows of material, including the effects (commodities, energy, transport, labour, emissions) of 'circularising' across various lifecycles. Once more this brings forth two questions. The first addresses the quality assurance of products, parts, and commodities, based on datafication and digitisation, leading to passive and active product passports (including questions about privacy and security). The second and more fundamental question is an exploration of the limits of circularity and sustainability, aiming to discover the ultimate balance.
4. Moving from an organisation-centric perspective towards one based on organising loops and supportive networks and institutions implies a fundamental change in dealing with issues such as commodities, risks, production, ownership, assurance, et cetera. The central research question is what kind of organisational science this requires.
5. A circular economy may only thrive when embedded in accommodating institutions such as fiscality, administration, laws, directives, and regulations. How such an institutional landscape will look and what processes are needed for this to take shape are the leading questions.

REFERENCES

Academy of European Law. (2022). *Extended Producer Responsibility (1/2)*. Waste Management: PPW, ELVs and WEES Directives. https://www.era-comm.eu/EU_waste_law/stand_alone/part_3/index.html.

Adamson, G. (2003). *Industrial strength design: How Brooks Stevens shaped your world*. Milwaukee Art Museum; The MIT Press.

Bakker, C., den Hollander, M., van Hinte, E., & Zijlstra, Y. (2014). *Products that last: Product design for circular business models* (2nd edn). TU Delft Library.

Benyus, J. M. (2002 [1997]). *Biomimicry: Innovation inspired by nature*. Harper Perennial.

Bocken, N. M. P., & Short, S. W. (2016). Towards a sufficiency-driven business model: Experiences and opportunities. *Environmental Innovation and Societal Transitions*. https://doi.org/10.1016/j.eist.2015.07.010.

Bocken, N. M., Short, S. W., Rana, P., & Evans, S. (2014). A literature and practice review to develop sustainable business model archetypes. *Journal of Cleaner Production*, *65*, 42–56.

Boulding, K. E. (1966). The economics of the coming spaceship earth. In H. Jarrett (ed.), *Environmental quality in a growing economy* (pp. 3–14). Johns Hopkins Press.

Coase, R. H. (1960). The problem of social cost. *Journal of Law and Economics*, *3*, 1–44.

Coyle, D. (2011). *The economics of enough: How to run the economy as if the future matters*. Princeton University Press. https://doi.org/10.1515/9781400838110.

Daly, H. E., Cobb, Jr., J. B., & Cobb, C. W. (1990). *For the common good: Redirecting the economy toward community, the environment, and a sustainable future*. Green Point.

Ellen MacArthur Foundation. (2013). *Towards the circular economy Vol. 2: Opportunities for the consumer goods sector* (p. 112). Ellen MacArthur Foundation. https:// www .elle nmacarthur foundation .org/ assets/ downloads/ publications/ TCE_Report-2013.pdf.

Ellen MacArthur Foundation. (2014). *Towards the circular economy Vol. 3: Accelerating the scale-up across global supply-chains* (p. 41). Ellen MacArthur Foundation. https:// www .elle nmacarthur foundation .org/ assets/ downloads/ publications/Towards-the-circular-economy-volume-3.pdf.

European Commission. (2019, 11 December). *The European Green Deal sets out how to make Europe the first climate-neutral continent by 2050, boosting the economy, improving people's health and quality of life, caring for nature, and leaving no one behind*. European Commission Press Release Database. https:// ec .europa .eu/ commission/presscorner/detail/en/ip_19_6691.

European Commission. (2020a). *First circular economy action plan*. Environment. https:// environment .ec .europa .eu/ topics/ circular -economy/ first -circular -economy -action-plan_nl.

European Commission. (2020b). *Programme for Environment and Climate Action (LIFE)*. European Commission. https:// commission .europa .eu/ funding -tenders/ find-funding/eu-funding-programmes/programme-environment-and-climate-action -life_en.

European Commission. (2020c, 11 March). *A new circular economy action plan for a cleaner and more competitive Europe*. EUR-Lex. https:// eur -lex .europa .eu/ resource.html?uri=cellar:9903b325-6388-11ca-b735-01aa75ed71a1.0017.02/DOC _1&format=PDF.

European Commission. (2021a). *Environmental footprint methods*. Green Business. https://green-business.ec.europa.eu/environmental-footprint-methods_en.

European Commission. (2021b, 25 January). *European Commission launches Green Consumption Pledge, first companies commit to concrete actions towards greater sustainability*. European Commission Press Corner. https:// ec .europa .eu/ commission/presscorner/detail/en/ip_21_182.

European Commission. (2021c, 14 July). *European Green Deal: Commission proposes transformation of EU economy and society to meet climate ambitions.* European Commission Press Corner. https://ec.europa.eu/commission/presscorner/detail/en/IP_21_3541.

European Commission. (2022, 22 June). *Sustainable products initiative.* European Commission. https:// ec .europa .eu/ info/ law/ better -regulation/ have -your -say/ initiatives/12567-Sustainable-products-initiative_en.

European Commission. (2023a). *2050 long-term strategy.* Climate Action. https://ec .europa.eu/clima/eu-action/climate-strategies-targets/2050-long-term-strategy_nl.

European Commission. (2023b, 22 March). *Rules promoting the repair of goods: Promoting repair improves the sustainable consumption of goods by consumers.* European Commission. https://commission.europa.eu/law/law-topic/consumer -protection-law/consumer-contract-law/rules-promoting-repair-goods_en.

European Union. (2015). *Closing the loop: Commission adopts ambitious new Circular Economy Package to boost competitiveness, create jobs and generate sustainable growth.* European Union. http://europa.eu/rapid/press-release_IP-15-6203_en.htm.

European Parliament. (2009). Establishing a framework for the setting of ecodesign requirements for energy-related products (recast), Directive 2009/125/EC of the European Parliament and of the Council (2009). http://data.europa.eu/eli/dir/2009/125/oj.

European Parliament. (2021). Establishing the framework for achieving climate neutrality and amending regulations, Regulation (EU) 2021/1119 of the European Parliament and of the Council (2021). http://data.europa.eu/eli/reg/2021/1119/oj.

Felber, C. (2011). *Die Gemeinwohl-Ökonomie: Das Wirtschaftsmodell der Zukunft* (Nachdr.). Deuticke im Zsolnay-Verl.

Friedman, M., & Friedman, R. D. (1980). *Free to choose: A personal statement* (1st edn). Harcourt Brace Jovanovich.

Gillabel, J., Manshoven, S., Grossi, F., Mortensen, L. F., & Coscieme, L. (2021). *Business models in a circular economy* (ETC/WMGE 2/2021). European Topic Centre on Waste and Materials in a Green Economy. https://www.eionet.europa.eu/etcs/etc-wmge/products/etc-wmge-reports/business-models-in-a-circular-economy.

Gorissen, L. (2022). *Building the future of innovation on millions of years of natural intelligence.*

Hickel, J. (2020). *Less is More* (1st edn). Penguin Random House.

Hurst, A. (2014). *The purpose economy: How your desire for impact, personal growth, and community is changing the world.* Elevate.

IPCC. (2022). *Climate Change 2022: Mitigation of climate change. Contribution of Working Group III to the Sixth Assessment Report of the Intergovernmental Panel on Climate Change* (P. R. Shukla, J. Skea, R. Slade, A. Alkhourdajie, R. van Diemen, D. McCollum, M. Pathak, S. Some, P. Vyas, R. Fradera, M. Belkacemi, A. Hasija, G. Lisboa, S. Luz, & J. Malley, eds). Cambridge University Press. doi: 10.1017/9781009157926.

Jonker, J., & Faber, N. (2021). *Organizing for sustainability: A guide to developing new business models.* Springer International Publishing. https://doi.org/10.1007/978 -3-030-78157-6.

Jonker, J., Faber, N., & Haaker, T. (2022). *Circular business models: A study to classify existing and emerging forms of value retention and creation.* Ministry of Economic Affairs and Climate Policy.

Jonker, J., Stegeman, H., & Faber, N. (2017). *The circular economy – Developments, concepts, and research in search for corresponding business models* [Working

Paper]. Radboud University, Nijmegen School of Management. https://pure.rug.nl/admin/files/238893669/WhitePaperTheCircularEconomy_INT_ebook.pdf.

Lacy, P., & Rutqvist, J. (2015). *Waste to wealth*. Palgrave-Macmillan.

Laloux, F., & Wilber, K. (2014). *Reinventing organizations* (1st edn). Nelson Parker.

London, B. (1932). *Ending the depression through planned obsolescence*. N.p.

Meadows, D. H., Meadows, D. L., & Randers, J. (1992). *Beyond the limits: Confronting global collapse envisioning a sustainable future*. Chelsea Green Publishing.

Meadows, D. H., Meadows, D. L., Randers, J., & Behrens III, W. W. (1972). *The limits to growth: A report for the Club of Rome's project on the predicament of mankind*. Universe Books.

Ministerie van Infrastructuur en Waterstaat. (2023). *Transitieagenda's per sector*. Nederland Circulair in 2050. https://www.nederlandcirculairin2050.nl/samenwerking/transitieagendas.

Mintzberg, H. (2015). *Rebalancing society: Radical renewal beyond left, right, and center*. Berret-Koehlers Publishers.

Nordic Innovation. (2023). *Nordic Circular Economy Playbook 2.0*. Nordic innovation. https://www.nordicinnovation.org/2022/nordic-circular-economy-playbook-20.

Nussbaum, M. (2013). *Creating capabilities*. Belknap Press.

Osterwalder, A., Pigneur, Y., & Clark, T. (2010). *Business model generation: A handbook for visionaries, game changers, and challengers*. Wiley.

Ostrom, E. (2010). Beyond markets and states: Polycentric governance of complex economic systems. *American Economic Review*, *100*(3), 641–672. https://doi.org/10.1257/aer.100.3.641.

Ostrom, E., Burger, J., Field, C. B., Norgaard, R. B., & Policansky, D. (1999). Revisiting the commons: Local lessons, global challenges. *Science*, *284*(5412), 278–282. https://doi.org/10.1126/science.284.5412.278.

Paris Agreement, No. 54113 (2015). https://treaties.un.org/pages/ViewDetails.aspx?src=TREATY&mtdsg_no=XXVII-7-d&chapter=27&clang=_en.

Pauli, G. (2010). *Blue economy – 10 years, 100 innovations, 100 million jobs*. Paradigm Publications.

Pelletier, N., Allacker, K., Manfredi, S., Chomkhamsri, K., & Maia de Souza, D. (2010). *Organisation Environmental Footprint (OEF) Guide* (No. N 070307/2009/552517). European Commission (EC), Joint Research Centre (JRC), Institute for Environment and Sustainability (IES). https://www.reteclima.it/wp-content/uploads/Organisation-Environmental-Footprint-OEF-Guide.pdf.

Persson, L., Carney Almroth, B. M., Collins, C. D., Cornell, S., de Wit, C. A., Diamond, M. L., Fantke, P., Hassellöv, M., MacLeod, M., Ryberg, M. W., Søgaard Jørgensen, P., Villarrubia-Gómez, P., Wang, Z., & Hauschild, M. Z. (2022). Outside the safe operating space of the planetary boundary for novel entities. *Environmental Science & Technology*, *56*(3), 1510–1521. https://doi.org/10.1021/acs.est.1c04158.

Porritt, J. (2007). *Capitalism as if the world matters*. Routledge.

Porter, M. E. (1985). *Competitive advantage: Creating and sustaining superior performance* (2nd edn). Free Press.

Raworth, K. (2017). *Doughnut economics: Seven ways to think like a 21st-century economist*. Chelsea Green Publishing.

Rittel, H. W. J., & Webber, M. M. (1973). Dilemmas in a general theory of planning. *Policy Sciences*, *4*(2), 155–169. https://doi.org/10.1007/BF01405730.

Rockström, J., Steffen, W. L., Noone, K., Persson, Å., Chapin III, F. S., Lambin, E., Lenton, T. M., Scheffer, M., Folke, C., Schellnhuber, H. J., Nykvist, B., de Wit, C., Hughes, T., van der Leeuw, S., Rodhe, H., Sörlin, S., Snyder, P. K., Costanza, R.,

Svedin, U., … Foley, J. (2009). Planetary boundaries: Exploring the safe operating space for humanity. *Ecology and Society*, *14*(2). http://pdxscholar.library.pdx.edu/iss_pub/64/.

Science Based Targets. (2023). *Ambitious corporate climate action.* Science Based Targets. https://sciencebasedtargets.org.

Sen, A. K. (1985). Well-being, agency and freedom. *The Journal of Philosophy*, *82*, 169–221. https://doi.org/10.2307/2026184.

Stahel, W. R. (1982). The product-life factor. In S. Grinton Orr (ed.), *Inquiry into the nature of sustainable societies: The role of the private sector* (pp. 72–104). HARC.

Stahel, W. R., & Reday, G. (1977). *The potential for substituting manpower for energy: Report to DG V for Social Affairs* (No. 76/13; Programme of Research and Actions on the Development of the Labour Market). Commission for European Communities.

Stevens, B. (1960, February). Planned obsolescence. *The Rotarian*, *96*(2), 12.

The Natural Step. (2021). *The Natural Step.* https://thenaturalstep.org.

TNO. (2023). *Circulaire Economie, milieu en duurzame chemische industrie.* TNO. https://www.tno.nl/nl/over-tno/organisatie/units/circulaire-economie-milieu/.

Tukker, A. (2004). Eight types of product–service system: Eight ways to sustainability? Experiences from SusProNet. *Business Strategy and the Environment*, *13*(4), 246–260. https://doi.org/10.1002/bse.414.

Tukker, A., & Tischner, U. (eds). (2006a). *New business for Old Europe: Product-service development, competitiveness and sustainability* (1st edn). Taylor and Francis.

Tukker, A., & Tischner, U. (2006b). Product-services as a research field: Past, present and future. Reflections from a decade of research. *Journal of Cleaner Production*, *14*(17), 1552–1556. https://doi.org/10.1016/j.jclepro.2006.01.022.

UN Climate Change. (2018, 22 October). *The Paris Agreement.* https://unfccc.int/process-and-meetings/the-paris-agreement/the-paris-agreement.

Vandermerwe, S., & Rada, J. (1988). Servitization of business: Adding value by adding services. *European Management Journal*, *6*(4), 314–324.

Vivarelli, M. (1991). The birth of new enterprises. *Small Business Economics*, *3*(3), 215–223. https://doi.org/10.1007/BF00400026.

von Carlowitz, H. C. (1732). *Sylvicultura oeconomica, oder haußwirthliche Nachricht und Naturmäßige Anweisung zur wilden Baum-Zucht.* Verlag Kessel.

WCED. (1987). *Our common future.* Oxford United Press.

Wikipedia. (2023). Greenhouse gas emissions. https://en.wikipedia.org/wiki/Greenhouse_gas_emissions.

4. The bioeconomy: a new productive and economic model for Latin America and the Caribbean

Elizabeth Hodson de Jaramillo and Adrián G. Rodríguez

1. HISTORICAL, CONCEPTUAL AND THEORETICAL DEVELOPMENT OF THE BIOECONOMY

1.1 Origin of the Concept

Nicholas Georgescu-Roegen is recognized as the first to propose an approach similar to what we now name either as bio-based economy or bioeconomy. He called it *bioeconomics*, indicating that 'The term is intended to make us bear in mind continuously the biological origin of the economic process and thus spotlight the problem of mankind's existence with a limited store of accessible resources, unevenly located and unequally appropriated' (Georgescu-Roegen 1977, p. 361).

Closely related concepts emerged at the turn of the century, which have shaped the trend that we will call here as the bioeconomy. Two major conceptual approaches can be identified. The first highlights the potential offered by fast knowledge advancement of biological sciences and technologies, especially modern biotechnologies; it has been designated as the *knowledge-based bio-economy*. Relevant policy developments under this approach have been carried out by the European Commission (2005), OECD (2009) and the White House (2012). The second approach, more in line with Georgescu-Roegen's original concept, emphasizes the potential of biological resources as an engine for development and it has been termed as the *bio-based economy*. Illustrative of this approach is also a policy document from the European Commission (2012).

The current most commonly-accepted understanding of the bioeconomy has emerged from the convergence between the two approaches and it has been advanced in the context of the Global Bioeconomy Summits, organized by the German Bioeconomy Council (GBC 2015, 2018) and the International Advisory Council on Global Bioeconomy (IACGB 2015, 2018, 2020a, 2020b). The communiqué from the 2018 Summit proposes that from a global perspective and general terms, 'bioeconomy is the production, utilization and conservation of biological resources, including related knowledge, science, technology, and innovation, to provide information, products, processes and services across all economic sectors aiming toward a sustainable economy' (IACGB 2018, p. 2). The definition recognizes both the role of biological resources (bio-based) and knowledge, science, technology and innovation (knowledge-based). This definition was adopted in the national bioeconomy strategies of Costa Rica (Gobierno de Costa Rica 2020) and Colombia (Gobierno de Colombia 2020). Table 4.1 provides a summary of bioeconomy-related definitions.

Biological resources are at the core of the bioeconomy. They are the basis for a new techno-economic paradigm for production and consumption as sources of materials and energy alternative to fossil resources.

1.2   Other Concepts Contributing to Shaping the Scope of the Bioeconomy

During the last two decades of the 20th century the concepts of industrial ecology/ecosystem (Frosch & Gallopoulos 1989) and industrial symbiosis (see Yap & Devlin 2017, for a discussion) emerged, as circular production approaches (see chapter on circular economy) in line with the circular nature of the bioeconomy. Both concepts refer to productive systems that seek to use the wastes generated in production and consumption in a way that eliminates or minimizes the losses of energy entailed in their discharge to the environment.

In addition to biological resources, more recent conceptualizations of the bioeconomy also highlight the role of biological systems, processes and principles (Table 4.1). They are the core elements of the concept of biomimicry (Vincent et al. 2006), which refers to the replication of biological systems, processes and principles in production processes (e.g. biomanufacturing;) or in the design of socio-technological solutions (e.g. temperature control, waste disposal, traffic control). Janine Benyus, promoter of the concept of biomimicry, for the last two decades has defined biomimicry as 'sustainable innovation inspired by nature' (Benyus 1997).

1.3   The Bioeconomy Today

At the beginning of the third decade of the 21st century we can say that the bioeconomy is about: (i) sustainable production, management and use of

a market economy; namely, purchase of artefacts to perform needed services versus leasing the flow of services from the artefacts (functional economy); access to artefacts versus their ownership (collaborative economy), whether we need to possess artefacts at all (sharing economy).

The bioeconomy is a market-based economy that does not prescribe on the purchase of goods versus the lease of their services. In fact, the bioeconomy intrinsically cares about how products are created to yield the highest possible use-value for the longest possible time using as little material and energy as possible and minimizing or eliminating waste, as it is promoted by the functional economy.

Moreover, even being market-based, the bioeconomy neither calls against or in favour of the principles of the collaborative or the sharing economies. The goods of the bioeconomy can be purchased or exchanged, owned or shared. What is important to the bioeconomy is what is their material content (bio-based) and how they are produced (minimizing or eliminating material and energy waste).

In fact, elements of these trends are consistent with some point that Georgescu-Roegen (1975, p. 378) includes in his *minimum bioeconomic programme*: fifth point, 'we must cure ourselves of the morbid craving for extravagant gadgetry', sixth point, 'we must also get rid of fashion', and seventh point, 'the necessity that durable goods be made still more durable by being designed so as to be repairable'.

2.3   The Bioeconomy and the Self-production Economy

The bioeconomy is also in line with the essence of the self-production economy: to produce yourself the goods you need to satisfy your needs. Especially when it comes to food, the most basic of all human needs. Sustainable urban and peri-urban agriculture, vertical agriculture as well as marketing mechanisms to shorten food chains (shorten the economic or physical distance between producers and consumers) are also socio-economic trends that can be accommodated within the new techno-economic paradigm of the bioeconomy, and which are also closely related with the idea of self-production. However, other features of the self-production economy are outside the scope of the bioeconomy, such as those associated with sustainable manufacturing through 3D printing type of technologies, except when the inputs are biomasses, either produced of or from waste.

3.   PRESENTATION OF VARIOUS CASES IN LATIN AMERICA AND THE CARIBBEAN (LAC) TO ILLUSTRATE THE TREND IN PRACTICE

The global concern for sustainability and the impacts of climate change that humankind is confronting are also present in Latin America and the Caribbean – LAC – where an increasing number of countries are adopting the bioeconomy as the smart choice for a sustainable productive model, with different levels of socio-economic impact.

The LAC region, with its rich natural resource endowments – land, water and biodiversity – is particularly well placed to both contribute to and benefit from the bioeconomy. Several countries are already on their way to making use of the numerous opportunities offered by the bioeconomy, with a particular emphasis on the agricultural and bioenergy sectors presently, factors of increasing strategic value for a bio-based world. The rapid agricultural transformation occurring in many countries, and the way that the region has rapidly evolved to become a world leader in the exploitation of the new agricultural technologies and in the bio-fuels markets, are clear signs of this potential. The sustainable use of biodiversity is also of increasing interest. The LAC region is very competitive as it concentrates the most important biodiversity hotspots of the world; seven of the 19 LAC countries are considered to be 'mega diverse' in terms of biodiversity resources (Brazil, Colombia, Mexico, Peru, Ecuador, Venezuela and Bolivia, but another three – Costa Rica, Panama and Guatemala – have important National Biodiversity Indexes (NBIs)). It also has a variety of cultures, which are of increasing strategic value for a bio-based world. This is a source of economic growth, and gives LAC the potential of becoming the world leader in offering the services that its ecosystems and biodiversity provide, and in return receiving new benefits from this conservation and sustainable management.

The LAC region is also a prominent player among global leaders that exploit the benefits of the new biotechnologies and the bioeconomy products – genetically modified organisms (GMO) and edited crops, as well as biofuels, are clear examples of this potential. The high intensity of use of biotechnological applications in the region's agricultural sector is, indeed, a great advantage for bioeconomy implementation (Trigo et al. 2014). The region's abundant resource patrimony has already served as the foundation for significant developments towards the development of a bio-based economy. The bioeconomy concept based on the diversification and increased efficiency of natural resources use is a response to the perceived environmental, social and economic challenges (Trigo 2011). There are several examples of biodiversity resource valorization in medicine, eco-intensification of agriculture, biotechnology applications in mature sectors such as mining, food and beverage production, biorefineries and ecosystem services (Sasson & Malpica 2018). The region is also a centre of origin and diversity of several species that sustain current world food supply (e.g. potato, sweet potato, maize, tomato, beans, cassava, peanuts, pineapple, cacao, chilli pepper and papaya, among others). Additionally, many plants with special compounds have been used for the biopharmaceutical, nutraceutical, cosmetic and environmental industries.

The region shows important developments in different areas (pathways) in Argentina, Brazil, Chile, Colombia, Costa Rica, Peru, Mexico, among other countries. Also, some countries have already developed dedicated national bioeconomy strategies (Colombia, Costa Rica) while others are in the process of doing so (e.g. Ecuador, Guatemala, Uruguay). Because of their different characteristics and conditions, each country and region must define and establish their own bioeconomy development plan (Henry et al. 2019). Given the high variability and heterogeneity of characteristics (biodiversity, social and cultural), several models of bioeconomy in LAC are being implemented, depending on the conditions of each country and even with local specificities. Any one of the bioeconomy models adopted is driven by the general objectives of more effective and efficient use of biological products and processes for achieving sustainability and specific societal goals including income increase.

Taking into account comparative advantages as well as relevant skills and capacities in the LAC region, the ALCUE-KBBE project (Latin America and the Caribbean Knowledge Based BioEconomy) identified six pathways for bioeconomy development. These pathways may overlap in some aspects, but together offer a holistic approach for achieving the stated purposes for the region and include: (i) biodiversity resources utilization and valorization (ii) ecointensification of agriculture, (iii) biotechnology applications, (iv) biorefineries and bioproducts, (v) value chain efficiency improvement and (vi) ecosystem services (Hodson 2014). In this regard, for example, some of the countries that plant biotechnological crops (Genetically Modified, GM) are also doing ecointensification of agriculture because of reduced or non-tillage and reduced use of agrochemicals, water and fuel, as well as improving their value chains, and probably carrying out activities in biorefineries or bioproducts. On the other hand, biodiversity resources valorization is often associated with, and complemented by, ecosystem services.

Presently, four of the countries in the region (Brazil, Argentina, Paraguay and Uruguay) are among the top ten producers of GM crops, with the associated eco-efficient agricultural practices, such as no-tillage, precision agriculture, integrated pest and nutrient managements, as well as bioinputs (biofertilizers, biological control) and organic agricultural approaches (ISAAA 2017). In relation to the biofuels market (biodiesel, bioethanol), LAC has become a leader, mainly with Brazil, Argentina and Colombia, and biogas production is expanding in almost all the countries (Trigo et al. 2014). Some examples of bioeconomy development in LAC countries are described in this section.

3.1   Argentina

Argentina is one of the leader countries in LAC in bioeconomy implementation. With different regions and productive systems, the country has several options of development for the bioeconomy model, which is underway as a political decision. The country has specific areas of strength, such as high biomass availability and scientific-technological capacities; as well as a long history of private institutions related to the agro-industrial sector. Advancing the consolidation of an effective and efficient bioeconomy would allow implementing a more balanced territorial development strategy in the relevant regions. Some significant opportunities are in the Central Pampean region where the confluence of quantity/quality of resources and infrastructure is more evident and there are important developments related to the aggregation of value in agribusiness chains and biofuels. The main areas of insertion are energy (biofuels) and food, which makes it a strategic component of global food security (Trigo et al. 2019). The country's leadership in biotechnology in LAC has allowed it to expand its portfolio of products and services. There is a network between the science and technology organizations, which allows them to articulate and make more efficient the results in developments in bioeconomy related to agriculture and agribusiness, food industry, fisheries and aquaculture, forestry and the paper industry, fibres and clothing, biochemistry and bioplastics, bioenergy, biopharmaceutical and biocosmetic industries, among others.

For Argentina, the bioeconomy is not a sector of the economy, but an industrial strategy crossing all the economy, which includes multiple sectors, traditional and new, that share the concept of the use of biological processes and resources as a central component of their production and service activities. In this context, traditional value chains lose much of their original meaning and change to the concept of value networks where raw materials are instrumental in different chains, depending on how relationships among demand, technology availability and the opportunity costs of resources involved in each particular situation occur. The use of cascade approaches and interrelations among chains are strategic to improve the efficiency of natural resource use, provide innovation options and new businesses, and reduce the potential conflict among alternative uses (Trigo et al. 2019).

Among the achievements materialized are development of biotechnology companies in several sectors; global pioneers in mass use and development of genetically modified organisms (GMO) for agricultural production;

massive use of environmentally friendly extensive agricultural production systems; and high dynamism in the production of vegetable oils, biofuels and biorefinery-derived industrial products.

The opportunities offered by the bioeconomy to Argentina will increase significantly in the coming decades, associated with the expected evolution of the food market and other traditional products, with increased population and income and their impact on the change of diets and food preferences. The expansion will also be encouraged by new demands for industrial goods and services, which emerge strongly given the interest in care for natural resources and the necessary minimization of the effects of economic activity on climate change (Trigo et al. 2019).

3.2   Brazil

Brazil has been promoting biotechnology and biofuel production for decades. The country shows a successful application of bioeconomy focused on obtaining bioenergy. There are several efforts looking for diverse mechanisms for partnerships, so that the small farmer is included in the developments and can benefit from the adoption of technologies. Bioeconomy is also considered key to contributing to SDGs.

Brazil has been a pioneer in the implementation of mixing ethanol and gasoline since the 1930s. At present, the requirements for the mixture are a minimum of 18% (E18) and a maximum of 27% (E27) in gasoline. Ethanol production has increased, reaching 28,000 million litres in 2016, placing the country second in the world ranking of major producers, after the United States. In terms of biodiesel, interest was raised in 1920 experimenting with renewable fuels, but the oil crisis in 1970 was the strongest boost. Brazilian biodiesel production for 2016 was 3.8 million cubic metres, which places Brazil among the three largest global producers (Oliveira 2019). In addition to biofuels, Brazil exports cane sugar and soya, mainly genetically modified crops (GM), being the second GM crop planter in the world, with 26% of the total area (ISAAA 2017). There is also interest and high potential in bio-based chemicals production, and the timber industry represents an additional growth market. Brazil has also committed itself to preventing the illegal clearing of rainforests by 2030.

The country intends to remain at the forefront of the use of renewable energy sources. Currently, it has one of the cleanest energy matrices on the planet: 39% of the energy consumed in Brazil comes from renewable sources, while the world average is 14%. Regarding bioenergy, sugarcane products are the most commonly used source since it supplies 16% of the energy consumed in the country, mainly in the form of ethanol for transport and bagasse for boiler combustion (Oliveira 2019).

Government documents consider bioeconomy issues under the label of the green economy, bioenergy development or biotechnology. The Action Plan for Science, Technology and Innovation (2016) includes bioeconomy and intends to produce and apply scientific and technological knowledge for the promotion of social, economic and environmental development. It has thematic lines defined according to the productive logic of bioindustries: biomass; processing and biorefineries; bioproducts, and the Brazilian Observatory in Bioeconomy. There is an emphasis on Blue Bioeconomy, highlighting the potential of marine resources, its by-products and marine compounds (German Bioeconomy Council 2018). On the other hand, the Brazilian Agricultural Research Corporation (EMBRAPA) is committed to bioeconomy development and has defined six lines of actions in bioeconomy. The lines are: biocontrol and biotechnological processes in the sustainable management of agricultural pests; biomass processing; renewable chemistry; green chemistry; environmental biotechnologies applied to the recovery of contaminated areas and to the valorization of waste from the industrial sector; and development and scale-up of biotechnological processes. Interesting developments are found in all of the above, both for extensive crops and for small farmers.

3.3   Chile

Although bioeconomy is not explicitly defined as a public policy in Chile, there are several public and private initiatives working in this direction, including the establishment of the Agency for Sustainability and Climate Change, as well as several programmes in '*Chile Transforma Alimentos*', where public-private cooperation is working for a productive and diversified economy. It focuses on 'the incorporation of sustainable technologies to develop new products from raw materials available, which stand out for their healthy composition and processing. Likewise, it intends to innovate in the packaging of products.' There are also biotechnological developments not totally integrated to the concept of bioeconomy (Doorn 2019).

A remarkable initiative, which has promoted bioeconomy development in Chile, is the Center for Systems Biotechnology (CSB), created by Fraunhofer Chile Research (FCR) in 2011, with the support of the Fraunhofer Institute for Molecular Biology and Applied Ecology (IME), Germany, as part of a programme by the Government of Chile to attract centres of excellence to the country. Between 2011 and 2021 the centre operated as a consortium and a strategic alliance among several universities, private companies and government agencies, focusing on agriculture, foods and ingredients, aquaculture and marine systems, and industrial sustainability, and had a platform for R&D services. In November 2021 the management and operation of the centre was transferred to the Andrés Bello University (UNAB), including equipment, researchers and ongoing projects.

During the ten years of operation under the aegis of FCR the centre's objective was to facilitate and promote the relationships between private companies and the academic world of knowledge, looking forward to strengthening national capabilities of the innovation ecosystem making use of the expertise skills of international entities with an important record in S&T development and transfer. An interesting point is that it is the first Fraunhofer's innovation model based in Latin America, assessing the innovation needs of the industry through the application of science and technology, in collaboration with universities. As an example, specifically in relation to agriculture, food and ingredients, the activities include incorporating technologies for more efficient production taking into account the preservation of natural resources and their sustainability, obtaining new food grade products and ingredients. Additional areas of interest are beekeeping and health of the bee, the implementation of intelligent crops with photovoltaic energy and use of sensors, and applied ecology for sustainable crop management. In food research, functional food development and the valorization of bioactive compounds from vegetable raw materials and waste from the agri-food sector; in biorefinery, the extraction of new bioingredients from agro-industrial residues, smart ingredients and controlled release of bioactive compounds (Doorn 2019).

3.4   Colombia

Colombia, with its immense biodiversity, has great potential for territorial development with social, environmental and economic sustainability. It is the second most mega-biodiverse country in the world with 51,330 species registered in the SiB Colombia (SiB Colombia: https://cifras.biodiversidad.co/). At present, the country is spending an appropriate time to advance the proposition of a new model of economic relations that allows access to a more prosperous and sustainable economy based on innovation: a bioeconomy model taking into account the specificities of each territory, with the development of new sustainable products and services, adding value based on scientific and technological knowledge.

There is a very favourable institutional environment for the bioeconomy model. As a precedent of policies to stimulate the bioeconomy, since 2011 with the 'Policy for the commercial development of biotechnology based on the sustainable use of biodiversity' the government has recognized the economic potential of biological resources. The 'Green Growth Policy' in 2018 prioritized the bioeconomy, as well the Mission of the Wise, an Advisory Council composed of national and international experts created in 2019 to provide a roadmap for the formulation, coordination and execution of a state policy for the development of Science, Technology and Innovation (CTI). The Mission recognized the bioeconomy as a framework that could support sustainable socio-economic development with a territorial approach (Misión Internacional de Sabios 2020).

Building upon the recommendation of The Mission, in December 2020 the Bioeconomy Mission was launched, as Colombia's National Bioeconomy Strategy, with the aim of providing solutions to the challenge of generating sustainable growth for a biodiverse, productive and equitable Colombia (Gobierno de Colombia 2020). The strategy identifies five strategic areas, namely: (i) biodiversity and ecosystem services; (ii) Colombia Bio-intelligent; (iii) productive and sustainable agriculture; (iv) biomass and green chemistry; and (v) health and wellness.

There are currently a good number of initiatives that underscore the potential and capacities for developing the bioeconomy in Colombia. In the academic sector, there are R&D activities that seek to propose sustainable solutions with the incorporation of knowledge and innovation both to agricultural production, as well as to the valorization of biodiversity resources and bioproducts of high added value. Work in progress also includes the processing of residual biomass, an aspect of great interest to the country because in addition to the recovery of co-products, the problem of soil and water pollution is addressed simultaneously.

In the agricultural sector, models that apply the principles of bioeconomy are under development. One of the most important examples is the obtention and use of bioinputs in the Colombian Corporation of Agricultural Research AgroSavia. These new bioproducts, (biofertilizers, biocontrol) are being used not only for so-called organic products, but also by producers who have incorporated them into conventional production systems, because they consider them to be a valuable tool to ensure the sustainability of their ventures and to minimize the negative impacts on the environment. Another example is the palm sector, which has been a key player in the development of the biofuels policy, given the role of palm oil as the main input for the production of biodiesel. The future of this sector may draw upon the generation of bioproducts, used as inputs for the chemical industry and for pharmaceutical, nutritional and biocosmetic products, as well as the creation of new bioservices, such as those associated with cellular medicine and stem cells.

There are also several instances of the use of S&T for the sustainable use of biodiversity and to face climate change, in line with the bioeconomy approach as a feasible option for territorial development and the conservation of natural resources. For example, the Amazonian Institute for Scientific Research (SINCHI) develops technologies to add value to primary resources and promotes sustainable bioenterprises and biobusinesses with products derived from Amazonian fruit trees and other timber and non-timber forest products, as well as their ecosystem services, generating environmental, social and economic sustainability for the Colombian Amazon. Among the developments, there are 28 natural ingredients, 25 food products (oils, pulps, flours, resins and pigments from microorganisms for use in food and cosmetics), and studies in the biodiversity of insects as an animal protein source (Bueno & Ritoré 2019). Another case of incorporating knowledge for the sustainable use of biodiversity and advances in circular bioeconomy is presented by the Centre for Research on Tropical Aromatic and Medicinal Plant Species – CENIVAM – based at the Industrial University of Santander (Colombia). It is focused on the development of an agro-industry of essential oils and natural ingredients from aromatic and medicinal plants cultivated in small farms. Developments of several commercial products obtained from essential oils to be used as ingredients in new consumer products – some of them patented – for cosmetics, care and cleaning, food and pharmaceutic industries are at various stages of Technological Readiness Level (TRL).

Due mainly to its agricultural tradition, the largest number of bioinnovative companies in the country are from the agricultural sector; in second place food and beverages (where the highest volume of exports is located); and third the pharmaceutical sector followed by bio-based cosmetics and grooming which is increasing rapidly. Concerning addition of value, the primary production sector, the most prominent is agriculture. In terms of intermediate products, chemical and energy – with good potential to initiate the transition to renewable energy and green chemistry. In relation to finished products, food is the most developed area, with high potential in cosmetics and pharmaceuticals. In summary, Colombia has very favourable conditions for the development of bioeconomy, taking into consideration several issues. The first one is the high availability of biomass associated with its condition of a tropical megadiverse country. It has a science and technology system in consolidation, mainly in biological sciences, engineering and ICTs. It also has the presence of one of the first experiences in key activities/sectors, such as the pharmaceutical industry, cosmetics, bioinputs, GMO use, biofuels, and food; and the presence of some business sectors with initiatives/experience in innovation (especially the agricultural sector).

3.5   Costa Rica

Costa Rica is at present a world leader in terms of environmental sustainability. There is high commitment among all the stakeholders and the society to be an international archetype of actions and accomplishments related to SDGs and the sustainability of the planet, moving to a green economy and promoting the sustainable use of natural resources. This inclusive participation has promoted the integration of biodiversity and traditional knowledge in addressing food security, increasing agrobiodiversity – which is an element of resilience – and, thus, contributing to adaptation to climate change (see below).

Historically, Costa Rica has a long tradition and has had clear policies in terms of the formulation and implementation of regulations and strategies associated with biodiversity conservation, environment protection and sustainability. The country pioneered the development of a Payment for Environmental Services Programme (PESP), which retributes forest-land owners in recognition of the ecosystem services their lands provide (Sánchez-Azofeifa 2007, Pagiola 2008, Le Coq et al. 2015). The programme was created under the 1996 Forestry Law, is partially funded by a tax on the consumption of fossil fuels, and recognizes the services of mitigation of greenhouse gases (fixation, reduction and storage of CO_2), and the protection of watersheds, biodiversity and scenic beauty.

The country has made significant investments in education, and in sustainability and related issues such as biodiversity conservation, bioprospection, climate change, deforestation, smart and sustainable agriculture, clean energy, and ecotourism. Building upon those initiatives and the experience of the PESP, in 2019 The National Decarbonisation Plan was launched, aiming to turn the country into a green, fossil GHG emission-free, resilient, and inclusive economy for the 21st century, creating a positive, innovative prospection of the future. This plan includes substantial changes in procedures associated with basic infrastructure and economic sectors such as the public and private transport, energy, industry, agriculture, integrated waste management, land use change, nature-based solutions as well as soil and forest management.

Costa Rica – vis-à-vis its size and population – has important S&T+I capacities, with more than 30 research centres in areas such as biological sciences, agricultural innovation, sustainability, and others relevant to the promotion of bioeconomy, in the three main public universities: The Costa Rica Institute of Technology (ITCR), the University of Costa Rica (UCR), and the National University of Costa Rica (UNA). These facilities include the National Center for High Technology (CENAT), an inter-university space dedicated to research and innovation, which integrates four laboratories in the areas of nanotechnology (LANOTEC), biotechnology innovations (CENINBIOT), environmental sciences (PRIAS) and advanced computing (CNCA) (Rodríguez-Vargas 2019).

The process of accession to the OECD has been a strong stimulus for defining policies and strategies for innovation and competitiveness (OECD 2017) and provided impetus for the elaboration of the National Bioeconomy Strategy – Costa Rica 2020–2030. The strategy aims at: (i) making Costa Rica a model country in sustainable development, taking advantage of its biological resources; (ii) making the bioeconomy one of the pillars of the productive transformation of Costa Rica, promoting innovation, value addition, diversification and sophistication of its economy; and (iii) promoting convergence between the country's wealth in biological resources and the use of national capacities in biological sciences for the valorization of that wealth (Gobierno de Costa Rica 2020). To support the implementation of the strategy an Inter-ministerial Committee for Bioeconomy has been established. To achieve those objectives five strategic axes are proposed: bioeconomy for rural development, biodiversity and development, biorefinery of residual biomass, advanced bioeconomy (e.g. bioentrepreneurship, biotechnology applications), and urban bioeconomy and green cities.

4. IMPLICATIONS OF THE TREND FOR THE DEVELOPMENT OF VALUE CREATION AND BUSINESS MODELS

Based on the type of biological inputs (natural and produced biomass, waste biomasses, elements of biodiversity, ecosystems services, and knowledge of biological processes and principles) we propose six categories to groups' business models (BMs) and value-creation streams: (i) sustainable biomass production; (ii) sustainable production and delivery of healthy food; (iii) biorefinery (bioenergy, bio-based materials) and biomanufacturing; (iv) conservation, knowledge and sustainable use of biodiversity; (v) bio-inspired design; and (vi) payment for ecosystem services. The characterization of BMs in each area proceeds identifying the main economic sectors, partners, resources, relevant innovation activities and consumers (see Table 4.2). The first two are traditional value-creation streams associated to primary activities and the food systems. The others are more innovative, especially the biorefinery concept, bio-inspired design and payment for ecosystems services.

4.1 Sustainable Biomass Production

Business models within this area relate to the sustainable production of the primary sectors of the bioeconomy; namely, crops, livestock, forestry, and fishing and aquaculture; the main partners are farmers, cattle, pig and poultry farmers, ranchers, shepherds, foresters, fishermen and fish farmers. Relevant bioeconomy-related innovations seek to increase productivity and the use of bio-based inputs, enhance the carrying capacity of carbon sinks (e.g. forests and soil) and strengthen adaptations to climate change. Crop and animal species' improvement, biomonitoring solution and the development of bio-based agricultural inputs are chief technological developments.

Three areas for BM development can be identified, associated with: (i) the sustainable intensification of agriculture (e.g. FAO 2011, Pretty & Pervez 2014, Millán et al. 2019); (ii) the forest bioeconomy (e.g. Ladu et al. 2019, Lovric et al. 2019); and (iii) the blue bioeconomy (e.g. EUMOFA 2018). In all cases BMs should include as primary goals improving productivity, adding value and diversifying the use of biomasses. From a sustainability perspective, special attention should be devoted to the needs and inclusion of small family farming and foresters and artisanal fishermen as well as avoiding land-use competition between the production of food and non-food biomasses.

4.2   Sustainable Production and Delivery of Healthy Food

Business models within this area are associated primarily with the food industry (including fresh and processed food) and relevant partners include those involved in processing, distribution and retail activities. Relevant bioeconomy-related innovations could be aimed at improving sensorial traits (e.g. flavour) and nutritional traits (e.g. biofortified and functional goods), pre-serving freshness, enhancing traceability, and improving or developing new bio-based processing methods (e.g. fermentation methods). Biotechnological application to enhance nutrition and other food attributes, new bio-based pack-aging materials, and the development of digital traceability applications are relevant technological developments that can pursue BM in this area.

4.3   Biorefinery (Bioenergy, Bio-based Materials and Biomolecules)

The biorefinery model allows the joint production of bioenergy and bio-based products, i.e. it relates to the transformation of biomass for direct non-food uses. According to the International Energy Agency there are two types of biorefineries depending on whether they are primarily oriented to produce bioenergy (e.g. fuels, electricity or power) and to valorize waste as a side activity; or to produce one or more bio-based product (e.g. feed, biomaterials or chemicals) and to valorize waste in energy generation as a secondary activity (Jungmeir 2014). In both cases the aim of BM is to maximize the economic profitability of the biomass chain.

The variety of products that can be obtained in a biorefinery depends on the variety of biomasses used and the type of technologies used in their transformation (e.g. Bentsen 2019). The more traditional models are those oriented to produce biofuels, for example, from sugarcane (e.g. Sherpa et al. 2017, Silva et al. 2016, Vaz Jr. 2017) and palm oil (e.g. Soh 2016, Silva et al. 2016, Sadhukhan et al. 2017). Other models have been proposed more recently; for example, the waste biorefinery model (e.g. Venkata Mohan et al. 2016, Venkata Mohan et al. 2018, Venkata Mohan et al. 2019a, Righi 2019), the lignocellulosic biorefinery (e.g. Hassan et al. 2019b, Sperandio & Ferreira Filho 2019, Cao et al. 2019, Temmes & Peck 2019), the seaweed and algal biorefinery models (e.g. Torres et al. 2019, Venkata Mohan et al. 2019b) and the urban biorefinery (e.g. Battista et al. 2019). There are also the concepts of large industrial scale (e.g. De Deswarte 2017, Sillanpää & Ncibi 2017) and small-scale (Visser & Ree 2017) biorefineries.

Biorefinery-related BM allows the integration of a variety of partners involved in the biomass management and transformation chains, covering all stages or specialized in specific tasks, from basic tasks such as waste collection and transportation to more sophisticated activities such as the provision of enzymes to be used in biomass conversion processes.

4.4 Bio-inspired Design

Biomimicry applications include a wide variety of areas such as architectural design (e.g. temperature and lighting control), waste reduction and the trans-formation of waste into useful products (e.g. through the biorefinery model), bioremediation and waste treatment, the development of new materials, vehicle design, the development of self-assembly processes, the use of CO_2, artificial photosynthesis, water capture, the designs of products to gradually degrade, and the design of transport and communication systems, among many others.[1] There is a growing body of technical literature about applications in several areas, such as miniaturization (e.g. Gorb & Gorb 2019), development of advanced materials (e.g. Meng et al. 2019, Capece et al. 2019, Sauerwein et al. 2019), aerodynamics (e.g. Hassan et al. 2019a) and fashion (Wood 2019), as well as reviews from an industry perspective (e.g. Richter 2019, Kohsaka et al. 2019).

Pauli (2011)[2] has proposed the concept of the blue economy in a sense that is intrinsically biomimicry-related, to allude to the development of industries inspired by the way nature makes use of physics and biochemistry to efficiently build, transform and recycle complex entities without waste or energy loss. He provides examples of innovations based on those principles in designing of temperature control systems for buildings, treating wastewater, processing of electronic and mining wastes, designing more aerodynamic cars, and using agricultural waste to produce food, beverages and fuels, among many others.

Biomimicry-related BM also can accommodate a diversity of heterogeneous partners, from rural and indigenous communities to advance design studios or

---

[1] See, for example, Janine Benyus' 12 sustainable design ideas from nature (https:// www .youtube .com/ watch ?v = n77BfxnVlyc), Monterey, California, February 2005; and Benyus', 'Biomimicry in action' (https://www.youtube.com/ watch?v=k_GFq12w5WU), TED Talk, Oxford, England, July 2009.

[2] Pauli (2011) includes 100 such examples; an updated list can be found at his webpage: https://www.theblueeconomy.org/

mechatronic labs. The range of potential customers is also wide as application can be found in most aspects of everyday life.

4.5   Conservation, Knowledge and Sustainable Use of Biodiversity

Article 2 of the United Nations Convention on Biological Diversity (UNCBD) (United Nations 1992) defines biological diversity – or biodiversity – as 'the variability among living organisms from all sources including, inter alia, terrestrial, marine and other aquatic ecosystems and the ecological complexes of which they are part; this includes diversity within species, between species and of ecosystems.'

We are interested in BM in the context of the UNCBD intended for the conservation, knowledge and sustainable use of biodiversity, including ecosystems, habitats, genetic materials and genetic resources, regardless of whether they are obtained from conservation areas or public or private germplasm collections. Also relevant are BMs related to agrobiodiversity.

Business models in country signatories of the UNCBD must comply with the rules set in the two protocols within the UNCBD: (i) The Nagoya Protocol on Access to Genetic Resources and the Fair and Equitable Sharing of Benefits Arising from their Utilization (ABS) to the Convention on Biological Diversity; and (ii) The Cartagena Protocol on Biosafety to the Convention on Biological Diversity.

4.6   Payment for Ecosystems Services

The Millennium Ecosystem Assessment (MEA) grouped ecosystem services (ES) into five broad categories: (i) provisioning ES, such as the production of food, freshwater, wood and fibres; (ii) regulating ES, such as the climate and food regulation and water purification; (iii) supporting ES, such as nutrient cycles, soil formation and crop pollination; and (iv) cultural ES, such as aesthetical, spiritual, educational and recreational benefits.

Business models based on the payment for ecosystems services (PES) have been motivated by global concerns, especially climate change. Probably the best known are the schemes of payment for ecosystems services and CO_2 emission trading mechanisms.

Table 4.2 *A framework for value creation and business models in the bioeconomy*

Sustainable biomass production

Base sectors	Partners	Resources	Relevant innovation activities	Consumers
Crops, livestock, forestry, fishing and aquaculture	Farmers, cattle, pig and poultry farmers, ranchers, shepherds, foresters, fishermen and fish farmers	Land, water, agricultural inputs, cows, poultry, fish	Crop and species improvement, biomonitoring, bioagricultural inputs, CO2 soil capture	Farmers, pig and poultry farmers, ranchers, foresters, fish farmers, agricultural input companies

Sustainable production and delivery of healthy food

Base sectors	Partners	Resources	Relevant innovation activities	Consumers
Crops, livestock, forestry, fishing and aquaculture, food industry	Local markets, wholesale markets, processors, distributors, retailers	Agricultural commodities, fresh food, fish, ingredients	Fermentation processes; ICTs and digital applications for traceability	Institutional and individual consumers

Biorefinery and production of bio-based materials

Base sectors	Partners	Resources	Relevant innovation activities	Consumers
Crops, livestock, forestry, fishing and aquaculture, food industry, municipalities	Waste collectors and transporters, providers of machinery and equipment	Grasses, fibres, wood, waste	Efficient waste collection, pre-treatment methods, bio-based routes for transformation	Electricity utilities, manufacturing companies, institutional and individual consumers

Bio-inspired design

Base sectors	Partners	Resources	Relevant innovation activities	Consumers

Sustainable biomass production				
Base sectors	Partners	Resources	Relevant innovation activities	Consumers
Packing industry, construction industry, transportation, manufacturing, robotics	Product and industrial designers, architects, urban planners	Information/ knowledge from biological processes and principles	Replication of biological principles and processes	Food processing companies, packing, construction and garment industries, city governments

Conservations, knowledge and sustainable use of biodiversity				
Base sectors	Partners	Resources	Relevant innovation activities	Consumers
Agriculture, forestry, conservation sector (public and private), biotechnology companies	Indigenous communities, family farmers, governments, biotechnology industry, pharmaceutical and cosmetic industries	Genes, biochemical elements, microorganisms	Bioprospecting for genetic materials, biotechnology applications in agriculture, food, pharmaceutic and cosmetical development	Conservation organizations, R&D biotechnology companies, agricultural input companies, pharmaceutical and cosmetic companies

Payment for ecosystem services				
Sectors	Partners	Resources	Relevant innovation activities	Consumers
Agriculture, water, tourism, forestry, biodiversity	Indigenous communities, family farmers, commercial farmers, financial sector	Ecosystems services (supporting, regulating, cultural)	Design of financial mechanisms	Investors, water and electricity utilities, GHG emitters

Source: The authors.

5.   IMPACT OF THE TREND REGARDING SOCIETAL, ECONOMIC AND ORGANIZATIONAL TRANSFORMATION AND TRANSITION IN LAC

The LAC region has a critical role to play in the global food security and environmental equilibrium. Bioeconomy expansion will make a substantial contribution to several of the SDGs such as hunger and poverty reduction, as well as in renewable energy and jobs and economic growth (see section 3). The bioeconomy in LAC has a dual set of objectives. At the global level, the region has a critical role in contributing to global food, fibre and energy balances, while improving environmental sustainability; and within the region's boundaries, the bioeconomy is a new source of opportunities for equitable growth through improved agricultural and biomass production (Trigo et al. 2014; Trigo et al. 2021). The processes for the promotion of a bioeconomy model for LAC are present in several countries and advancing according to market conditions based on the specific local characteristics, resources and modes of insertion on the international markets, responding to global challenges such as declining resources, climate change and global demand for sustainable products and services.

The transition towards a knowledge-based bioeconomy is also highly dependent on the level of applicability of new technology developments in specific sectors of the Latin American economy. The expected socio-economic impact can be very high in mature sectors, where value chains are well established (Sasson & Malpica 2018). New approaches look towards more environmentally friendly agricultural systems producing 'more with less', which in the long run will be achieved using biotechnology advances such as improved resistances or tolerances to biotic and abiotic stresses, new functionalities, new bioproducts, and uses of biological resources (see section 4). Some examples of bioeconomy activities based in knowledge and advances in biological sciences include the use of biomass to produce biofuels in biorefineries, or the utilization of microbial enzymes in various food and textile industries, as well as value chains, which include, in addition to the obtention of useful products, the reuse of residues and by-products. The main issue is the increase in knowledge incorporation into agriculture and biomass production. A successful transition to the bioeconomy will require both an intensive effort at human resources development and improved mechanisms for social participation. Implementation of the bioeconomy model requires not only an improved technological base, which in turn reflects in a rearrangement of the scientific skills base for research and development, but also the productive and management levels as bioeconomy strategies (Trigo et al. 2019).

From the different experiences of bioeconomy developments in LAC (see section 3), it is clear that the implementation of bioeconomy systems requires, additionally to a solid scientific and technological base, strong policies supporting it, as an integral part of the country's development plans, including investment allocation. There is also a need for deep changes not only in the productive systems, but also in the social behaviour, attitudes and habits related to demand, market, use and disposal of the products and services. Likewise, policies and regulations are crucial to help to promote and guide new processes, and to manage the transition costs, from the unsustainable fossil-based systems, to the new systems with environmental, social and economic sustainability. Recommendations include the establishment of international mechanisms for knowledge coordination and exchange.

There is close relationship between bioeconomy and climate change management and adaptation; effects on health; digitization and converging technologies (bio, nano, computing); communication and public confidence in transformative sciences and technologies; interdisciplinary education and training at all levels; biodiversity as a resource and basis of bioeconomy; marine and ocean bioeconomy; innovative sources of financing; and bioeconomy in cities.

6.   ASSESSMENT OF THE 'SUSTAINABILITY'

Environmental deterioration, degradation of natural resources and climate change are the utmost current challenges. Ecosystems' health and integrity have been affected by the extraction and overuse of natural resources for production and transformation in many productive systems and economic activities including the waste generated (Dasgupta 2021). In order to improve sustainability, the global economic system has to undergo radical transformation processes. Probably the most clear and smart answer to this challenge is through the circular bioeconomy model for the sustainable production and use of resources and waste streams and their transformation into bioproducts, with added value such as food, feed, bio-based products, biomaterials and bioenergy. The fulfilment of the Sustainable Development Goals (SDGs) in an economy more respectful of the environment is not an option, it is the greatest current responsibility of humanity. It is fundamental to promote human health, environmental health, social health and economic health. Several innovations based on science are crucial for maintaining healthy soils and water, to protect from degradation or restore natural resources, and to conserve biodiversity and increase agrobiodiversity in local communities (von Braun et al. 2021).

The use of SDGs as indicators for bioeconomy monitoring and evaluation facilitates the determination of the associations between the bioeconomy and the 2030 Agenda for Sustainable Development (Calicioglu & Bogdanski 2021). The bioeconomy economy can play a fundamental role in the decarbonization of the planet. How we produce and consume food has profound implications for the health of people, animals, plants and the planet itself. Science, technology and innovation have the potential to turn these unsustainable practices into more environmentally friendly and sustainable productive systems, while creating livelihood opportunities and reducing negative impacts. The adverse environmental and social impacts of current productive systems are mainly due to lack of attention paid to scientific alerts by policy makers, regulations, low levels of science investments and an absence of communication among scientists and with the society in general.

Transitioning towards a sustainable productive system requires transformative changes in food production – the major driver of terrestrial biodiversity decline – in decarbonizing our energy systems – contributors of climate change – and drastically changing consumption and production patterns aligning environmental objectives along entire global supply chains (Dasgupta 2021). The most important global activity looking forward to transforming food systems into sustainable ones and combating climate change during the last two years was the Food Systems Summit 2021 (FSS-2021) (https://www.un.org/en/food-systems-summit). The rationale of this approach is that 'Healthier, more inclusive, sustainable and equitable food systems have the power to catalyse the achievement of all 17 Sustainable Development Goals by 2030 in every country.' Part of the documents from the Scientific Group of the FSS-2021 included specific proposals for the sustainable, inclusive transformation of food systems (von Braun et al. 2021, Hodson et al. 2021). It is clear that there is a need to boost global broad support and commitment for technical, political and social cooperation to implement SDGs, climate agendas and food systems transformation in a holistic process. To achieve this goal, policy innovations, institutional innovations and technology innovations are required urgently, as well as public and private investments.

The bioeconomy provides a systemic framework to enhance the transformation towards nature-positive food systems through the stimulation of synergies among the main UN environmental agreements, i.e. the United Nations Framework Convention on Climate Change (UNFCCC), the Convention on Biological Diversity (CBD), and the United Nations Convention to Combat Desertification (UNCCD) (e.g. IPCC 2019, chap. 6). These synergies can be realized in nature-based solutions (NBS). In fact, NBS are the route of the bioeconomy for synergy among the Rio conventions and post-COVID-19 pandemic recovery.

'Science and innovations for food systems transformation and summit actions' (von Braun et al. 2021) concentrates on the key role of science and knowledge for more sustainable, equitable and resilient food systems, which must be pursued working together with policy makers, public and private sectors, scientists, NGOs and with grassroots organizations of marginalized groups. It identifies seven strategic science-driven innovations for a successful transformation of the food systems that need the strengthening of research cooperation between academy and indigenous peoples, to increase investments on S&T+I, and to establish pathways towards strong science-policy interfaces.

Adequate resource management practices for soil and water will contribute to promote sustainable food systems and are part of ecosystem services. For this, the bioeconomy strategies focus on value chains with integrated cycles, which increase efficiency and recycling through products and co-products in different biological systems. Using new S&T to add value to biological resources leads to more profitable and sustainable markets; therefore future scientific and technological developments can increase the portfolio of bio-products, developed from local biodiversity, in keeping with a circular bio-economy approach (Trigo et al. 2021). The document 'Boost nature positive production' (Hodson et al. 2021) proposes actions and S&T advancements for the transformation of the current 'nature negative' food systems, to food systems that conserve, protect and regenerate natural resources and the natural environment including biodiversity. Bioscience and digital opportunities for innovations include precision agriculture and use of drones for crop production and management, satellite technologies, data science and artificial intelligence, robotics, electronic and biological sensors, genetic engineering, genome editing, alternative protein (including more plant-based and insect-derived protein) sources, diverse micronutrient sources, cell factories, microbiome and soil and plant health technologies, plant nutrition technologies, and animal production and health technologies. Innovations include restoration and maintenance of soil health, increasing agrobiodiversity using local adapted crops, breeding local and underutilized crops, and the use of traditional knowledge to adapt the innovations to the local capacities, conditions and resources.

7.   THE WAY FORWARD

Bioeconomy is receiving increasing attention as an alternative to a global transition to sustainable fossil-free development for its potential to make important contributions to environmental and economic transformation, help conserve or restore habitats, improve knowledge on biodiversity, valorize livelihoods, increase social participation and societal renovation, and going beyond the commoditization of nature (Bastos Lima & Palme 2021). The sustainable and circular bioeconomy has a major role to play here in aligning the economy with the biosphere (IACGB 2020a). Bioeconomy responds to the environmental challenges the world is facing, oriented to reduce the dependence on natural resources, transform manufacturing, promote sustainable production of renewable plant, microbial and animal resources and their conversion into food, feed, materials, bio-based products and bioenergy, while growing new jobs and industries. It is a model that encompasses the environment (natural world, biological resources, and their interactions with human activity), as well as biotechnologies (use of biological organisms, processes or systems to obtain goods and services) and their convergence with digital and nanotechnologies. It strengthens the eco-efficiency of processes and the use of recycled carbon to reduce the use of fossil carbon. It is transversal, regional and interdisciplinary.

The circular bioeconomy model for territorial efficient conversion of resources into value-added products has been recognized as the best choice for SDGs making important contributions to the health and nutrition of a growing population, sustainable provision of food, energy, water and raw materials, as well as soil, climate and environmental protection (IACGB 2020a). The concept excludes the false dichotomy between productive development and sustainability. The sustainable production model of the circular bioeconomy has been proposed as the new strategy for reactivation and reindustrialization, considering changing political contexts such as international power structures, promoting resilience, facing zoonotic and epizootic diseases, biodiversity loss and natural resources degradation (IACGB 2020b). Bioeconomy is not inherently sustainable because it is based on natural resources; it requires the articulated integration of a sustainable supply chain, sustainable appropriate transformation processes and sustainable high-value bioproducts, biomaterials or bioenergy with appropriate trade systems (Tan & Lamers 2021).

A sustainable bioeconomy requires sustainable supply chains and appropriate transforming biotechnologies for processing renewable resources into high value added bioproducts, materials and bioenergy (Tan & Lamers 2021). Biotechnology is one of the key enabling technologies to sustain the circular bioeconomy, offering solutions for an efficient and sustainable production of plant and microbial biomasses; production of bioenergy from (waste) bio-masses; bioremediation and environmental protection; transformation through green chemistry; agri-food processes, integrated value chains in the circular economy (Trigo et al. 2021). In addition, biotechnology also brings solutions to improve the post-harvest processing and thus optimize the bioeconomy sector as a whole. Composting and residual biomass transformation by micro-organisms are crucial for the valorization of waste. Biotechnology and other converging technologies should provide support to the development of the bio-based industries to ensure sustainability of the sector and to reduce possible negative environmental impacts.

Nevertheless, to promote the advances and bioscience innovations and direct them to be a factor of sustainability is not enough; it is fundamental to adapt them to local conditions, resources and capacities, to make them available and accessible to the regional community especially smallholders, and to use them to enhance local and traditional knowledge (von Braun et al. 2021). In order to ensure the sustainability, resilience and adaptability of the selected supply chains, there is a need to maintain permanent investments in bioeconomy development for the establishment of new, innovative, diversified and decentralized value chains and the adaption of old ones. The bioeconomy's maintenance lies in its diversity, adaptability and close interactions with local and rural communities (IACGB 2020b).

The challenges ahead for humanity are multiple, complex and interconnected. Dealing with them requires systemic thinking and acting, and the bioeconomy provides such an approach. There is no second planet. The bioeconomy can allow us to preserve the only one we have.

REFERENCES

Bastos Lima, M. G. & Palme, U. (2021). The bioeconomy–biodiversity nexus: Enhancing or undermining nature's contributions to people? *Conservation*, 2(1), 7–25. https://doi.org/10.3390/conservation2010002.

Battista, F., Frison, N., Pavan, P., Cavinato, C., Gottardo, M., Fatone, F., Eusebi, A. L., Majone, M., Zeppilli, M., Valentino, F., Fino, D., Tommasi, T. & Bolzonella, D. (2019). Food wastes and sewage sludge as feedstock for an urban biorefinery producing biofuels and added value bio-products. *Journal of Chemical Technology and Biotechnology*, 95(2), 328–338. doi.org/10.1002/jctb.6096.

Bentsen, N. S. (2019). Biomass for biorefineries: Availability and costs. In: Bastidas-Oyanedel, J. R. & Schmidt, J. (eds), *Biorefinery* (pp. 37–48). Springer. https://doi.org/10.1007/978-3-030-10961-5_2.

Benyus, J. M. (1997). *Biomimicry: Innovation inspired by nature*. Morrow.

Bueno, J. & Ritoré, S. (2019). Bioprospecting model for a new Colombia drug discovery initiative in the pharmaceutical industry. In: Pardo Martínez, C., Cotte Poveda, A., Fletscher Moreno, S. (eds), *Analysis of science, technology, and innovation in emerging economies*. Palgrave Macmillan. https://doi.org/10.1007/978-3-030-13578-2_3.

Calicioglu, Ö. & Bogdanski, A. (2021). Linking the bioeconomy to the 2030 sustainable development agenda: Can SDG indicators be used to monitor progress towards a sustainable bioeconomy? *New Biotechnology*, 61, 40–49. https://doi.org/https://doi.org/10.1016/j.nbt.2020.10.010.

Cao, Y., Chen, S. S., Zhang, S., Ok, Y. S., Matsagar, B. M., Wu, K. C.-W. & Tsang, D. C. W. (2019). Advances in lignin valorization towards bio-based chemicals and fuels: Lignin biorefinery. *Bioresource Technology*, 291, 121878. https://doi.org/10.1016/j.biortech.2019.121878.

Capece, S., Buono, M., Cascone, F., Egido-Villarreal, J. & Caputo, F. (2019). Biomimetic design and advanced materials for innovative systems. *Materials Science Forum*, 957, 445–454. https://doi.org/10.4028/www.scientific.net/MSF.957.445.

Dasgupta, P. (2021). *The economics of biodiversity: The Dasgupta Review*. London: HM Treasury. https://www.gov.uk/government/publications/final-report-the-economics-of-biodiversity-the-dasgupta-review.

De Deswarte, F. (2017). Biorefining in the UK: Perspectives on opportunities, challenges, the future. *Biofuels, Bioproducts and Biorefining*, 11(1), 12–14. https://doi.org/10.1002/bbb.1748.

Doorn, M. (2019). Bioeconomy in Chile. In: Hodson de Jaramillo, E., Henry, G. & Trigo, E. (eds), *Bioeconomy. New framework for sustainable growth in Latin America*. Editorial Pontificia Universidad Javeriana, Bogotá.

El-Chichakli, B., von Braun, J., Lang, C., Barben, D. & Philp, J. (2016). Policy: Five cornerstones of a global bioeconomy. *Nature*, 535(7611), 221–223. https://doi.org/10.1038/535221a.

EUMOFA – European Market Observatory for Fisheries and Aquaculture Products. (2018). Blue bioeconomy, situation report and perspectives. European Union, Brussels.

European Commission. (2005). New perspectives on the knowledge-based bio-economy. European Commission, Brussels.

European Commission. (2012). Innovating for sustainable growth: A bioeconomy for Europe. Directorate-General for Research and Innovation. European Commission, Brussels. http:// ec .europa .eu/ research/ bioeconomy/ pdf/ b ioeconomyc ommunicati onstrategy_b5_brochure_web.pdf.

European Commission. (2018). A sustainable bioeconomy for Europe: Strengthening the connection between economy, society and the environment: Updated bioeconomy strategy. Directorate-General for Research and Innovation. https://data.europa .eu/doi/10.2777/478385.

European Council. (2007). En route to the knowledge-based bio-economy. German Presidency of the Council of the European Union, Cologne, Germany. https:// dechema.de/dechema_media/Downloads/Positionspapiere/Cologne_Paper.pdf.

FAO. (2011). Save and grow: A policymaker's guide to the sustainable intensification of smallholder crop production. FAO, Rome. http://www.fao.org/3/i2215e/i2215e .pdf.

Frosch, R. A. & Gallopoulos, N. E. (1989). Strategies for manufacturing. *Scientific American*, 261(3), 144–152. DOI:10.1038/scientificamerican0989–144

GBC – German Bioeconomy Council. (2015). Global Bioeconomy Summit, conference report – for a sustainable global bioeconomy. Berlin. https://gbs2020.net/wp -content/uploads/2021/10/GBS-2015_Report_final_neu_2.pdf.

GBC – German Bioeconomy Council. (2018). Global Bioeconomy Summit 2018, conference report, Innovation in the global bioeconomy for sustainable and inclusive transformation and wellbeing. Berlin. https://gbs2020.net/wp-content/uploads/2021/ 10/GBS_2018_Report_web.pdf.

Georgescu-Roegen, N. (1975). Energy and economic myth. *Southern Economic Journal*, XLI, 347–381.

Georgescu-Roegen, N. (1977). Inequality, limits and growth from a bioeconomic viewpoint. *Review of Social Economy*, XXXV, 3, 361–375.

Gobierno de Colombia. (2020). Bioeconomía para una Colombia Potencia viva y diversa: Hacia una sociedad impulsada por el Conocimiento. Bogotá, Colombia.

Gobierno de Costa Rica. (2020). Estrategia Nacional de Bioeconomía – Costa Rica 2020–2030. Ministerio de Ciencia, Tecnología y Telecomunicaciones, San José, Costa Rica.

Gorb, S. N. & Gorb, E. V. (2019). Aquatic insects as a source for biomimetics. In: Del-Claro, K. & Guillermo, R. (eds), *Aquatic insects*. Springer. https://link.springer .com/chapter/10.1007/978-3-030-16327-3_17.

Hassan, J., Anindo, R., Kaushik, C. & Prasad, K. D. V. Y. (2019a). Mimicking insect wings: The roadmap to bioinspiration. ACS Biomater. Sci. Eng. https://doi.org/10 .1021/acsbiomaterials.9b00217.

Hassan, Shady S., S. S., Williams, G. A., Jaiswal, A. K. (2019b). Lignocellulosic biorefineries in Europe: Current state and prospects. *Trends in Biotechnology*, 37(3), 231–234. https://doi.org/10.1016/j.tibtech.2018.07.002.

Henry, G., Hodson de Jaramillo, E., Aramendis, R., Trigo, E. & Rankin, S. (2019). Introduction. In: Hodson de Jaramillo, E., Henry, G. & Trigo, E. (eds), *Bioeconomy. New framework for sustainable growth in Latin America*. Editorial Pontificia

Universidad Javeriana, Bogotá. https://repository.javeriana.edu.co/handle/10554/12190/discover.

Hodson de Jaramillo, E. (ed). (2014). *Towards a Latin America and Caribbean knowledge-based bio-economy in partnership with Europe*. Editorial Pontificia Universidad Javeriana.

Hodson, E., Niggli, U., Kaoru, K., Lal, R. & Sadoff, C. (2021). Boost nature positive production: A paper on Action Track 3. The Scientific Group for the UN Food System Summit 2021. https://dx.doi.org/10.48565/scfss2021-q794.

IACGB – GBS Global Bioeconomy Summit. (2015). Making bioeconomy work for sustainable development. Communiqué of the Global Bioeconomy Summit 2015. Berlin, Germany.

IACGB – GBS Global Bioeconomy Summit. (2018). Innovation in the global bioeconomy for sustainable and inclusive transformation and wellbeing. Communiqué of the Global Bioeconomy Summit 2018. Berlin, Germany.

IACGB – GBS Global Bioeconomy Summit. (2020a). Expanding the sustainable bioeconomy –Vision and way forward. Communiqué of the Global Bioeconomy Summit 2020. https://gbs2020.net/wp-content/uploads/2020/11/GBS2020_IACGB-Communique.pdf.

IACGB – GBS Global Bioeconomy Summit. (2020b). Global Bioeconomy Summit 2020 conference report – Expanding the bioeconomy. Berlin. https://gbs2020.net/wp-content/uploads/2021/02/GBS_2020_Report_final.pdf.

IPCC – (Intergovernmental Panel on Climate Change). (2019). Climate change and land: An IPCC special report on climate change desertification, land degradation, sustainable land management, food security, and greenhouse gas fluxes in terrestrial ecosystems [P. R. Shukla, J. Skea, E. Calvo Buendia, V. Masson-Delmotte, H.-O. Pörtner, D. C. Roberts, P. Zhai, R. Slade, S. Connors, R. van Diemen, M. Ferrat, E. Haughey, S. Luz, S. Neogi, M. Pathak, J. Petzold, J. Portugal Pereira, P. Vyas, E. Huntley, K. Kissick, M. Belkacemi, J. Malley (eds)].

ISAAA. (2017). Global status of commercialized biotech/GM crops in 2017: Biotech crop adoption surges as economic benefits accumulate in 22 years. ISAAA Brief No. 53. ISAAA: Ithaca, New York.

Jungmeir, G. (2014). The biorefinery fact sheet. IEA Bioenergy Task 42 Biorefining. International Energy Agency, Paris, France.

Kohsaka, R., Fujihira, Y. & Uchiyama, Y. (2019). Biomimetics for business? Industry perceptions and patent application. *Journal of Science and Technology Policy Management*, 10(3), 597–616. https://doi.org/10.1108/JSTPM-05-2018-0052.

Ladu, L., Imbert, E., Quitzow, R. & Morone, P. (2019). The role of the policy mix in the transition toward a circular forest bioeconomy. *Forest Policy and Economics*, 101937, https://doi.org/10.1016/j.forpol.2019.05.023.

Le Coq, J.-F., Froger, G., Pesche, D., Legrand, T. & Saenz, F. (2015). Understanding the governance of the payment for environmental services programme in Costa Rica: A policy process perspective. *Ecosystem Services*, 16, 253–265. https://doi.org/10.1016/j.ecoser.2015.10.003.

Lovrić, M., Lovrić, N. & Mavsar, R. (2019). Mapping forest-based bioeconomy research in Europe. *Forest Policy and Economics*. https://doi.org/10.1016/j.forpol.2019.01.019.

Meng, F., Liu, Q., Wang, X., Tan, D., Xue, L. & Barnes, W. J. P. (2019). Tree frog adhesion biomimetics: Opportunities for the development of new, smart adhesives that adhere under wet conditions. *Philosophical Transactions of the Royal Society*

A: *Mathematical, Physical and Engineering Sciences*, 377(2150). http://doi.org/10 .1098/rsta.2019.0131.

Millán, R., Schröder, P. & Sæbø, A (2019). Editorial: Options for transition of land towards intensive and sustainable agricultural systems. *Front. Plant Sci.*, 10(346). DOI: 10.3389/fpls.2019.00346.

Misión Internacional de Sabios. (2020). Colombia hacia las fronteras del conocimiento. Síntesis de las propuestas Volumen 2. https://minciencias.gov.co/sites/default/files/ upload/paginas/ volumen_2_-sintesis_de_propuestas.pdf.

OECD – Organization for Economic Cooperation and Development. (2009). The bioeconomy to 2030: Designing a policy agenda. OECD. https://doi.org/10.1787/ 9789264056886-en.

OECD – Organization for Economic Cooperation and Development. (2017). Reviews of Innovation Policy: Costa Rica 2017. OECD Publishing, Paris. http://dx.doi.org/10 .1787/9789264271654-en.

OECD – Organization for Economic Cooperation and Development. (2018). Realising the circular bioeconomy. OECD Science, Technology and Industry Policy Papers No. 60. https://doi.org/10.1787/31bb2345-en.

Oliveira, A. G. (2019). Bioeconomy in Brazil: Overview. In: Hodson de Jaramillo, E., Henry, G. & Trigo, E. (eds), *Bioeconomy. New framework for sustainable growth in Latin America*. Editorial Pontificia Universidad Javeriana, Bogotá.

Pagiola, S. (2008). Payments for environmental services in Costa Rica. *Ecological Economics*, 65(4), 712–724. https://doi.org/10.1016/j.ecolecon.2007.07.033.

Pauli, G. (2011). *La economía azul*. (Traducción de Ambrosio García Leal de la 1ra edición en inglés, *The Blue Economy: 10 years, 100 innovations, 100 million jobs*, Paradigm Publications, 2010), Tusquets Editores, Bogotá, Colombia.

Pretty, J. & Pervez, B. Z. (2014). Invited review: Sustainable intensification in agricultural systems. *Annals of Botany*, 114, 1571–1596. DOI: 10.1093/aob/mcu205. www .aob.oxfordjournals.org.

Richter, E. (2019). Modern biomimicries. *SN Applied Sciences*, 1(9), 979. https://doi .org/10.1007/s42452–019–0811-y.

Righi, S. (2019). Life cycle assessments of waste-based biorefineries – A critical review. In: Basosi, R., Cellura, M., Longo, S. & Parisi, M. (eds), *Life cycle assessment of energy systems and sustainable energy technologies. Green energy and technology*. Springer. https://doi.org/10.1007/978-3-319-96971-8_1.

Rodríguez, A., Mondaini, A. & Hitschfeld, M. A. (2017). Bioeconomía en América Latina y el Caribe Contexto global y regional y perspectivas. Serie Desarrollo Productivo No. 215, LC/TS.2017/96. CEPAL, Santiago de Chile. https://repositorio .cepal.org/bitstream/handle/11362/42427/1/ S1701022_es.pdf.

Rodríguez-Vargas, A. G. (2019). Bioeconomy in Costa Rica. In: Hodson de Jaramillo, E., Henry, G. & Trigo, E. (eds), *Bioeconomy. New framework for sustainable growth in Latin America*. Editorial Pontificia Universidad Javeriana, Bogotá. https:// repository.javeriana.edu.co/handle/10554/12190/discover.

Sadhukhan, J., Martinez-Hernandez, E., Murphy, R. J., Ng D. K. S, Hassim, M. H., Ng K. S., Kin, W. Y., Fahani, J. I., Leung Pah Hang, M. Y. & Andiappan, V. (2017). Role of bioenergy, biorefinery and bioeconomy in sustainable development: Strategic pathways for Malaysia. *Renewable and Sustainable Energy Reviews*. https://doi.org/10.1016/j.rser.2017.06.007.

Sánchez-Azofeifa, G. A., Pfaff, A., Robalino, J. A. & Boomhower, J. P. (2007). Costa Rica's payment for environmental services program: Intention, implementation, and impact. *Conservation Biology*, 21(5), 1165–1173. https:// doi .org/ 10 .1111/ j .1523 -1739.2007.00751.x.

Sasson, A. & Malpica, C. (2018). Bioeconomy in Latin America. *New Biotechnology*, 40, 40–45. https://doi.org/10.1016/j.nbt.2017.07.007.

Sauerwein, M., Doubrovski, Z., Balkenende, R. & Bakker, C. E. (2019). Exploring the potential of additive manufacturing for product design in a circular economy. *Journal of Cleaner Production*, 226, 1138–1149. https://doi.org/10.1016/j.jclepro .2019.04.108.

Sherpa, K. C., Rajak, R. C., Banerjee, R. & Banerjee, R. (2017). Sugarcane: A potential agricultural crop for bioeconomy through biorefinery. In: A. Kuila (ed.), *Lignocellulosic biomass production and industrial applications* (pp. 171–196). John Wiley & Sons, Inc. https://doi.org/10.1002/9781119323686.ch8.

Sillanpää, M. & Ncibi, C. (2017). Biorefineries: Industrial-scale production paving the way for bioeconomy. In: *A sustainable bioeconomy: The Green Industrial Revolution* (pp. 233–270). DOI: 10.1007/978–3-319–55637–6_7.

Silva, E., Escobar, J., Garcia-Nunez, J. A. & Barrera, J. (2016). Bioenergía y bior-refinerías para caña de azúcar y palma de aceite. *Palmas*, 37 (Especial Tomo II), 119–136.

Soh, L. (2016). Biocombustibles de segunda generación de la biomasa de palma de aceite. *Palmas*, 37 (Especial Tomo II), 137–148.

Sperandio, G. B. & Ferreira Filho, E. X. (2019). Fungal co-cultures in the lignocellulosic biorefinery context: A review. *International Biodeterioration & Biodegradation*, 142, 109–123. https://doi.org/10.1016/j.ibiod.2019.05.014.

Tan, E. & Lamers, P. (2021). Circular bioeconomy concepts – A perspective. *Frontiers in Sustainability*, 2, 701509. https://doi.org/10.3389/frsus.2021.701509.

Temmes, A. & Peck, P. (2019). Do forest biorefineries fit with working principles of a circular bioeconomy? A case of Finnish and Swedish initiatives. *Forest Policy and Economics*. https://doi.org/10.1016/j.forpol.2019.03.013.

Torres, M. D., Kraan, S. & Domínguez, H. (2019). Seaweed biorefinery. *Rev Environ Sci Biotechnol*. https://doi.org/10.1007/s11157-019-09496-y.

Trigo, E. (2011). The bioeconomy in Latin America and the Caribbean: Towards a soci-oeconomic research agenda. LAC Regional IAAE Inter-conference Symposium on the Bio-economy, 19–20 September 2011, CIAT, Cali, Colombia.

Trigo, E., Regúnaga, M., Costa, R. & Coremberg, A. (2019). Bioeconomy in Argentina: Scope, current situation, and sustainable development opportunities. In: Hodson de Jaramillo, E., Henry, G. & Trigo, E. (eds), *Bioeconomy. New framework for sustainable growth in Latin America*. Editorial Pontificia Universidad Javeriana, Bogotá. https://repository.javeriana.edu.co/handle/10554/12190/discover.

Trigo, E. J., Henry, G., Sanders, J., Schurr, U., Ingelbrecht, I., Revel, C., Santana, C. & Rocha, P. (2014). Towards bioeconomy development in Latin America and the Caribbean. In: Hodson de Jaramillo, E. (ed.), *Towards a Latin America and Caribbean knowledge-based bio-economy in partnership with Europe*. Editorial Pontificia Universidad Javeriana.

Trigo, E., Chavarria, H., Pray, C., Smyth, S. J., Torroba, A., Wesseler, J., Zilberman, D. & Martinez, J. F. (2021). The bioeconomy and food systems transformation: Food Systems Summit Brief Prepared by Research Partners of the Scientific Group. http:// doi.org/10.48565/scfss2021-w513.

United Nations. (1992). Convention on Biological Diversity. https://www.cbd.int/doc/ legal/cbd-en.pdf.

Vaz Jr., S. (2017). Sugarcane-biorefinery. *Advances in Biochemical Engineering/ Biotechnology*, 166, 1–12. DOI: 10.1007/10_2016_70.

Venkata Mohan, S., Chiranjeevi, P., Dahiya, S. & Kumar, A. N. (2018). Waste derived bioeconomy in India: A perspective. *New Biotechnology*, 40, 60–69. https://doi.org/ 10.1016/j.nbt.2017.06.006.

Venkata Mohan, S., Dahiya, S., Amulya, K., Katakojwala, R. & Vanitha, T. K. (2019a). Can circular bioeconomy be fueled by waste biorefineries – A closer look. *Bioresource Technology Reports*, 7, 100277. https://doi.org/10.1016/j.biteb.2019 .100277.

Venkata Mohan, S., Hemalatha, M., Chakraborty, D., Chatterjee, S., Ranadheer, P. & Kona, R. (2019b). Algal biorefinery models with self-sustainable closed loop approach: Trends and prospective for blue-bioeconomy. *Bioresource Technology*, 295, 122128. https://doi.org/10.1016/j.biortech.2019.122128.

Venkata Mohan, S., Nikhil, G. N., Chiranjeevi, P., Nagendranatha Reddy, C., Rohit, M. V., Kumar, A. N. & Sarkar, O. (2016). Waste biorefinery models towards sustainable circular bioeconomy: Critical review and future perspectives. *Bioresource Technology*, 215, 2–12. https://doi.org/10.1016/j.biortech.2016.03.130.

Vincent, J. F. V., Bogatyreva, O. A., Bogatyrev, N. R., Bowyer, A. & Pahl, A.-K. (2006). Biomimetics: Its practice and theory. *Journal of The Royal Society Interface*, 3(9), 471–482. https://doi.org/10.1098/rsif.2006.0127.

Visser, C. L. M. de & Ree, R. van. (2017). *Small-scale biorefining*. Wageningen University and Research.

von Braun, J., Afsana, K., Fresco, L. O. & Hassan, M. (eds). (2021). Science and innovations for food systems transformation and summit actions. Papers by the Scientific Group and its partners in support of the UN Food Systems Summit. https:// sc-fss2021.org/wp-content/uploads/2021/09/ScGroup_Reader_UNFSS2021.pdf.

The White House. (2012). *National bioeconomy blueprint*. The White House, Washington DC.

Wood, J. (2019). Bioinspiration in fashion – A review. *Biomimetics*, 4(1), 16. https:// doi.org/10.3390/biomimetics4010016.

Yap, N. T. & Devlin, J. F. (2017). Explaining industrial symbiosis emergence, development, and disruption: A multilevel analytical framework. *Journal of Industrial Ecology*, 21(1), 6–15.

5. The collaborative and sharing economy: underlying trends, values and tensions

Arnoud Lagendijk and Mark A. Wiering

---

1. TRENDS AND THEIR LINKAGES: BRAVE ATTEMPTS TO DEMARCATE DIFFERENT PHENOMENA WITHIN THE COLLABORATIVE AND SHARING ECONOMY

As Šiuškaitė et al. (2019) discuss, the collaborative and sharing economy can build on nearly half a century's development of societal initiatives and business models. The 1970s gave rise to the concept of collaborative consumption (Felson & Spaeth, 1978), which was popularised by the seminal work of Botsman and Rogers (2010) when the first digital innovations became visible (Šiuškaitė et al., 2019, p. 374). Next, in the 1990s, Internet technology was introduced and spread, with both profound social and economic implications. This ushered in an era of digitalisation, platform-based business models and a wave of business and social innovation. Then, in the view of Šiuškaitė et al. (2019), from around 2010 a divide emerged between the concepts of the sharing economy and collaborative consumption. This divide occurred around the issue of profit-making, with (real) sharing embracing non-profit, and collaborative consumption embracing profit. However, by this time the variety in practices in the field of the collaborative and sharing economy, and underlying idea and motives, had become enormous. This also resulted in a proliferation of definitions and categorisations. To shed some light on this complex development, we will present three 'founding' trends: (1) the sharing economy seeking utility, (2) digital platforms, and (3) initiatives seeking mutuality and solidarity, in which goods and services are considered as 'new commons'.

In this section, we will discuss the three trends which, in our reading, constitute the landscape of collaborative and sharing economy. This landscape consists of three overlapping circles, resulting in a more fine-grained division, pictured and elaborated in Figure 5.1. In doing so, we try to be more precise than the way the literature uses the term 'collaborative economy'. For instance, in their seminal work, Botsman and Rogers (2010) use 'collaborative economy' as the umbrella term for utility-based and commons-based collaborative consumption, production, education and finance (cf. Stokes et al., 2014) that we distinguish below (they use 'collaborative consumption' for the part that we describe here under trend 1).

1.1   Trend 1: Sharing as an Instrument for Collective Utility

In their seminal paper, Felson and Spaeth (1978) saw sharing practices and collaborative consumption as routine activities occurring within social groups, such as families, friends, neighbours, etc. This collective consumption stemmed primarily from functional interdependencies that shape social interaction. Utility thus stems not only from personal preferences, but also from the need for social interaction and, consequently, the rise of group preferences. These needs are twofold. Felson and Spaeth (1978) emphasise the way social interaction within the group creates specific collaborative consumption behaviour. Apart from access to goods and services, this includes the wish of individuals to join group activities and be part of community life. Meeting this social need is considered a utility in itself. One area in which such collective consumptions continue to grow is neighbourhood security. The most manifest form of security consists of gated communities, a phenomenon with a long history and recently accelerating. Supported by digital technology, there is also a growing market of neighbourhood watch applications.

Trends in utility have been accompanied by moves towards scaling. Over time, the scope of collaborative consumption has shifted and scaled from local communities to larger groups of customers. Rather than social bonds, interdependencies became mediated through a third party, an intermediary firm orchestrating transactions between peers. Sharing practices and collaborative consumption thus shifted from social routines fixed in time and place, to a new business and market reality in which firms explored and developed new business models based on (peer-to-peer) P2P interaction resulting in new forms of access (Bardhi & Eckhardt, 2012). At the core of this understanding of the sharing economy is the increased utility it brings to consumers and users. Moreover, many intermediaries have grown into multinational companies, thus scaling 'sharing' to national and global levels. In doing so, they have turned into viable and threatening alternative business models for conventional, dyadic markets. Examples are the impact of Uber and Lyft in the taxi market, Airbnb in the hotel market, and crowdfunding in the financial market.

Against this background, definitions of the collaborative and sharing economy range from narrow to broad. Frenken (2017, p. 3), for instance, defines the sharing economy as 'consumers granting each other temporary access to their underused physical assets ("idle capacity"), possibly for money'. The use of idle capacity only covers a part of the broader sharing phenomenon, however. While it is not easy to draw exact boundaries, the collaborative and sharing economies, as defined above, also encompass the shared use of goods provided by businesses rather than P2P (such as on-street bikes and scooters), collective production and distribution (e.g. energy) (Plewnia, 2019). An even broader definition also includes second-hand use and the exchange of immaterial stuff (like ideas). While such boundaries go too far in our view, it is useful to mark out the importance of P2P in the economy at large, and how it has given rise to a blooming sharing economy, however circumscribed.

The main tenet of sharing and collaborative consumption, in summary, is that it goes beyond conventional dyadic (seller-buyer) transactions (Perren & Grauerholz, 2015). Collaborative consumption is either multiple or triadic. Multiple means that consumers consist of a peer group using a collective, social mechanism for acquiring and using a good/service. Examples include a family car, a shared holiday home booked by friends and a street's tool bank. Triadic means that a consumer acquires access to a good/service in the possession of a 'peer' through an intermediary agent. Although peers often make some form of social contact, arranging access here mostly includes a formal (legal and pecuniary) P2P arrangement for the temporary use of an item. Examples are Airbnb, ZipCar or Snappcar. Moreover, rather than a group activity, 'collaboration' then turns into a utility-based business technique overhauling an entire market. In the words of Sundararajan (2013, p. 2): 'The terms "collaborative consumption" and "sharing economy" might seem more reminiscent of flower power than of Gordon Gekko, but the business threats they embody are very real.' Such utility-based sharing and collaborative consumption presents an important trend, hence, which has benefited from digitalisation. It also partly contrasts to, but also overlaps with, a 'commons-based' collaborative economy. We will now turn to the trends of digitalisation and the embracing of the commons.

1.2   Trend 2: Digital Sharing Platforms

The main boost for the shift in collaborative consumption from social groups to 'peer to peer' (P2P) mediated transactions has been digitalisation and the 'platform economy'. In her seminal paper 'Debating the sharing economy', Schor (2016) tightly connects the sharing economy to the use of digital platforms. It is the development and proliferation of digital access and platforms that spurred and overhauled collaborative consumption. From a communal washing machine in the basement of the apartment block, the ridesharing to ease the burden of the daily commute, the family- and friends-based consumption of cars, homes, gardens, and joint leisure trips (Felson & Spaeth,

1978), digitalisation boosted the sharing and (re)circulation of a much wider set of goods and services, involving much larger groups of customers. Without doing away with the significance of interaction between peers, digitalisation revolutionised access. Not only did digitalisation allow the sharing of assets such as cars, homes, private gardens, etc., to extend from family, friends and neighbours to a much wider peer network; it also made it possible for business providers to bring new services to the market, through creating advanced technologies allowing peers to share assets and knowledge in sophisticated and frequent ways (Sundararajan, 2013). Famous examples are Airbnb, Uber or Snappcar, or neighbourhood apps such as Peerby (local tool-sharing) and Nextdoor (neighbourhood communication). In particular, the rise of digital apps enabled widespread P2P transactions for goods and services with a much-enhanced utility for both provider and customer. Moreover, besides common items such as homes and cars, platforms have proliferated for 3D printers, clothing, pets, (moto)bikes, and all kinds of untapped talent.

The scaling of the peer group, and the widening of the scope of goods/ services has turned the debate on 'sharing' and collaborative consumption from an issue of consumer behaviour and social practice to one of economic change, as captured by notions of 'sharing economy', 'platform economy', 'gig economy', etc. In market terms, what is of particular interest is how the fertile combination of collaborative consumption and digitalisation has given rise to a whole new world of business models. The crux of these models is that they join a more open approach to collaborative consumption (beyond family, friends and neighbours) with advanced, hyper-productive digital technologies of transacting, payment and business operations. As the growth and reach of sharing apps shows, the impact of these new business models cannot be underestimated.

While digitalisation presents a major force, one should note that collaborative consumption does not fully coincide with the digital platform economy. On the one hand, platform-based applications have developed alongside more traditional, group-based collaborative forms of consumption such as ridesharing, communal laundry, and family and friends' outings. While these group-based forms also stand to benefit from digital communication, their continuing success stems from their rooting in local social practices. A substantive part of the collaborative economy, hence, remains non-digital. On the other hand, digital platforms also work outside of the collaborative economy. Many goods and services now rented and hired to customers through digital platforms remain dyadic, and hence do not involve P2P sharing. Examples are the business-to-consumer (B2C) booking sites for tourist accommodation, flights and event tickets, car and bike rental, and the resale of second-hand goods. Because the rise and impact of these digital business models has been immense, it is presented as a revolutionary shift to an 'on-demand' economy.

Although many accounts have also included digital booking and reselling under a broad umbrella of the collaborative and sharing economy, we prefer to keep them out, as we will show later.

1.3   Trend 3: 'Commons'-based Sharing and Producing

Early proponents grounded the sharing economy in a narrative on basic values, notably sustainability, solidarity, democratisation and a move away from individual possession (Heinrichs, 2013). This grounding, in turn, stemmed from a growing interest in the 'commons' and collaboration as core means of social and economic governance. In line with both economic and urban perspectives on collaboration, the commons are understood here as a way to better organise the shared utilisation of scarce goods and resources (Ostrom et al., 1999; Sennett, 2012). The rising attention for sharing presents a counterweight against the largely individualistic, market oriented, consumer-oriented patterns in our societies that we gradually created and fine-tuned over the last decades (Graeber, 2012). So, critically, where sharing in collaborative consumption is primarily understood in *instrumental terms*, based on the utility of sharing and social bonding, the collaborative economy adopts a *valued-based perspective*, pointing out the significance of the commons and solidarity. Besides collaborative consumption, this idea of sharing also entails collective production, such as in collective craft workshops or, in current times, 'hackerspaces'.

What troubles the debate is that, in the literature, the utility-based and commons-based trends present an area of overlap as well as divide. That overlap sits in applications where sharing enhancing collective utility is organised through communal (non-profit) business or organisational models. The original Couchsurfing presents an emblematic case, as will be explained later. The divide arises where sharing just becomes a commercial P2P affair, detached from social bonding or communal values. In a provocative statement titled 'The sharing economy isn't about sharing at all', Eckhardt and Bardhi (2015) brought home the message that the sharing economy, first and foremost, entailed a profit-making business model combining access-based consumer utility and extreme operational efficiency. For the consumer, platform trading gives, to quote, the 'convenient and cost-effective access to valued resources, flexibility, and freedom from the financial, social, and emotional obligations embedded in ownership and sharing' (Eckhardt & Bardhi, 2015, p. 898). This is not to say that utility-based access has no wider social benefits. Better access enhances efficiency, and hence welfare, at the level of society. It also contributes to sustainability, although this may be countered by a rise in demand enabled by increased access. Increasing demand, in effect, appears to be a major aspiration of access-based business models, through the invitation to travel more, to stay more at other places, view more, etc. Indeed, through this 'sharing economy', we can also access more stuff (Botsman & Rogers, 2010). In doing so, we seem to meet our tendency towards addictive and compulsive consumption far more than engaging in the ethical and moral debates triggering the original ideas on sharing. Perren and Grauerholz (2015, p. 143) thus see that a major issue is 'whether the so-called "sharing economy" is a manifestation of the empowered and entrepreneurial consumer or just the latest form of contemporary capitalist exploitation'. In the words of Le Tellier (2014), 'the sharing economy isn't about sharing, [i]t's about making as many quick bucks as possible'.

Accordingly, the domain of sharing splits between communal sharing and what Belk (2014, p. 14) labels as 'pseudo sharing'. In business terms, this brings about a basic divide between 'non-profit' and 'for-profit'. We should admit, however, that the borders between non-profit and for-profit are rather fuzzy. There are many for-profit companies embracing, to some extent, value-based business models. We can think of the rise of social enterprises. Examples are Couchsurfing (after its capitalisation in 2011) and ZipCar (Sundararajan, 2013). Also, communal models often outsource sharing applications to for-profit companies, as our example of bike-sharing will show. Digitalisation plays an important role here, because it has driven much sharing in the hands of 'high-tech' businesses and 'big-tech' corporations, adding for-profit aspects to non-profit transactions. Accordingly, the most marked non-profit activities remain in non-digitised commons-based collaborative and sharing practices, such as 'street level' tool libraries and timebanks, and in the domain of collaborative production (energy cooperatives, makerspaces etc.).

We capture the richness and diversity of the sharing and collaborative economy twofold. First, we present a more traditional and straightforward picture (see Figure 5.1) built upon the triangle of platform, provider and consumer, with providers and consumers being businesses or (peer-)citizens. This is further divided into the for-profit versus non-profit spectrum. Examples of P2P platform-based hiring activities are digitalised provisions of private-owned rental assets like rooms, car rides or tools, with for-profit intermediaries such as Uber and Airbnb. This entails not-for-profit intermediaries: (original) Couchsurfing, bike-sharing, or P2P services such as Repair Café. A service like Peerby is somewhere in-between as this service is not making profit in itself, however, it adds additional services for profit. Examples of B2C include digitalised provision of business-owned, locally provided rental goods like 'docked' cars (Greenwheels), scooters (Bolt), and coworking space (seats2meet), and (for-profit) versus communal bike-sharing (Vélib-Paris, Velo-Antwerpen, not for profit). Finally, B2B hiring activities entail platform-based sharing as lending or exchanging information between businesses without profit base (cooperation on waste management, of different

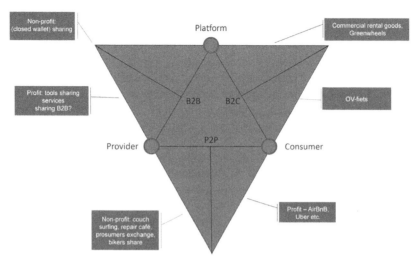

Figure 5.1   Overview of sharing organisational models, with examples

companies – Le Deux Rives project in Paris, or an Artificial Intelligence-based digital freight network, for more efficient freight transport – Convoy) or with profit-based market parties (Yard Club, renting idle equipment for construction companies, taken over by Caterpillar).

Second, drawing three overlapping circles representing our three trends creates a landscape with six segments of the collaborative and sharing economy, plus two outliers (see Figure 5.2). The outliers do not meet our middle-range definition in which we demand more than idle capacity, and exclude second-hand markets and platform booking. Core segments:

1. Utility-based sharing as part of long-standing social practices, grounded in collective utility and social needs, without platform technology; the crux here is a business model based on triad or multiple parties (groups, communities) rather than just the buyer-seller dyad. Neighbourhood security presents a growing market.
2. Sharing and collaborative consumption driven by aspirations to shift to an economy rooted in values of the commons; here utility meets mutuality. While this section includes some of the earlier examples of 'sharing-in', like tools- and timebanks, it largely remains a small-scale local phenomenon.
3. Sharing spaces or creating collaborative production deeply rooted in values of the common; this entails the world of physical (and hence localised) makerspaces and hackerspaces, manifesting considerable growth and development.

4. Platform-based collaborative production, in the form of digital maker-spaces and hackerspaces (as 'commons'), like digital map-making, also manifesting some growth.
5. 'Sharing' platform-based collaborative consumption, in which all trends of a peers-based market, values of the commons and digital technology, come together; while this can be seen as a pivotal site of the collaborative and sharing economy, we also see that organisations that started here have either disappeared or turned into full-fledged for-profit companies (like Couchsurfing).
6. For-profit ('pseudo-sharing') platform-based sharing; this is the site of the emblematic, world-conquering companies meeting the utility of sharing houses, cars, etc. This is offering new, rapidly expanding domains for capitalist growth.

Outliers:

7. Exchange of products through digital platforms run by a for-profit inter-mediary, without P2P sharing; this entails platform delivery and booking of commercial goods, as well as the digital second-hand market. This also presents a major growth market. However, because of the absence of sharing, it is not part of the collaborative and sharing economy.
8. Conventional markets for renting, leasing and reselling, like car hiring and leasing, bike renting, and travel, accommodation bookings in tourism, flea markets and car boot sales; while (in our view) even less part of collab-orative and sharing economy, these activities remain highly popular, and even dominant.

Overlooking our landscape gives the broad impression that developments move away from the centre, towards more for-profit (segments 6 and 7), and one non-profit or 'sharing in' segment (3). To further understand this centrifugal movement, we will look into the development of business models based on business-to-business (B2B), B2C and P2P exchange, in two steps. As a second step, the remainder of the chapter will zoom in further on three cases, two focusing on the intersections of utility and commons in collabo-rative consumption and sharing, and the third one focusing on collaboration production. The cases entail bike-sharing, Couchsurfing and collaborative energy production.

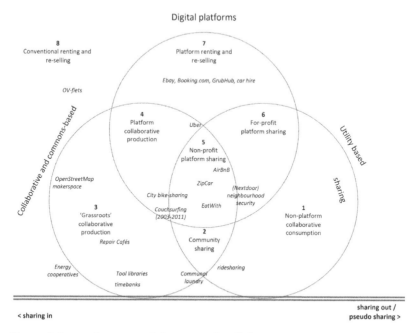

Figure 5.2   Overview of sharing and collaborative economy

2.   VALUE CREATION AND BUSINESS MODELS: EXAMPLES

2.1   Case 1: Bike-sharing as a Case of Commons–Utility and Platform-based Collaborative Consumption

Bike-sharing presents a prominent, global case manifesting the influence of all trends explored so far. These trends, moreover, combine in different ways, underscoring the scattering, and even centrifugal tendencies. We will explore here how these trends have promoted a business model of value creation that, through combining profit and non-profit (Figure 5.1), sits at the middle of our trends (Figure 5.2, segments 5, 6, 8).

In many ways, bike-sharing can be seen as emblematic for the intersection between the commons-based collaborative economy, utility-based sharing, and digital platforms. Notably in dense urban areas, the idea of having easy access to a bike enabling a quick ride from one place in town to another is highly appealing. Besides reducing car congestion and dominance, riding a bike is more flexible, and often quicker, than using public transport; it may also be more cost-effective (Teixeira et al., 2021). So, this brings together the commons and the utility of sharing. The user group consists of inhabitants and visitors subscribing to the system of the communal use of a pool of bikes. Moreover, sharing bikes meets certain technical challenges, such as access control, theft protection, easy adaptation of saddle heights, and the management of availability across space. This then benefits from a digital platform, combined with a locking system to protect the bike and verify users' identification. These issues often demand a public-private business model in which municipalities ally with commercial providers.

So, what has happened in practice? Affected by these trends, many cities around the world, as part of communal policies, have built up local, high-tech systems of bike-sharing (https:// en .wikipedia .org/ wiki/ Bicycle -sharing_system). The systems usually consist of docking stations distributed throughout the city, accessible through digital apps and cards, with subscriptions organised through local councils. There have also been many trials with systems without docking stations, where bikes can be left across a certain urban space. While this clearly increases flexibility, it also meets major problems of illegal parking, cycle loss and management. Large-scale docking systems are available in Paris (Vélib), Antwerp (Velo); dockless services abound in Chinese cities such as Beijing (Sun, 2018). Often, the systems receive substantial subsidies, allowing the bikes to be available for low fees. Subsidies are also needed for maintenance and repairs. The systems are run by commercial companies, such as JCDecaux, Motivate and Lyft. In Asian cities, investing in urban bike-sharing became a popular target of venture capitalists (Sun, 2018). This resulted in massive investments in large docking stations and digital platforms.

While the creation of the systems could benefit from a wave of attention and financing, maintaining the system turned out to be a major challenge. The exemplary case is Vélib, the system in Paris. After a successful launch in 2007, and an enormous growth in the following years, the system collapsed in 2017. The performance of the system was impressive, with, at its peak, around 1,400 docking stations across the central districts of Paris, with 14,500 bikes, and almost 89,000 daily rides. However, far more than expected, the system suffered from theft, vandalism and attrition. While exact levels of losses remain open to dispute, this problem has affected many systems worldwide. For instance, an attempt to install a rental system of e-bikes at our own campus in Nijmegen halted because most bikes, despite heavy locks and GPS, quickly disappeared abroad without affordable means of retrieval. Nevertheless, the Paris system has been revived under a new company and has learnt better how to cope with maintenance issues. This contrasts with many bike-sharing schemes in Asia, which have been seriously cut resulting in dumps of excess bikes.

A special case is the Netherlands. Despite the high modal share of bike-riding, access to on-street bike-sharing systems in the Netherlands remains quite limited. This is even more remarkable given that the idea of bike-sharing as a city-wide system originated in Amsterdam in the early 1960s, as part of the hippy movement (Ploeger & Oldenziel, 2020). The initial idea was to put thousands of white-painted bikes for free use in cycle parks across the city. The plan was conceived, and even briefly piloted, by Provo (hippy) member Schimmelpennink. However, because the council refused to adopt the plan, it never materialised. Schimmelpennink tried again in 2000, now with digital technology. However, due to theft, vandalism and rapid obsoletion of the digital technology, the idea folded again. Also, other bikeshare initiatives in Amsterdam, as well as other Dutch cities, never got beyond the pilot phase. So, ironically, the country with the highest modal share of biking is not taking part in the bike-sharing revolution.

It is often said that the market for bike-sharing is limited in the Netherlands due to the high ownership of bikes. While that may be true for demand close to home, it does not apply for travellers. On arrival in a new city, access to a bike can be very handy. Such access is available, but only at railway stations, through the system of 'OV fiets' (PT bike) (Ploeger & Oldenziel, 2020). These bikes are available, often in large quantities, at the cycle parking facilities at the railway stations. In the (pre-COVID-19) top year of 2019, the system reached around 15,000 per day nationally. Most bikes are accessed from the stations' bike parking staff using the public-transport chip-card and some bikes are accessible through lockers. Bikes need to be returned to the rental site. Because of that, and because the system does not rely on open-air docking stations, maintenance costs are lower, although far from negligible. While the system's efficiency and accessibility are enhanced by the use of digital technology, it basically resembles a conventional, and long-standing, service of station-based bike-renting.

So, in sum, many cities host emblematic bike-sharing systems manifesting our threefold trends towards a communal, collective utility, digitalised economy (segment 5), complemented with major commercial investments (6). The Dutch case, however, continues to be dominated by more conventional means of bike-renting, albeit with the use of digital technology.

2.2   Case 2: Couchsurfing from 'Non-profit' to 'Profit'

Very often, sharing platforms evolved from communal to commercial. An example is Couchsurfing, the freely available sharing alternative for Airbnb, based on trust and social aims (Figure 5.2, segment 5/6). This alternative hospitality network was consciously drawn on 'notions of openness and the ideals of the commons' (Marton et al., 2017, p. 1528). It was based on the voluntary work and dedication of many volunteers with the ideal of open-source projects like Wikipedia (Gigaom.com, 2015) and promoted cosmopolitan openness and cultural exchange to strangers (Marton et al., 2017). A vivid account of the site's glory days, 2006–2011, reads as follows:

> Many consider this period the golden era of Couchsurfing. Nobody made any money from the site, it was funded purely by donations and 100% a labour of love by travellers around the world. 'Hosting' and 'surfing' quickly became dictionary terms in the backpacker community. And the community was rich. Any time you were in a new city you could just post in the groups, who is around this afternoon? And instantly you'd have awesome people to hang out and explore with. I started travelling full time in 2011 and was neck deep in the backpacking community. Couchsurfing was central to the culture. It was everywhere. (https://brenontheroad .com/the-end-of-couchsurfing/)

Unfortunately, after a slow but steady rise of subscribers, the platform system suffered from serious server, hard drive and back-up problems in June 2006. After a community-driven restart the lead partners decided to put restrictions on the open-source code and demanded non-disclosure agreements. In 2011, after a rejection of an application for a non-profit, charitable status, it was decided to change to a for-profit, investment-based business model, to professionalise Couchsurfing while trying to preserve the spirit of the service. The site started to charge fees, and, during the COVID-19 crisis, a full paywall required users to pay a monthly subscription. Although new, free sites immediately started to emerge ('WarmShowers', 'BeWelcome', 'Trustroots', 'MovingWorlds', for example), the benefit of a single, high-reach, high-density platform was gone. The debate continues as to whether Couchsurfing has been captured by global capital, only interested in profit-making, or whether the open model was unsustainable due to mounting technical and organisational demands.

2.3   Case 3: Communal, Collaborative Energy Production and Sharing (Windpark Nijmegen-Betuwe)

The ideal of a commons-based collaborative economy has given rise to communal, collaborative production (Figure 5.2, segment 3). This trend is illustrated by the wave of energy cooperatives in the Netherlands, where citizens cooperatively work on creating renewables (wind, solar or biomass) to contribute to the Dutch energy transition. Energy cooperatives have been around since the 1970s in the Netherlands, but it was only after the economic crisis of 2008–2009 that these initiatives took flight, from 40 in 2009 to 340 in 2016 and 676 in 2021 (Oteman et al., 2017; Schwencke, 2021). Almost three-quarters of all cooperatives work on solar projects, amounting to almost a thousand solar projects in 2021. About 12% of cooperatives are setting up wind parks and others are investigating and co-creating new local heat systems (on the basis of geothermal power, sun, air or water); some cooperatives are developing other renewable energy sources such as river hydropower (Schwencke, 2021). Considering these developments, we will zoom in onto a local case, namely Windpark Nijmegen-Betuwe (WPN).

WPN presents a successful initiative of cooperative energy production. By the end of 2012, a regional Dutch environmental NGO (Natuur en Milieu Gelderland) and a local wind farm developer shared their plans for a cooperative wind farm within the municipality of Nijmegen, a city keen to promote greening initiatives for its population. A large energy company had recently abandoned the development of a wind farm along the A15, and the NGO and wind farm developer wanted to take over this plan, on a cooperative basis. The municipality, as the landowner, gave permission 'on the condition that a professional development foundation would realise the wind farm, together with the cooperative yet to be established' (National Program Regional Energy Strategy, interview with one of the initiators, 5 February 2021).

The initiators set up a professional foundation (Wiek-II) and an energy cooperative. With the help of a professional communication and crowdfunding campaign, some seed money and a lot of voluntary enthusiasm, the energy cooperative WPN grew rapidly. During the spring and summer of 2013 more than 1,000 people signed up to become shareholders and the cooperative was able to invest in the wind farm at a risk of about 2 million Euros. Together with a loan from the provincial development agency, sufficient equity was created to borrow the remaining budget. The municipality of Nijmegen was prepared to pay for the zoning plan procedure and environmental impact assessment.

After this first phase, a national subsidy was granted (SDE) and construction of the wind farm could begin. Since then, the farm has been supplying green power to about 7,000 households distributed through a (smaller) energy company. Project revenues helped to create an environmental fund, set up to assist the neighbouring residents, many of whom had initially protested against the wind park. The energy cooperative wants to function as a revolving fund: revenues are partly skimmed to invest in new projects. In 2021, the cooperative created a solar farm of 17,000 PV solar panels. The cooperative's ambition is to create 'a new energy landscape' with innovative forms of electricity storage and local heat systems.

The cooperative and the foundation invested a great deal in participation with local residents, through a lot of talking, coffees and beers, notably during open days for the wind-park organisation and residents' meetings. This resulted, amongst other things, in 'the greening of a square, the preservation of a cherry orchard and the activities of a community theatre', as well as various forms of individual compensation (National Program Regional Energy Strategy interview, 2022). The residents of a nearby smaller hamlet, who initially opposed the park, 'have become good friends'; they even built a solar park in the neighbourhood themselves (National Program Regional Energy Strategy, interview, 2022). So, what this case teaches us is that the 'commons' as a basis for the collaborative economy requires hard work. That starts with transparency and dialogue, both outside and inside the cooperative, with continuous communication on progress, setbacks and adaptation. Notably in the case of resistance, much work should be devoted to a separate process for, and engagement with, neighbouring residents. In the case of Windpark Nijmegen-Betuwe, this engagement also drew on collective utility, involving financial deals.

3. IMPACT OF THE SHARING AND COLLABORATIVE ECONOMY

It is difficult to underestimate the impact of the sharing and collaborative economy, in all its varieties. Considering the for-profit parts, the global sharing economy was valued at USD 113,000 million in 2021 and is expected to rise to USD 600,000 million in 2027 (www.globenewswire.com, 14 October 2022). Digital sharing platforms have changed the way we understand firms and (marketing) channel providers; they have changed (or accelerated the change in) systems of transaction, the institutions of quality control as well as the regulations accompanying new business models, e.g. in lodging or transportation. The sharing and collaborative economy has changed labour markets and their conditions, in positive terms (opening up jobs for low-income groups, increasing demand for jobs) and in negative terms (replacing permanent jobs for temporary, on-demand labour, e.g. through freelance platforms) (Schor, 2016; Ciulli & Kolk, 2019). The impact on sustainability is very difficult to measure, not least because of this growing economic share and accelerated speed of societal and economic activities and transactions.

Pouri and Hilty (Pouri, 2021; Pouri & Hilty, 2021) gave a useful overview of eight 'impact types' of the sharing economy on resource consumption (as part of sustainability). First, there are optimization effects because of increased utility (with 1) direct optimization and 2) cross-activity effects). Next, they point to other effects, such as 3) induction – increased use of the resource leads to use of related sources, car use leads to use of fuel and infrastructure. Then, there is 4) direct and 5) indirect substitution (e.g. Zipcar replacing conventional car services – direct – or replacing the use of public transport – indirect and less sustainable), also 6) direct and 7) indirect rebound effects (e.g. affordable accommodation offered by Airbnb enables guests to use more of these services and travel more or when savings are used to spent on air travel). Finally they mention 8) the 'degradation' effect, which addresses the condition that increased utility and use leads to faster degradation, e.g. scooters wearing out faster in sharing schemes; this also connects to the danger of misuse and mishandling of services and resources, or to downright vandalism and destructiveness of shared or 'commons' goods. In sum, to estimate the impact of the sustainability of sharing activities we have to look at their consumption and other consumptions connected to them, with these impact types (Pouri, 2021, p. 2).

4.   CONCLUSION: CAN THE ASPIRATIONS OF SHARING AND COLLABORATIVE ECONOMY BE KEPT TOGETHER?

The sharing and collaborative economy encompasses a broad range of activities under a variety of definitions and approaches. We have tried to map these approaches and categorise the initiatives by drawing on three trends: 1) the instrumental aspiration for collective utility; 2) digitalization; and 3) (the return to) the aim of collaboration and contributing to mutuality and the 'commons' (Figure 5.1), through the development of business models (P2P, B2C and B2B) and financial models. We have discussed three cases more closely: bike-sharing, Couchsurfing and energy cooperatives.

Conceptually, the discussion is somewhat troubled as scholars are using different labels for the same phenomena (e.g. collaborative consumption and sharing economy) or are emphasising specific elements and specific activities or groups under the umbrella of the sharing economy. We have tried to map different trends and create clearer divisions, but any attempt to do so is vulnerable and open for discussion. In the end, while acknowledging this diverse landscape, we embrace Helen Goulden and Rachel Botsman's comprehensive understanding of the *collaborative economy*, as 'a new way of thinking about business, exchange, value and community'. While its definitions are varied and parameters continue to evolve, activities and models within the collaborative economy enable access instead of ownership, encourage decentralised networks over centralised institutions, and unlock wealth (with and without money). They make use of idle assets and create new marketplaces. In doing so, many also challenge traditional ways of doing business, rules, and regulations' (Stokes et al., 2014, p. 7).

Under this broad umbrella, however, we detect centrifugal forces, drivers, ambitions and developments. Profound idea(l)s regarding the sharing and collaborative economy meet drives towards business expansion, market capture and profit-making. This produces centrifugal forces that swing us out of the overlapping segments joining 'utility' and 'commons-based sharing'. Activities in pivotal segment & (Figure 5.2), combining the three trends, show a tendency to become more profit-oriented (Figure 5.2, segment 6). The exemplary case here is Couchsurfing. This platform, although it reached a larger scale, had difficulties surviving as a non-profit platform because of technical problems and other issues of professionalisation. Lacking a suitable financial model for such a large platform, it was largely dependent on voluntary work and the spirit of the commons, which also asks a lot of the initiators and involved employees. The centrifugal tendency also applies to community initiatives (Figure 5.2, segment 2, outside platform technology), which tend to remain quite limited, and surpassed by commercial apps supporting neighbourhood communication and security (e.g. Nextdoor). For instance, Peerby, a low-access tool-sharing platform, still exists, but is seeking ways to survive by creating more profit-based additional activities. Our bike-sharing case shows a mixed pattern. There are many community-supported urban bike-sharing systems, but it takes a major effort to sustain them, which often requires a role for commercial companies. Old-fashioned rental schemes with some digital support (such as OV fiets) seem more viable. So, why is it so difficult to share goods and services, for free, or almost for free, on larger scales with platform technology? Why is it apparently so difficult to survive as social enterprises or non-profit, trust-based platforms? How is it that sharing 'for free' in an open commons-based environment appears such a strange, distrusted phenomenon in our liberal market economy? Why would we rather pay for a more professional, more commercial and less personal Airbnb service than an open access, commons-based and free service of Couchsurfing? Accordingly, the initial aims of sharing idle capacity in light of sustainability and the creation of new commons, with the help of digital platforms, prove to be hard to meet.

Moreover, the incredible popularity of the more well-known sharing activities such as Airbnb and Uber raise major concerns regarding sustainability. Rebound effects of this sharing of so-called idle capacity cause more traffic, more rental activities and more economic exchange. This might be 'good for the economy' but has profound consequences for environmental sustainability and urban liveability. So, a major dilemma looms for the collaborative and sharing economy. On the one hand, the rise of new, sharing-based business models has had the effect of extending the sharing economy beyond the notion of *idle capacity*. In this way, platform technology has revolutionised traditional rental companies leasing out vehicles, and the sharing of tools, holiday accommodation and other items. It also goes beyond platform-based business models and has given rise to community initiatives that are genuinely devoted to contributing to a fairer, more sustainable economy. On the other hand, there is nothing inherent in the exploitation of idle capacity, or even in P2P transacting, which drives business in the direction of the commons sustainability and social enterprise. What's more, to assess the effects of the sharing and collaborative economy is even more difficult because our societies and economies are changing rapidly due to the same changes that were underpinning the sharing and collaborative economy. These changes include a general shift from production to services, ownership to access and increased digitalisation, especially after COVID-19, affecting every household and business. The aspiration to become more 'collaborative' and 'sharing-in' will remain a major challenge.

REFERENCES

Bardhi, F. & Eckhardt, G. M. (2012). Access-based consumption: The case of car sharing. *Journal of Consumer Research, 39*(4), 881–898.

Belk, R. (2014). Sharing versus pseudo-sharing in Web 2.0. *The Anthropologist, 18*(1), 7–23.

Botsman, R. & Rogers, R. (2010). *What's mine is yours. The rise of collaborative consumption.* Harper-Collins Publishers.

Ciulli, F. & Kolk, A. (2019). Incumbents and business model innovation for the sharing economy: Implications for sustainability. *Journal of Cleaner Production, 214*, 995–1010.

Eckhardt, G. M. & Bardhi, F. (2015). The sharing economy isn't about sharing at all. *Harvard Business Review, 28*(1), 881–898.

Felson, M. & Spaeth, J. L. (1978). Community structure and collaborative consumption: A routine activity approach. *American Behavioral Scientist, 21*(4), 614–624.

Frenken, K. (2017). Political economies and environmental futures for the sharing economy. *Philosophical Transactions of the Royal Society A: Mathematical, Physical and Engineering Sciences, 375*(2095), 20160367.

Graeber, D. (2012). *Debt: The first 5000 years.* Penguin UK.

Heinrichs, H. (2013). Sharing economy: A potential new pathway to sustainability. *Gaia, 22*(4), 228.

Le Tellier, A. (2014). The sharing economy isn't 'collaborative consumption', it's 'disaster capitalism'. *Los Angeles Times, 5.* https://www.latimes.com/opinion/opinion-la/la-ol-sharing-economy-collaborative-consumption-disaster-capitalism-20140604-story.html.

Marton, A., Constantiou, I. & Lagoudakos, G. (2017). Openness and legitimacy building in the sharing economy: An exploratory case study about CouchSurfing. *Proceedings of the 50th Hawaii International Conference on System Sciences.*

National Program Regional Energy Strategy (website) Energy Participation, interview with one of the initiators of windpark Nijmegen-Betuwe. https://www.energieparticipatie.nl/community/praktijkverhalen/hoe-de-buren-van-windpark-nijmegen-betuwe-vrienden-werden.

Ostrom, E., Burger, J., Field, C. B., Norgaard, R. B. & Policansky, D. (1999). Revisiting the commons: Local lessons, global challenges. *Science, 284*(5412), 278–282.

Oteman, M., Kooij, H.-J. & Wiering, M. A. (2017). Pioneering renewable energy in an economic energy policy system: The history and development of Dutch grassroots initiatives. *Sustainability, 9*(4), 550.

Perren, R. & Grauerholz, L. (2015). Collaborative consumption. *International Encyclopedia of the Social & Behavioral Sciences, 4*(2).

Plewnia, F. (2019). The energy system and the sharing economy: Interfaces and overlaps and what to learn from them. *Energies, 12*(3), 339.

Ploeger, J. & Oldenziel, R. (2020). The sociotechnical roots of smart mobility: Bike sharing since 1965. *The Journal of Transport History, 41*(2), 134–159.

Pouri, M. J. (2021). Eight impacts of the digital sharing economy on resource consumption. *Resources, Conservation, and Recycling, 168*, 105434–105434.

Pouri, M. J. & Hilty, L. M. (2021). The digital sharing economy: A confluence of technical and social sharing. *Environmental Innovation and Societal Transitions*, *38*, 127–139.

Schor, J. (2016). Debating the sharing economy. *Journal of Self-governance and Management Economics*, *4*(3), 7–22.

Schwencke, A. M. (2021). *Lokale Energie Monitor 2021*. Hier Opgewekt. https://www .hieropgewekt.nl/uploads/inline/Lokale_Energie_Monitor_2017_3.pdf.

Sennett, R. (2012). *Together: The rituals, pleasures and politics of cooperation*. Yale University Press.

Šiuškaitė, D., Pilinkienė, V. & Žvirdauskas, D. (2019). The conceptualization of the sharing economy as a business model. *Engineering Economics*, *30*(3), 373–381.

Stokes, K., Clarence, E., Anderson, L. & Rinne, A. (2014). *Making sense of the UK collaborative economy* (Vol. 49). Nesta London.

Sun, Y. (2018). Sharing and riding: How the dockless bike sharing scheme in China shapes the city. *Urban Science*, *2*(3), 68.

Sundararajan, A. (2013). From Zipcar to the sharing economy. *Harvard Business Review*. https://hbr.org/2013/01/from-zipcar-to-the-sharing-eco.

Teixeira, J. F., Silva, C. & Moura e Sá, F. (2021). Empirical evidence on the impacts of bikesharing: A literature review. *Transport Reviews*, *41*(3), 329–351.

6. The self-production economy

Peter Troxler

1. INTRODUCTION

The world, as we know it, consists of nature, humans and things. Things are the tools, machines, infrastructures and contraptions the human race was able to make in a much richer way than any other species on earth. Making things at scale, industrial production, is humanity's achievement of the industrial revolution of the 19th century. The 20th century has seen developments on industrialisation through mechanisation (Giedion, 1948), and automation (Noble, 1984) and smart machines (Zuboff, 1988). The full-blown digital transformation of industrial production in both its aspects, the design of things and the manufacturing of things is the most recent phase of these developments.

Industrial development drawing from the promise of digital transformation gets promoted in various national programmes, such as "Smart Industry" (Netherlands), "Industrie 4.0" (Germany), "Future of Manufacturing" (UK), "Piano Nazionale Industria 4.0" (Italy), "La Nouvelle France Industrielle" (France), "Industria Conectada 4.0" (Spain), "Factories of the Future" (Europe), "Advanced Manufacturing Partnership" (USA) and "Made in China 2015" (China), to name a few.[1] A new industrial revolution is said to be on its way.[2] It is supposed to bring a full-blown digitalisation[3] of industrial manufac-

---

[1] For an overview of some of the policies, see e.g. Liao et al. (2017, 2018).

[2] Depending on which sources one refers to, this is the third industrial revolution (Rifkin, 2011), the fourth as in Industrie 4.0 (National Academy of Science and Engineering, 2013) or the fifth (Marsh, 2013).

[3] Literature discerns three levels of turning technologies and systems digital – digitisation, digitalisation, and digital transformation. Digitisation is described as a technical process in Saarikko et al. (2020). Digitisation is the conversion from analogue to digital formats, for example, paper forms to webforms. Digitalisation is defined as a socio-technical process by Saarikko et al. (2020). OECD (2020) state that digitalisation is the use of digital technologies and data as well as interconnections that result in new activities or changes to existing activities. Digitalisation is referred to as a development of technology to achieve transac-

turing – repeating and extending the vision of the ideas of computer integrated manufacturing (CIM) of the 1980s and 1990s.[4]

However, government policies on the digitalisation of manufacturing appear to neglect one inherent affordance of digitalisation. Through digitalisation, the tools of the trade become accessible to people outside the guilds of trade professionals. This is happening in manufacturing, too, as it has happened in music, encyclopaedias and news, although to a much lesser extent. Euchner and Gershenfeld (2015) posit that this aspect of the next revolution in manufacturing "has the really interesting implication of turning consumers into creators and, as a result, into competitors of incumbent companies".[5] These competitors of incumbent companies represent a new branch of manufacturing: the self-production of goods. In this self-production economy local resources could be utilised in a circular manner and at local facilities – production hubs – that could serve as a third kind of manufacturing infrastructure. These hubs would thrive on collaboration and the sharing of knowledge and machinery. They bring together technological, social and knowledge resources to form a new manufacturing ecosystem that ties into the various other aspects of a new economy.

Fuelled by the ubiquitous availability of cheap 3D printers and the proliferation of fab labs and maker spaces, manufacturing has also been turned into a technical pastime. Almost as a by-product of industrial digitalisation, this revival of hobbyist "making" promises to democratise invention; "making" allows people to express their creativity through technology. Everybody, so the slogan goes, can "make (almost) anything" and is empowered to invent and build technical contraptions the current markets don't provide for. "Makers" represent the personification of the reversal of industrial division of labour

---

tional operational efficiencies, or local advantages (Iosad, 2020). Digital transformation is described as a socio-cultural process in Saarikko et al. (2020). According to Iosad (2020), digital transformation is the cultural, organisational and operational change of an organisation, industry or ecosystem through a smart integration of digital technologies, processes and competencies across all levels and functions in a staged way. It is not primarily about technology adoption. It is first and foremost about transforming the mindset and culture of an organisation to ensure that technology can be deployed as a multiplier of impact. The concept of digital transformation goes beyond digitalisation and must also be understood as a profound and radical process of change that directs businesses and organisations in new directions and brings them to a completely different level of effectiveness (Wilms et al., 2017). The process of digital transformation must be seen as a long-term and iterative process.

[4] For an overview, see e.g. Meudt et al. (2017).
[5] Euchner and Gershenfeld (2015, p. 18).

which was a product of scientific management.[6] They invent, design and manufacture, or paraphrasing the words of Petroski, they "hypothesize about assemblages of plastic and electronics that they arrange into a world of their own making".[7]

This chapter investigates the emergence of the self-production economy, its enablers and affordances. While globalisation and digitalisation potentially render any phenomenon ubiquitous, the geopolitical scope of the chapter is mainly on the global North for reasons of concision and accuracy. In terms of economic sectors, the chapter focuses on the manufacturing of consumer goods rather than food and other consumables, while occasionally including professional goods in the analysis. Also, for conciseness the chapter does not delve into the issue of the self-production of energy.[8] The chapter will start with an introduction of the predecessors of the self-production economy, followed by a description of its genesis. It will then analyse the main enablers of the self-production economy – its technologies, factories, communities and markets – and the affordances of the self-production economy in terms of societal, economic and organisational impact and its contribution to a transition to a new economy. The chapter concludes with an informed interpretation of the phenomenon of self-production and an outlook on further analysis and development.

---

[6] In *The principles of scientific management*, Frederic Winslow Taylor (1911) argued that for each element of work, a method must be scientifically developed on how to perform that element of work in the most effective way. Workers need to be trained according to this method. Taylor also advocates a separation between management and (manual) workers, the former develop the method and train the workers, the latter execute the method.

[7] In his book *To engineer is human: The role of failure in successful design*, Henry Petroski describes the scientific method of engineers: "Engineers hypothesize about assemblages of concrete and steel that they arrange into a world of their own making" (Petroski, 2018, p. 43).

[8] "[G]reat economic transformations in history occur when new communication technology converges with new energy systems", according to Rifkin (2011, p. 35). Over the course of the publication of this book, the issue of energy has moved from one of the drivers of economic transformations to center stage in political and economic discussion. The energy transition envisaged by Rifkin as distributed storage technology and "continuous, reliable supply of green energy to meet demand" (ibid., p. 71) has taken center stage in view of accelerating climate change (IPCC, 2023). Alongside decentralised, distributed and small-scale approaches to the self-production of energy, traditional, centralised approaches are pursued too. The intricate interplay of central infrastructures and decentral, "inverse" infrastructures (Egyedi & Mehos, 2012) forms an intriguing field of study – technically, socially and economically – that is, alas, beyond the scope of this chapter.

2. THE DEVELOPMENT OF THE SELF-PRODUCTION ECONOMY

Self-production – also called "do-it yourself" (DIY) – is not a new phenomenon per se. Atkinson defines it as a 19th-century invention: "it emerged from a perceived need to 'keep idle hands busy'. In the hours following a long working day, it acted only to bring the Victorian work ethic from the factory into the home" (Atkinson, 2011, p. 26).

In the early 20th century, magazines such as *Popular Mechanics* in the US featured automotive, home, outdoor, electronics, science, do-it-yourself and technology topics. During wartimes, self-sufficiency and repairing tools and machinery often was a sheer necessity. In the post-war boom, DIY became anew a pastime, promoted, for example, in Germany through the magazine *Selbst ist der Mann*, directed mainly at male adults and promoting home decoration, furniture making and all sorts of technical subjects.

In the US American counterculture of the 1960s, the *Whole Earth Catalogue* promoted self-sufficiency, ecology, alternative pedagogy and DIY, alongside reviews and recommendations of everyday tools. With its religiously inspired opening sentence, "[w]e are as gods and might as well get good at it" (Brand, 1968, p. 3), it set a theme that got repurposed decades later. The *Whole Earth Catalogue* is said to have served as a source of inspiration for the likes of Steve Jobs and Kevin Kelly. The *Whole Earth Catalogue* can be seen as a seminal publication for the Californian ideology, "this unexpected collision of right-wing neo-liberalism, counter-culture radicalism and technological determinism" (Barbrook & Cameron, 1995, para. 9). The "power-to-the-people" rhetoric of the counterculture of the 1960s played a significant role in fostering DIY. Technology was seen as an opportunity of emancipation and the belief that it could empower individuals and make them able to deinstitutionalise society (Lindtner et al., 2014).

More radically, in punk culture, DIY was associated with anti-establishment, anti-consumerist and anti-corporatist ideals. In technology, computers and electronics, a hacker subculture emerged. Initially, the word "hacker" came to use in places like MIT as a tech slang, meaning "one who works like a hack at writing and experimenting with software, who enjoys computer programming for its own sake". Soon, hack also signified a creative prank, and later, hacking became synonymous with (illegally) entering a computer system. Hacking, spearheaded by the Chaos Computer Club, brought the DIY approach to information security research. Hacklabs and hackerspaces emerged when personal computers became available.[9] DIY, as Cramer (2019) notes, "has always been conservative *and* anti-conservative" (emphasis in the original), romantic and reactionary, extreme left and extreme right, Unabomber and Home Depot shopper.

Collectively owned and used workshops where people share tools and knowledge – what today one would call self-production hubs – have also been around for decades. In the 1940s in Turkey, several agricultural schools were established, the village institutes, teaching basic literacy and numeracy as well as agriculture, construction, and arts and crafts. In communist Czechoslovakia, the Svazarm were publicly accessible spaces equipped for the mechanical repair of agricultural and military machinery and radios (P. Stratil, personal communication, 3 May 2019). In East Germany, so-called stations for young naturalists and technicians (Stationen Junger Naturforscher und Techniker) existed as part of the Vladimir Lenin All-Union Pioneer Organization (Sipos & Franzl, 2020).

In the mid-1980s, the Greater London Council supported community-based prototyping workshops. Called "Technology Networks", they were a short-lived answer to increasing unemployment and the demise of industry in the UK in these times. Their purpose was to provide physical spaces, access to shared machine tools, and assistance from technical staff to local communities, workers and co-operative enterprises so they could develop prototypes for new industrial products such as energy saving devices for refrigerators, toys for schools, or electric bicycles. Some of those found developers and investors in the UK and other countries. Another stream of activities, though, was more oriented towards social mobilisation. Eventually, funding for Technology Networks was withdrawn under Margaret Thatcher, and they are largely forgotten now.

More recently, the "Haus der Eigenarbeit" (house of your own work) in Munich opened in 1987. Hackerspace c-base in Berlin started in 1995; it is said to be "the mother of all hackerspaces" and served as a model for similar spaces, mainly in the US and in Europe.

The early years of the 21st century can be seen as a particularly important period for the genesis of the self-production economy of durable consumer goods. Under a new name – making – several technical, social and commercial developments coincided.

---

[9]   Hacklabs and hackerspaces differ in political agenda and social critique, the former being more politically oriented and oriented towards the development of critical knowledge, the latter more leisurely and oriented towards socialising (maxigas, 2012).

In 2005, the RepRap project was founded by Adrian Bowyer at the University of Bath, UK, with the promise to create a rapid prototyping machine (aka 3D printer) that could reproduce itself. In the same year, Massimo Banzi and David Cuartielles presented their first Arduino boards, easily programmable microcontrollers with accessible analogue and digital inputs and outputs that quickly became famous with artists for interactive installations and found uses in engineering and DIY for the creation of all sorts of interactive objects.[10]

Also in 2005, Neil Gershenfeld published his book *FAB* in which he promised personal fabrication as "the coming revolution on your desktop" (Gershenfeld, 2005). The book served as a companion for many to set up fabrication laboratories, "fab labs", according to the recipe developed at MIT, that would become one of the backbones of the self-production economy. Mark Frauenfelder and Dale Dougherthy of O'Reilly Media launched *Make:* magazine, which quickly became the publication to go to if one wanted to learn about self-production. Eric Wilhelm launched Instructables, a website where makers could share instructions on how they realised their projects.[11]

Indeed, the year 2005 can be rendered as the "year zero of making" (Boeva & Troxler, 2021, p. 226). In 2006, two more self-production milestones followed. *Make:* organised its first "Maker Faire", a gathering, festival and market where makers would gather, give talks, follow workshops and sell the goods they made. Jim Newton and Ridge McGhee opened the first TechShop location in Menlo Park, California.

There are a few surprising details in the language and metaphors used to promote these developments – what I like to call linguistic elements of bio-mimicry, theo-mimicry[12] and the American Dream.

The RepRap builds on the metaphor of self-reproduction, an inherent quality of biological entities (biomimicry). Similarly, the famous FabAcademy, Neil Gershenfeld's online training for the aspiring maker, makes extensive reference to artificial biology in terms of assembler robots that make large

---

[10] Some of these events were just turning points in a longer development. Arduino, for example, started as a fork of Hernando Barragán's master thesis project *Wiring* (Barragán, 2004) – Barragán graduated from the Interaction Design Institute Ivrea (IDII) in Italy in late 2004 under the supervision of Massimo Banzi (Barragán, 2016).

[11] Again, there appears to be a hidden predecessor: Gershenfeld's fab labs evolved from an initiative by Shrinath Kalbag, the founder of an Ashram type institute in India to promote non-formal education for rural youths and who adopted some of Gershenfeld's tools in 2002 (Kulkarni, 2016).

[12] The only reference to "theo-mimicry" we could find was this LinkedIn post by John E. Betterson Jr. https://www.linkedin.com/pulse/theomimicry-perspective -christian-leadership-behavior-betterson-jr-/.

structures from little pieces, meta-materials (materials that can change their structure under the influence of light, UV or heat, also known as 4D-printing) and synthetic genomes and cells that actually grow and divide.[13]

The initiators of *Make* and TechShop repeatedly stressed that "man is made to make", "all of us are makers" and "making engages us fully and deeply as human beings, and it satisfies our creative souls". This rhetoric was echoed by US presidents Obama and Trump alike, rendering "making" and the "maker movement" as something deeply rooted in US American culture, as an almost magic source of creativity and innovation for rebuilding America's economy capable of reviving the "American Dream".

On the one hand, the rhetoric of "man is made to make" has something strikingly spiritual to it. Mark Hatch, co-founder and CEO of TechShop, explicitly relates the concept of "maker" to religion when he states that "God is a maker, and he made us in his image. [W]e may not know much about God or humans, but we do know one thing for sure: we were made to make" (Hatch, 2014, p. 12); the theme of theo-mimicry that sounds vaguely familiar from the *Whole Earth Catalogue*.

On the other hand, that rhetoric reminds strongly of US propaganda from the 1950s and 1960s, as, for instance, produced by General Motors: "As makers of today, and shapers for tomorrow we Americans seem to share an inborn understanding of how to go about making the things we want – whether we're reaching for the moon, hobbying in the home, doing our part on a convenience to be enjoyed or preparing a tasty titbit, we're all of us makers" (Handy (Jam) Organization, 1960, sec. 0:02:38–0:02:54). Reviving the sounds and imagery of the post-war years appears like an attempt to conjure up a new economic boom after the shocks of the dot.com crash, 9/11, and the collapse of Lehman Brothers in the wake of the subprime market crisis – only stopping short of the recent revival of the 1980s slogan "make America great again".[14]

Depending on what one understands by "production", there are many other areas of self-production outside the production of physical goods that constitutes part of the self-production economy in a wider sense – think of

---

[13]   The slides of the introductory session of Neil Gershenfeld's course "How to make (almost) anything" at MIT in 2021 are available at http://ng.cba.mit.edu/show/script/21.09.fab.html.

[14]   The slogan "Make America great again" appears to have first been used by Republican senator Alexander Wiley in 1940 (*Congressional Record: Proceedings and Debates of the 76th Congress Third Session*, 1940, p. 12393). Ronald Reagan used it in his 1980 presidential campaign and nomination acceptance speech (*Acceptance of the Republican Nomination for President*, 1980). It has become part of pop culture in the context of Donald Trump's campaign for the US presidency since 2012 ('Make America Great Again', 2023; Trump, 2015).

the production of software (Couture et al., 2021), of encyclopaedic content (Haider & Sundin, 2021), of cartography (Fish, 2021), of education (Panayotis & Pantazis, 2021), of the urban fabric (Anastasopoulos, 2021), bio-based production (Meyer, 2021), the provision of network infrastructure (Shaffer, 2021), the decentralised and distributed self-production of energy (Inês et al., 2020; Mazzola et al., 2020; Nayeripour et al., 2020), and so on. For the sake of clarity and conciseness, this chapter focuses on the self-production of physical goods.

3. SELF-PRODUCTION

The self-production economy is strongly tied to the other six trends of a new economy. At its core is the availability of digital design and manufacturing technology to a wide range of individuals. Such technology allows for advanced DIY, cost-effective industrial-grade manufacturing of one-of-a-kind products. The self-production economy thrives on a digital infrastructure for designing, with individuals collaborating and sharing globally, and on physical infrastructures for manufacturing – shared and local – to turn the digital designs into material products.

The self-production economy relies on elements of the collaborative economy, particularly regarding the access to information and knowledge and the availability and willingness of participants in the self-production economy to share these with others. Collaboration supports the processes of continuous improvement and collective innovation and maintains the flow of creativity. Exchanges are typically based on mutuality and reputation.

As collaboration is carried out to a large extent on digital platforms that increasingly not only allow the exchange of designs but also interaction with and on designs – up to the extent of collectively designing online – the self-production economy is part of the Internet of Things and services economy. Data and metadata are generated along the design and manufacturing processes; however, their additional value is not yet understood.[15]

Local manufacturing hubs are often created as shared assets, collectively owned manufacturing equipment and collectively rented spaces. This element

---

[15] In 2018, Microsoft acquired GitHub, one of the most prominent sharing platforms for software and increasingly elements of hardware (such as bills-of-material); Autodesk, best known for its design software AutoCAD for architecture, engineering, construction and manufacturing, acquired public-facing online platforms such as Instructables (sharing of making instructions) in 2011 and TinkerCAD (entry-level computer aided design (CAD) platform) in 2013. These acquisitions indicate that incumbent multinationals suspect to find value in having access to user-generated data.

of the sharing economy is a common enabler for achieving cost-effectiveness in the self-production economy. Industry-grade production equipment requires industry-grade utilisation, which in a market-of-one situation can only be achieved collectively.

Manufacturing in the self-production economy hence becomes a function one accesses rather than a capacity one owns. While the self-production economy still largely produces consumables, it relies on the function of turning bits into atoms, digital designs into material products. That means that local manufacturing hubs need to be able to connect to the collaborative design infrastructure; this is the functional value proposition of these hubs.

The digital designs and local manufacturing hubs of the self-production economy allow for and require products to be redesigned for manufacturing from local materials, therefore reducing the need for shipping raw materials and final products over large distances, minimising the use of non-renewable fuels for transportation. Also, decisions on which materials to use are largely handed down to the "makers" who can choose for renewable, recycled or bio-based materials as they see fit. In that way, the self-production economy interacts closely with the circular economy and offers a pathway to become part of the bio-based economy when "makers" substitute wood panels for acrylic sheet material or bio-based PLA-filament for ABS made from petroleum.

4.　　VALUE CREATION IN THE SELF-PRODUCTION ECONOMY

The following sections will be looking at four essential aspects of the self-production economy that enable value creation and the establishment of business models. The first aspect of value creation is digitalisation, the generative mechanism of the self-production economy – the technologies of self-production. Second are the places where self-production happens – the factories of self-production. Third, the economic exchanges of self-production – the markets of self-production; and, fourth, the social exchanges or communities – the social practices of self-production. In conclusion, we will discuss how these aspects of value creation can be leveraged in business models, whether or not related to other economic trends.

5.　　TECHNOLOGIES OF SELF-PRODUCTION

Digitalisation of technology is the major generative force in the current industrial revolution. Turning existing industrial operations into digitally controlled processes is just one layer of digitalisation of technology. The digital, if programmed adequately, can take over a large proportion of codified craftsmanship. This creates a second layer of digitalisation of technology, it makes technology accessible to lay people. A third layer in digitalisation is that it liberates technology to a large extent from the need to mechanically connect to it and so eliminates the need of physical proximity and enables collaboration on a potentially global scale. Let's examine the three layers.

An early example that demonstrates well the first layer is the typesetting system LaTeX, initially released in 1984. The writer uses plain text to input text, with mark-up codes for structuring and formatting their text. The typesetting engine then transforms this text into a well-formatted output that meticulously follows typographers' conventions. LaTeX produces typographically much more satisfying documents than the average user of Word would be able to produce despite all the fancy what-you-see-is-what-you-get (WYSIWYG) possibilities in Word. Essentially, thanks to digitalisation the machine can do the repetitive, tedious part of typesetting that would require the notorious 10,000 hours of practice to learn.

To illustrate layers two and three, we return to examples of other industries before manufacturing that have been exposed to and changed by the generative force of digitalisation – music, encyclopaedias and news (Troxler & Woensel, 2016). Digitalisation of music production and delivery in the internet era has fundamentally changed as studios had to make room for computers, musicians for samples, and record shops for online streaming services. Wikipedia has replaced expert writers and editors employed by well-known publishing houses with crowd sourcing of content and lateral governance of editing processes, outgrowing printed encyclopaedias in volume, depth, recency and use. In news, from print to radio and TV, digitalisation has handed over the tools of the trade to self-appointed authorities, amateurs and impostors, increasing speed of reporting (up to real-time self-reporting), increasing the diversity in opinion, creating a level playing field for information and propaganda, fake and real news, and providing platforms for charlatans on all sides of the political spectrum. Particularly in news, speed of reporting and analysis – always a key characteristic of the trade – has been exaggerated through digitalisation to cater for an increasing thirst for instant gratification and a propensity to the extreme, the latter reinforced by the algorithms of some of the distribution platforms. Of the eight "generatives [of] better than free" proposed by Kevin Kelly (2008) five have been deprived of their immediate capacity to generate monetary income – immediacy, personalisation, interpretation, accessibility, and findability.

These three examples of music distribution, creation and curating of encyclopaedic content, and the production of fast-paced news depict a development that builds on the possibilities of digital and internet technology – a technology that requires little central control for the release of content and allows for participation and collaboration across continents and time zones. But disruptive change did only arise with various social practices developed around this technology that embraces the absence of central monitoring of content, for good and for bad, and allows for individual and even idiosyncratic contribution. The algorithms of the distribution platforms – which are designed to control or rather manipulate the attention of the consumers by keeping them longer on the platform to increase exposure to advertorial content – became technological manifestations of these social practices.

For manufacturing, the generative forces of digitalisation also render the tools of the trade to amateurs and potentially open them up for global collaboration. Different from the production of content that can be delivered fully digitally (as in music, encyclopaedias and news), manufacturing requires some sort of materialisation in the delivery process. The Star Trek Replicator has become the common metaphor used for such a materialisation device and the "distant endpoint of the Industrial Revolution" (Saadia, 2016, para. 6). While such a machine, claimed to be able to reconfigure arbitrary molecules into new materials, briefly made its appearances in the press,[16] current manufacturing technology remains much more limited to physically transforming existing raw materials.

The closest apparatus to a Star Trek Replicator is undoubtedly the 3D printer, a machine that is capable of taking in material in some raw form, as liquid, powder or filament, and transforming it into almost unlimited shapes and forms.[17] This capacity has rendered the 3D printer the icon of the new industrial revolution. The instructions for the printing device are of digital origin and can be created remotely and collectively – as can digital music, digital encyclopaedias and digital news. Some sort of digital platform can facilitate digital creation and distribution – tools like TinkerCAD (an online 3D design software) and Thingiverse (a platform to showcase and share 3D design files) are readily available. Printing off a 3D design from Thingiverse has in a sense become the manufacturing equivalent of copy-pasting texts and video clips and might be the closest to instant gratification in manufacturing.

So, in summary, from the technologies of self-production, we can derive three lines, or vectors, of value creation:

• Encapsulate expert knowledge or know-how in digital tools.

---

[16] A company called "mattershift", a start-up with alumni from MIT and Yale promised to make it possible to 3D print literally anything by recombining molecules. Its website has gone from promising "Field programmable, Angstrom-scale separation, catalysis, and nano electro mechanical systems (NEMS) – Enabling molecular factories to radically transform how we make fuels, fertilizer, materials, and food" (*MatterShift*, 2018) to telling silence, its (Twitter/) X feed fell silent on the day of the publication of the Forbes article (Mack, 2018).

[17] For a good overview see Lipson & Kurman (2013).

- Democratise production or content creation through crowd sourcing and crowd-curation.
- Separate geographically the place of content creation or design from the place of physical content manufacturing and ship "recipes", not products.

6. FACTORIES OF SELF-PRODUCTION

The factories of self-production – self-production hubs – are publicly accessible workshops with a range of prototyping and manufacturing equipment – ranging from simple hand tools to sophisticated, digitally controlled machinery: machines for woodworking, metal working, forges, ceramics workshops, sewing and embroidery machines and weaving looms for textile work, and on the high-tech end: laser cutters, CNC routers, 3D printers and so on. Many such places offer electronics workbenches with signal generators, oscilloscopes and soldering equipment. Apart from manufacturing infrastructure, some places include shared office space, meeting rooms, even cafés or event areas.

In terms of their historic and ideological positioning, spaces differ considerably. There are at least five different types of self-production factories:

- Traditional hobbyist workshops, stemming from pre-"year-zero-of-making" initiatives – for example, the 'offene Werkstätten' (open workshops) in Germany. These might be provided by DIY hardware stores or found at community centres.
- Spaces that stand in the tradition of hacklabs and hackerspaces that have their origin in computer hacking, be it political (hacklabs) or leisurely (hackerspaces).[18] Many times, such spaces are related to other counterculture activities such as squats.
- Fab labs that follow the paradigm established by Neil Gershenfeld and Sherry Lassiter at MIT with the aim of "empowering inventors through sharing of capacities, people, and projects" (Fab Charter), often with a distinctive educational flavour. Such spaces are often found at educational institutions and public libraries.
- Maker spaces which pretty much adhere to the Californian ideology of "Make": the idea that hedonistic self-production leads to freedom and therefore (commercial) success. They might try to tap into people's free time and money for creating business from making. Such spaces are logical extensions to start-up incubators and accelerators.

---

[18] For details of the differentiation between hacklabs and hackerspaces, see note 7 above.

- Shared machine shops aimed at professional makers that operate as some kind of collective micro factory. Best-known is the former chain of TechShops that existed in the US between 2006 and 2018.[19] Examples of professional shared machine shops can often be found in business parks.[20]

Few of these five types have so far been able to prove that their mainly recreational way of self-production adds to the economy in any sustained and substantial way. Their business models – independent of ideological position – remain based on the perceived added value their members (users, customers) attribute to the space. This can range from free-to-all, volunteer-run spaces located in squats to high-end paid-membership clubs in to-be-gentrified A-locations and on university campuses.

Due to equipment and space available, the self-production factories do not lend themselves easily to manufacturing on any sizeable scale. In general, their remit remains the production of prototypes, one-offs, and (very) small, early series. This is certainly sufficient for self-production by a small number of individuals. However, overall capacity is too limited to provide for self-production for everyone.

Self-production factories promise to be places to 'make (almost) anything' (Gershenfeld, 2005). At the same time, Gershenfeld suggests a basic inventory of consumables consisting of resistors, capacitors, chokes, diodes, transistors, motor divers, LEDs, connectors, screws, acrylic, plaster, casting materials, vinyl sheets, laminates, fabrics, coatings, plywood, ball bearings, etc. The slogan of 'make (almost) anything' suggests a certain depth of manufacturing that totally eschews the realm of self-production – as Thomas Thwaites has demonstrated with his toaster project.[21]

---

[19]   The overseas locations of TechShop in Paris and Tokyo closed down as well. TechShop Abu Dhabi became Makerspace Al Zeina. TechShop Lille is the only remaining location carrying the TechShop branding.

[20]   Interesting examples in the Netherlands include WerkSpoor, Utrecht, De Wasserij, Rotterdam, Keilewerf, Rotterdam, or 3D Makers Zone, Haarlem. Many cities have established plans for "urban manufacturing", e.g. Los Angeles, New York, London, Vienna, Brussels and Rotterdam (*Cities of Making*, 2018; *Foundries of the Future*, 2020).

[21]   In *The toaster project*, Thwaites aimed to manufacture a common household appliance from scratch: a toaster. The project was inspired by a quote from Douglas Adams' *Mostly harmless* (1992): "Left to his own devices he couldn't build a toaster. He could just about make a sandwich and that was it" (p. 89). After dismantling a commercially available toaster (bought at Argos for £3.99), Thwaites set out to build a toaster using raw materials like copper, iron, nickel and plastic. It took Thwaites nine months to complete the project, and he spent about

Even when it comes to designing products – a necessary predecessor to actually manufacturing them – a large proportion of self-production is based on pre-existing designs that get propagated on YouTube and platforms such as Thingiverse.com (online, crowd sourced) or *Make:* magazine (print and online, edited). Makers reproduce these designs, often adapting them to their taste, needs or own affordances.

Despite the digitally encoded manufacturing knowledge, self-production still requires a certain skill set of makers – designing, manufacturing, electronics, coding – which is not that easy to acquire. Online instructions provide step-by-step instructions which often are incomplete, faulty or only valid under some specific circumstances – e.g. having access to a US American rather than a European or even African supply of parts and materials. They rarely furnish the conceptual understanding of "proper" craftsmanship that training delivers. And they tend to cover up the things that might or will go wrong in manufacturing.

So, in summary, from the factories of self-production, we can derive four lines, or vectors, of value creation:

- Shared equipment.
- Supply of materials and parts.
- Skill set of makers as guidance and support services.
- The combination of guidance and supply as commodification in terms of kits, workshops, etc.

7.   MARKETS OF SELF-PRODUCTION

According to Neil Gershenfeld (2006), fab labs enable the "market of one" – for goods that are not available (and probably never economically will be) under the mass-manufacturing paradigm.[22] The actual markets of self-production

---

£1,000 – and when he plugged it in: "for about five seconds, the toaster toasted, but then, unfortunately, the element kind of melted itself" (Thwaites, 2010, sec. 10:19–10:28).

[22] This so Gershenfeld holds for the global North (the "developed world" in his words). For the global South (the "developing world") the market is one of "providing solutions to local problems". As discussed above, we are not going to discuss that latter aspect of the self-production economy – though we feel it is relevant to notice that indeed in the global South there thrives a different kind of self-production economy, e.g. Jugaad in India or the Suame Magazine in Ghana. They create self-production solutions to local needs in ways that have become almost unthinkable in 21st-century Europe and North America. In the global North, the notion of the "market of one" as a characterisation of the market of

are rather collective endeavours, the most prominent being the "maker faires". Established in San Mateo, San Francisco, in 2006, this operation of O'Reilly's Maker Media found franchisees and imitators on all continents. Part festival, part conference, part market, those events serve as a podium to promote Maker Media's self-production ideology, as a platform for makers to showcase their projects, and as a marketplace for anyone from lobbyist to purveyors of software, machines, tools, supplies and kits to flog their merchandise to aspiring makers.

The "faire" image is of course chosen on purpose. It blends in with the revival of the self-sufficient, self-provisioning pre- and early industrial society, the romantic vision of great America unfettered by globalisation and dependence on (foreign) fuel reserves, raw materials, industrial goods and commodities. The maker faire narrative corresponds to restoring the narrative of the "American Maker".[23]

As part of Make's international franchising and colonisation, maker faires have spilled all over the globe – and sometimes integrated into different national narratives. In Germany, technology hobby publisher Heise has engaged in an overall franchising agreement with O'Reilly's Maker Media to promote making, publish *Make:* magazine and run two "maker faires" in the country. However, Heise worked hard on relating *Make:* to the German culture in which engineering can be seen as one of the defining elements of national identity. This included publishing in-depth articles on technical issues (which have found an eager audience in the US, much to the surprise of Maker Media) and aligning maker projects with the legal environment in Germany, which is in certain aspects radically different to the situation in the US (Hepp, 2018).

There are other obvious markets for self-production. The best-known online platform for promoting and selling products is Etsy (and similar platforms like (defunct) DawandDa and Selekkt in Germany, Folksy in the UK or Artesanum in Spain that serve as online markets for selling products). On other platforms, such as MakeXYZ.com and 3Dhubs.com, makers rather market their skills

---

self-production is euphemistic, at best; and it is loaded with the ideology of the strong individualism of Randian descent that dominates the current US-American discourse of self-production and fuels the Californian ideology.

[23] "Maker faires" are modelled after traditional country fairs – agricultural shows that provided local people with an opportunity to celebrate achievements and enjoy a break away from day-to-day routine with a combination of serious competition and light entertainment. These annual shows acknowledged and rewarded the hard work and skill of primary producers – similarly "maker faires" acknowledge and reward the "work" of self-producing makers. Country fairs provided a venue for rural families to socialise – and so do "maker faires" for makers to meet.

and capacities. The latter platform, however, has moved on from being a platform for makers to becoming one of the world's largest professional 3D print services.

In self-production, not only products, tools and capacities are exchanged, but also "knowledge" – recipes, instructions and tutorials on how to self-produce. The medium of choice for knowledge markets in self-production is the internet, and various platforms to exchange (manufacturing) designs and instructions have been developed. Some of these platforms are (or have initially been) related to a specific technology. For instance, Arduino used to host a wiki with numerous Arduino-related projects;[24] 3D printer manufacturer MakerBot Industries set up the platform Thingiverse.com for their customer to share 3D designs; Instructables.com, founded independently in 2005 and owned by Autodesk since 2011, is a website that allows its (registered) users to create and upload descriptions of their do-it-yourself projects; wikiHow.com, founded the same year, serves similar purposes (although its contents sometimes tends to veer off the pure self-production realm, see e.g. Scherker (2013)). WikiFactory has been set up as a social platform for collaborative product development, offering online 3D design software (CAD) and document storage. It operates a mix of business-to-business and business-to-consumer services.

So, in summary, from the markets of self-production, we can derive four lines, or vectors, of value creation:

- Events, markets and gatherings like the maker fairs.
- Marketing of goods and skills.
- Sharing, collaboration and co-creation platforms.
- Self-production as a business-to-business service.

8.   SOCIAL PRACTICES OF SELF-PRODUCTION

While digital technology is a strong generative force, and self-production needs its factories for manufacturing and its markets, there is a final ingredient: the people and their communities related to self-production. As in the other examples mentioned earlier, music, encyclopaedias, and news, the social practices into which a technology gets adopted play an important role. Aizu and Kumon (2013) have theorised that the third wave of the industrial revolution coincides with the first wave of the information revolution. A "new social fab movement will allow people to interact more creatively with physical objects, be it art, appliances, gadgets or daily commodities" (p. 14).

---

[24] Arduino stopped using a wiki for security and maintainability reasons (Icipriani, 2018).

Given the various social and historical backgrounds in which the factories of self-production entered – from traditional community workshops to high-end tech start-up incubators – there is a variety of social practices self-production ties into. However, evangelists of self-production – and many analysts as well – have tried to establish a narrative of a single collective social practice under the label "maker movement". On proper consideration, it becomes clear that this "movement" is mainly a mediated projection, "a deft rhetorical strategy: by construing anything whatsoever as 'making,' its proponents gain substantial momentum" (Jenkins & Bogost, 2015, p. 30).[25]

At least four different social practices have been identified in the self-production economy (Troxler, 2017):

- A mainly bourgeois pastime that employs revolutionary rhetoric as a token act of rebellion (e.g. Chris Anderson's (2014) *Makers: the new industrial revolution*) but at heart remains just a new form of entertainment (the "movement") consumed by a mainly white, 40-plus-aged population of well-educated, married fathers with kids, a job and a house of their own.[26]
- An innovation in technology or STEM (science, technology, engineering and maths) education, loosely based on the constructionist pedagogy of Seymour Papert (Harel & Papert, 1991) who worked on introducing computational thinking to schoolchildren by using early computer and computer-controlled toys. As "maker education" this practice has gained traction in modern pedagogy.
- A modern renaissance reuniting the liberal arts with science and engineering using contemporary tools and approaching that fusion of two distant disciplines in a playful but also critical manner, being able to transgress the rigidity of engineering while eschewing the conditions of contemporary artistic production – critical making (Bogers & Chiappini, 2019).
- The practice of a new industrial revolution, consisting of new, agile engineering tactics in product development, and with the potential to counteract

---

[25] Based on a broad media ethnography of the core organisational figures behind Maker Media, several maker events and makerspaces, Hepp (2018) concludes that the entire "maker movement" is a curated franchise strategy with the term "maker" conveying that anyone can belong to this diverse community. According to Hepp, a more appropriate description of the "maker movement" would be "a pioneer community with intimate connections to the corporate world and the political class maintained by a globally spread organisational elite".

[26] Readership demographics of *Make:* magazine: eight in ten readers are male, median age 44, median household income $106,000, married, homeowners with children under 17. Ninety-seven per cent attended college, 4/10 hold post-graduate degrees, 83% are employed (Dougherty & Karlin Associates LLC, 2012, p. 24).

dysfunctional implications of extant industrial constellations, such as designed obsolescence, unsustainable use of materials, gendered design of technology and its enshrined reinforcement of social inequality (Baier et al., 2016).

Self-production manifests itself often as a combination of those social practices, their intersections and their extensions into other territories. The contractionary diversity of practices and apparent absence of a single, simple social model of self-production need not be a disadvantage or interpreted as a weakness of the concept. Rather, it is a sign of an emerging socio-technical phenomenon that interacts with a diversity of current constellations. From transition theory (Geels, 2002; Geels & Schot, 2007) it is known that radical innovations need relatively insulated "incubation rooms" or niches to evolve. Radical innovations incubated in niches interact with the existing socio-technical regimes – entertainment, education, (hybrid) arts, industry (and its revolutions). They might be able to form certain sorts of symbiosis or move into specific growing markets. Rather than "revolutions", the transition from radical niche innovations into mainstream socio-technical regimes are reconfiguration processes that affect technologies, production networks (or factories), markets, and user groups and user practices (Geels, 2002, p. 1272).

So, in summary, from the technologies of self-production, we can derive three lines, or vectors, of value creation:

- Social fabrication as "do it with others" (DIWO).
- Co-existing practices and their intersection.
- Niches for transition where there is a specific growing market.

9.   BUSINESS MODELS

There are many business model opportunities for providing the infrastructure and equipment for the self-production economy. Any exploitation of one of the value creation vectors mentioned above can become the foundation of a business model. There are three examples of this business model strategy.

First, there are the platforms, such as the sharing platforms Instructables and WikiFactory, and the online 3D design platforms TinkerCAD and Google SketchUp. They are not primarily operating as crowd-sourcing platforms. Rather, they are built around the prospect of datafication of the self-production, which is evident in the case of Google and in the case of Autodesk who bought both Instructables and TinkerCAD.

Second, many ventures in the self-production economy exhibit business models that combine various value creation vectors, a phenomenon we call business model portfolio (Wolf & Troxler, 2016). In fact, successful fab labs and maker spaces are not just operating as factories of self-production – providing equipment and guidance – but might offer business-to-business services as well and engage in activities of social fabrication. They participate in maker fairs and operate their own repository of projects that were released at the location in question – as "fab moments" (Määttä & Troxler, 2011), for example. Ultimaker, the Dutch 3D printer manufacturer, has equally set up a platform for sharing designs, and it has set up a programme to supply its own materials, together with partners, and to certify third party materials for use with its printers.

Third, there are business models based on the smart combination of different trends in a new economy where self-production acts as a boundary object around which other trends can find meaningful manifestations. One example is the concept of Repair Cafés. Repair Cafés are regularly held meetings where people are invited to show up with their broken consumer goods to get help with fixing them. People with expertise in, for instance, electronics, 3D design and 3D printing, etc., attend the gatherings to help with finding and identifying faults and devising solutions to fix the problems. A Repair Café is primarily a manifestation of the circular economy. A maker space as venue for a Repair Café with its electronics and manufacturing infrastructure provides the perfect setting to deploy these activities – as a factory of self-production.

9.1   Self-production and Socio-economic Transitions

Beyond its relevance for value creation and business models at the firm level, the effects of the trend of the self-production economy can also be found at higher levels. Where properties of the self-production economy meet the capabilities of larger groups of economic participants, new societal, economic and organisational configurations are generated. These new configurations first appear as innovation in niches from where they potentially transit to the general level of the institutions and infrastructures of a society at large.

New societal configurations stem from the way people use the underlying, digital design and manufacturing technologies of the self-production economy. Being personally involved in designing everyday products can stimulate the understanding that every design decision is a decision of a designer. Shapes and functions of products are not given by nature but created by humans. So, products, and basically any technology, is man-made. Design decisions are not purely rational, they are based on assumptions, theories and beliefs. Different assumptions and beliefs could lead to different decisions, and hence to different products and technologies.

Being personally involved in manufacturing everyday products can stimulate the understanding that manufacturing is often a wasteful process that leaves scraps and rejects behind. This, in turn, can encourage people to reduce, reuse scrap or recycle waste, or select materials that are easier to recycle. So, self-producing products can expose people to the questions of materials, their source and their lifecycle, which are fundamental to the understanding of the circular economy.

Evangelists of the "maker movement" are never tired of stressing the satisfaction that stems from self-production. Experiences in maker education, which one basically could see as self-production in the classroom, confirm this effect. While evidence might be anecdotal, self-production can emotionally contribute to pride and self-esteem, particularly as it can be seen as a different type of accomplishment than more traditional dimensions such as wealth or status in society, or reading, writing and arithmetic in school.

New economic configurations stem from the various routes of value creation and business model innovation made possible by self-production and their wider bearing on the economy. The self-production economy is able to serve a market of one at reasonable cost – thanks to involvement of the "maker" – and with industry-grade quality – thanks to digital design platforms and manufacturing equipment.

Moving manufacturing capacity from centralised factories to local manufacturing hubs has a direct impact on the logistic flow of materials and goods. It is likely that fewer goods will be transported across long distances. Localised manufacturing has the potential to increase the use of local materials and to lower the CO_2 footprint of products.[27] A network of local manufacturing hubs can be expected to balance differences in demand more easily.

Hubs and individuals in the self-production economy have proved to be fast, flexible and adaptive in responding to supply chain stresses and failures. Their more generic production equipment might be slower per piece, but working in alliance and being placed locally they are able to outpace global supply chains. Local self-production, i.e. the ability to design and manufacture locally, also increases the capacity of adaptation of products, the needs of local users and the affordances of a local economy.

New organisational configurations stem from the way work is done in the self-production economy. Above, we touched a few times on the division of labour, or rather its reversal. One, the "maker" as a prosumer is the rever-

---

[27] Brody and Pureswaran (2013) demonstrated in a simulation for hearing aids, mobile phones, industrial displays and washing machines that localised production, using 3D printing, intelligent robotics and open-source electronics, can result in an average 23% unit cost benefit and reduce barriers to entry in manufacturing by an astounding 90%. However, they calculated mixed results for carbon footprint, down 67% and 8% respectively for hearing aids and mobile phones, up 1% and 9% respectively for industrial displays and washing machines.

sal of the division between producer and consumer; two, self-production entails the reversal of the division between design and manufacturing; three, self-production is based on the reversal of Taylor's division between manager and worker.

Local self-production hubs working in alliance and the global co-creation and exchange of digital designs requires a new way of coordination. This new way of coordination has to follow the way participants in the self-production economy relate to each other – through networks. So, the way of coordination must be horizontal, or lateral.[28]

Copying others' designs and sharing one's own is an accepted practice and is an encouraged strategy in self-production. To be efficient, copying and sharing cannot be burdensome transactions that have to be negotiated between individuals as they occur, as is the case with traditional intellectual property regimes. Copying and sharing requires a system where intellectual property rights do not stand in the way of innovation. While abolishing the notion of intellectual property seems an unlikely step, open-source configurations such as Creative Commons and open-source software and hardware are the norm in the self-production economy.

Finally, there is *combined social, economic and organisational configuration* in the self-production economy. This is the configuration of common pool resources or commons. The commons are actually a re-entrant in the economy, a configuration of collective stewardship for shared resources. Such a configuration is, first, a new social configuration as it contains actors who are able and willing to self-organise. Second, it is a new economic configuration, as the actors create and share collectively owned resources – knowledge, machines, buildings and land, even materials. Third, it is an organisational configuration, as it requires processes, protocols and infrastructures that enable collaboration, self-organisation and the stewardship of resources.

10.   THE FUTURE OF SELF-PRODUCTION

Elements of self-production have made their appearance in the current economic system as technologies, factories, markets and social practices. They can function in the current environment, and many of them have proved to be able to survive. Those who did not survive were depending on the injection of external money, be it venture capital or state subsidies, but did not manage to create a compelling enough narrative to keep these funds flowing (see vignette "Failed self-production giants of California"). Those who survived

---

[28]   Jeremy Rifkin describes this phenomenon in the second part of *The third industrial revolution* (2011) as "lateral power".

found ways to involve communities in an economically sustainable way. That also means that the technologies, factories, markets and social practices of self-production are still evolving and have not yet reached a state of maturity. However, their self-production has achieved a couple of relevant milestones. The makers' response to COVID-19 (see vignette "3D printed face shields") is the first global case that allowed makers to step out of the character of consenting nerds who produce funny things for maker fairs. The fact that there is a German standards institute specification for open-source hardware (see vignette "Open-source hardware") points towards broad acceptance of the open-source principle.

There are many fields where self-production needs development. It is not only the evolving social practices of self-production (as illustrated in the vignette "iManufacture") and the development of new business models (see vignette "Digital maker-entrepreneurs"). Development is also required in the technologies of self-production and in the materials used. Many industrial manufacturing processes still require a steep learning curve, even if fully digitalised according to current standards. Robotics, which could assist self-production in handling and assembly, is just entering the field of safely usable devices with what is called co-bots; traditional industrial robots are still to be considered industrial hazards if not controlled properly. Many materials used in self-production still are too specific and too limited in applications. Particularly in electronics, the industry tends to cram more functionality onto one single chip, with proprietary firmware and closed development systems, and does not facilitate the reuse of components.

All these challenges solved and ready to grow, the path to growth for self-production lies not in scaling up. Symbolically, there are no economies of scale in 3D printing; rather, a large production volume in 3D printing is achieved by assembling a large number of 3D printers. The same holds for self-production as a socio-technical phenomenon. Self-production scales out, it grows in the network by multiplying, rather than by units growing bigger. Scaling out, or lateral growth, is not yet very well understood, let alone taught in business schools. "Big fish eats small fish" is still the dominant paradigm in business. However, biological evidence points towards the advantages of shoals of small fish, too. Furthermore, while the term self-production seems to carry the notion of the market of one, the "self" in self-production is actually a collective self. It is DIWO (do it with others), rather than DIY (do it yourself) – as the case of 3D printed face shields has shown. Collective self-production is therefore aligned with the ideals of a new economy.

Self-production cannot thrive on itself. It is intrinsically entangled with the other trends of a new economy, as shown above.

11.   VIGNETTES

11.1   Open-source Hardware

In 2017, Danish high-end audio manufacturer Bang & Olufsen (B&O) partnered with Swiss electronics developer Modul 9 to allow owners of its vintage loudspeakers to use them with contemporary wireless audio technology. The result of this cooperation was the BeoCreate board, an electronic device to which the vintage speakers get connected and which turns them into current-times wireless speakers. The BeoCreate, however, is not just a black box device. It has been designed to work with the open-source hardware board Raspberry Pi, which allows users of the BeoCreate to optimise the digital audio processing on the board according to their individual needs and taste. While this might not be an average use case, it is certainly technology that appeals at least to some audiophiles.

Denmark has seen several open-source hardware (OSH) initiatives. In 2018, the Danish Design Centre worked with eight manufacturing companies to help them open source some of their products and services. The project called Remodel centred around involving a community of users as co-developers in designing hardware. They are also involved in a follow-up project with universities from Germany, France and the UK and SME partners from more countries to further develop business models and software solutions to foster collaboration between SMEs, maker communities and consumers in sectors as diverse as eco-friendly mobility, consumer electronics and built-to-order furniture. Open-source hardware is the infrastructure underpinning these endeavours.

In Switzerland, the European Organization for Nuclear Research, better known as CERN, home of the Large Hadron Collider, has been using principles of open-source hardware for a decade to develop the bespoke electronics they require to carry out intricate time measurements on elementary particles. One example is the White Rabbit Project, technology to synchronise electronics with sub-nanosecond accuracy and a precision of a few picoseconds. It has since become an industry standard and has been adopted for bespoke uses in telecommunications, financial markets, smart grids, the space industry and quantum computing. The reason for CERN to adopt an open-source approach was that they could much more easily involve a larger group of companies and organisations to contribute to the development of hardware and software for the White Rabbit devices.

While sharing advanced technology in an open-source manner might seem revolutionary in the 21st century, one should not forget, that in the 18th and 19th centuries many technologies – including aeroplanes, steam engines, clock works and steel mills – were initially advanced collectively; inventions and developments shared through handbooks and journals. It was only the aggressive patenting efforts of some individual industrialists that oftentimes stopped collective innovation for the benefit of a single patent-holder. It is encouraging that the German standards institute (DIN, Deutsches Institut für Normung) produced a specification for the documentation of open-source hardware (Bonvoisin, 2020; *DIN SPEC 3105–1*, 2020; *DIN SPEC 3105–2*, 2020). Such a specification, or DIN Spec, is often an early predecessor of a full standard.

11.2   Failed Self-production Giants of California

Two Californian ventures dominated the first decade of making – Maker Media with *Make:* magazine and the "maker faires", and TechShop, a chain of DIY manufacturing studios. Both ventures went bankrupt with no warning in 2017 (TechShop) and 2019 (Maker Media). Some TechShop locations reopened under new names and ownerships.[29] Maker Media resurfaced as an LLC, a private limited liability company, supported by a membership community. It continues to publish *Make:* magazine and other operations like the "maker faires".

Make: magazine's first issue appeared in January 2005. Its main founder, publisher and public figure was O'Reilly co-founder Dale Dougherty. In 2013, Maker Media Inc. was set up as a separate entity and subsidiary of O'Reilly. In 2014, German media house Heise Group set up Maker Media GmbH as a franchise of Maker Media for the German-speaking market. In 2006, the first "maker faire" was held at the San Mateo Fairgrounds, California. The "maker faire" brand was licensed through a franchising scheme across the globe. *Make:* became not only the brand, but the curator of what making entailed.[30] It projected the image of the "maker" – initially white male until publicly criticised – their attitude and their interests, while leaving it up to individuals to self-identify as "makers". In June 2019, Maker Media Inc. laid off all staff due to lack of financial resources – and probably with no compelling narrative to attract funding or sponsoring from venture capitalists and big tech. The same

---

[29] Only Leroy Merlin TechShop in Lille, France, more commonly known as Les Ateliers Leroy Merlin, still carries the TechShop name and logo. It is a public-private partnership between the University of Lille and French DIY stores chain Leroy Merlin (https://www.techshop-lille.fr/).

[30] Hepp (2018) argues that Dale Dougherty played an important role in the co-construction of what is called the "maker movement". Rather than a social movement, he considers the "maker movement" as a pioneer community, created by an organisational elite in which Maker Media played a crucial role.

month, it resurfaced as Maker Media LLC and established a membership community, which allowed it to recuperate the brands and continue its operations.

The first DIY manufacturing studio under the name TechShop opened in Menlo Park, California, in 2006. Until its sudden demise in 2017, TechShop established ten studios in the United States, and four international licensees to the brand in Japan, Abu Dhabi, Paris and Lille. Equipment included both conventional and digitally controlled manufacturing machines, electronics labs and a variety of plastics fabrication equipment. TechShop aimed at fostering invention and entrepreneurship – a flagship product was the Dodo iPad case that was even used by Barack Obama. It operated as a chain of membership-based, open-access, do-it-yourself (DIY) manufacturing studios. The initial costs of setting up a workshop were often paid by NGOs such as the US Veteran Organizations or public and private partners – city councils and corporates like Ford. With no warning, TechShop filed for immediate liquidation on 15 November 2017. TechShop had run out of cash and was unable to raise additional funds.[31]

Both ventures were considered flagships of the "maker movement", the self-production economy of the late 2000s and early 2010s. Both ventures failed to sustain their business models – corporate and public sponsorship, licensing – and to attract funding to extend them. Neither subscriptions nor membership fees were generating sufficient cash flow to keep the businesses running. Maker Media Inc. and TechShop Inc. ventured into the self-production economy without understanding its economics. Exposed to the financial realities of the start-up market, they failed.

11.3   3D Printed Face Shields: Makers' Response to COVID-19

It was on Friday 13 March 2020 when in a hospital in Brescia one particular part of a breathing apparatus broke down – a valve that changes speed and pressure in the airflow, named "venturi" after its inventor. However, there were no replacement parts available. One of the doctors was friends with the founder of a fab lab and tech journalist, Massimo Temporelli (Corsini et al., 2021; Sher, 2020), who in turn managed to find an engineer at Isinnova, a company specialising in 3D printed prototypes. Within only 24 hours Isinnova was able to reproduce the part. The story made headlines in the European and global press, and fab labs and 3D printing were inextricably linked to fixing supply chain tribulations for healthcare.

---

[31]   International licensing deals had not been established and were not affected by the closure of TechShop, such as the initiative between BMW and the Technical University of Munich (Barcucci, 2017, p. 6).

So, when there was an immediate surge in the demand for personal protective equipment in care and other public facing professions, such as police or bus drivers, many makers immediately came into action. One item in high demand was visors or face shields, used as an alternative to face masks. One particular type of face shield was very popular among makers. It was designed by Josef Průša, a manufacturer of 3D printers well known and admired among makers for their strong open-source strategy. Self-organising groups of makers started to defeat global supply chains by producing supplies locally, all around the world. These groups met typically on some internet platform and started to organise themselves in ad-hoc national networks, in a few cases stimulated by government initiatives, such as the "WirvsVirus" (we against the virus) hackathon in Germany.

In many cases, makers were directly and closely interacting with the users of their products, the front-line workers. This direct contact led to small improvements of the initial face shield designs, which were then shared and discussed. Some of the makers started to involve small industry partners to mass produce what they initially 3D printed. Others, however, orchestrated armies of volunteers with their own 3D printers to produce the parts. So, in the UK, one initiative was able to produce 185,000 face shields within the timespan of only ten weeks – with a combined printing time of over 60 years.

The realisation that by joining together and self-organising they could manufacture meaningful products for others, rather than just quirky stuff for themselves, quickly became part of the narrative of the self-assumed "maker movement" and the press reporting on it. Press coverage waned. However, after the end of the first wave of COVID-19, many of these initiatives ebbed away. Regular supply chains were back in action. Funding issues could not be solved. Regulatory regimes, particularly in the medical sector, proved to be barriers too high for makers to properly enter the market.

The makers' response was a reaction to a window of opportunity. It brought to the fore the dominant design of the face shield, its socially networked 3D printing technology added onto existing manufacturing capacity, and they were developing a niche market. In their very practical responses, makers indeed realised a new socio-technical configuration in organising themselves, in putting social resources and technical means to good use. All these elements are possible ingredients for a transition (Geels, 2002) – however, they are not a guarantee that this transition will actually happen. While respecting safe procedures and products in emergency circumstances, makers did not attempt to reconfigure the regulatory regime. Yet indeed, they established what Chalet et al. (2021) call "a digital archipelago of making" (p. 94) that was "impressively demonstrating the potential of civic innovation" (Richterich, 2020, p. 166).

11.4   iManufacture (Scenario)

iManufacture is a fictive but fully-fledged maker space. It was initially set up with the idea to stimulate technical invention and new start-ups by a group of mostly male friends – architects, designers, engineers, software developers and consultants. Over the years, iManufacture has seen a steady growth in the number of members. A small group of its members have started an initiative "STEAM fathers"; as their kids started to attend middle school, they found that the schools did not do enough for the kids to develop an interest in science, technology, engineering, arts and mathematics (STEAM). So, they developed various initiatives – an after-school programme, a summer school and eventually a STEAM-week during school hours. This last programme could be realised when the school hired a couple of new teachers: Rob, a science teacher, and Claire, his girlfriend, an arts teacher.

Claire was also a community activist who in her spare time spent hours at a Repair Café – a place where people gathered once a month to repair defective consumer goods to actively fight planned obsolescence. The community that Claire was part of engaged in several other activities. Members could take part in urban gardening, in citizen science or in new, experimental forms of community governance. They had started to pool the power tools some of the community members owned, so other community members could borrow them when, for instance, embarking on a home improvement project.

The community also developed an interest in recycling and alternative modes of energy generation. Together with local furniture maker "The Cabinartry" they hope to develop a small biomass energy plant that could process organic food waste and wood scraps. The furniture maker, in turn, operates as the regional manufacturing hub for Opendesk. London-based Opendesk is a design platform that specialises in designing office furniture that is produced locally through a network of furniture makers, while the design files were initially available to download for free for personal use.

One of the founding cabinet makers at The Cabinartry, Jane, is also a practising sculptor and wood artist. Jane is moderately famous in her field, particularly for her sculptures which resonate with the theme of the circular economy. It is this fame that has landed her a surprising assignment with the number one national manufacturer of office furniture: they asked Jane to develop a conceptual piece that should illustrate how office furniture could be rendered completely circular.

11.5   Digital Maker-entrepreneurs

Received logic posits that creators, designers and inventors should protect their intellectual property to create value from it. Therefore, open source appears counterintuitive, despite being practised. With colleagues Laura Guggiari and Patricia Wolf, we studied maker-entrepreneurs in open-source 3D printing and how they designed their business models. We were interested to understand how one could earn a living from a co-created idea. Therefore, we started with the 3D print design sharing platform Thingiverse. We carefully selected Thingiverse users who were very actively using the platform to share designs and reuse designs other users shared. From these heavy users, we chose only those who had their own business, and after a careful selection process, we ended up with 11 companies who agreed to take part in a multiple case study consisting of the analysis of publicly available profiles and websites and individual in-depth interviews with the owners of the businesses.

In multiple iterations, we analysed the business models of the 11 cases. In the first round of analysis, we discovered five salient business models the companies were using: (1) participation in online brokerage and sales platforms, (2) direct sale of objects via web shops, (3) 3D printer retail, (4) customised prototyping for industry or private clients, (5) research and education activities. Strikingly, nine of the 11 companies were using not one, but two or even – one on each count – three or four business models. So, what we found in practice is that maker-entrepreneurs typically operated a portfolio of business models.

Then we analysed the business models as activity systems, as proposed by Zott & Amit (2010, p. 217). A business model is a system of activities performed by the focal firm and its partners, suppliers and customers. Its architecture is described in terms of three elements: content (what the activities are), structure (how the activities are carried out), and governance. Traditionally, there are four sources of value creation (or themes in Zott & Amits' terminology): novelty, lock-in, complementarities, and efficiency. Indeed, in the 11 cases, we mostly found that the business models were built on traditional elements and themes. Yet, we also found business model innovation in these cases. Reciprocity and fairness were explicitly mentioned as governance principles. We also found additional design themes (drivers of value creation), namely altruism, serving the community, and hedonism, doing what one likes to do oneself (Wolf & Troxler, 2016).

Through an additional analysis using activity theory (Blackler, 1993; Engeström, 1987, 2000) we were able to uncover two additional features of the business models of these maker-entrepreneurs. First, and pretty much in line with the idea of the self-production economy, those entrepreneurs combined design and manufacturing skills in their ventures, something that many professional artists and designers don't do (they tend to outsource manufacturing to specialists). Second, the notion of community was central to their business models in terms of working with a designer community, in terms of forming a community on the one hand with their customers, on the other hand with their suppliers, and in terms of considering the business itself as a community (Troxler & Wolf, 2017). Therefore, we called those business models community-based, rather than the community-oriented business models of incumbent industry.

REFERENCES

Adams, D. (1992). *Mostly harmless: The hitch hiker's guide to the galaxy 5*. Pan.

Aizu, I. & Kumon, S. (2013, August 23). The impact of social fabrication in the New Stage of Information Society using InfoSocionomics Framework. *Proceedings of the Fab9 Research Papers Stream*. Fab9, Yokohama.

Anastasopoulos, N. (2021). Commoning the urban. In M. O'Neil, C. Pentzold & S. Toupin (eds), *The handbook of peer production* (pp. 268–281). Wiley.

Anderson, C. (2014). *Makers: The new industrial revolution*. Random House.

Atkinson, P. (2011). Orchestral manoeuvres in design. In In B. Able, L. Evers, R. Klaassen & P. Troxler (eds), *Open design now. Why design cannot remain exclusive* (pp. 24–31). BIS Publishers.

Baier, A., Hansing, T., Müller, C. & Werner, K. (2016). Die Welt reparieren Open Source und Selbermachen als postkapitalistische Praxis. transcript Verlag.

Barbrook, R. & Cameron, A. (1995, 1 September). The Californian Ideology | Mute. *Mute*, *1*(3). http://www.metamute.org/editorial/articles/californian-ideology.

Barcucci, S. (2017). Report on p2p knowledge exchange. PP1 MakerSpace Garching visit (p. 14). FabLabNet.

Barragán, H. (2004). *Wiring: Prototyping physical interaction design* [Interaction Design Institute Ivrea]. http:// people .interactionivrea .org/ h .barragan/ thesis/ thesis _low_res.pdf.

Barragán, H. (2016). *The untold history of Arduino*. https://arduinohistory.github.io/.

Blackler, F. (1993). Knowledge and the theory of organizations: Organizations as activity systems and the reframing of management. *Journal of Management Studies*, *30*(6), 863–884.

Boeva, Y. & Troxler, P. (2021). Makers. In M. O'Neil, C. Pentzold & S. Toupin (eds), *The handbook of peer production* (pp. 225–237). John Wiley & Sons. https://doi.org/ 10.1002/9781119537151.ch17.

Bogers, L. & Chiappini, L. (2019). *The critical makers reader: (Un)learning technology*. Institute of Network Cultures.

Bonvoisin, J. (2020, 27 August). DIN SPEC 3105 explained. *Journal of Open Hardware*. https://journalopenhw.medium.com/din-spec-3105-explained-2cce6134c207.

Brand, S. (1968). *Whole Earth catalog*.

Brody, P. & Pureswaran, V. (2013). *The new software-defined supply chain*. IBM Institute for Business. https://www.ibm.com/downloads/cas/JQP1DK0L.

Chalet, L., Dutilleul, M. & Fages, V. (2021). Des visières à haut débit: Un regard sociologique sur la mobilisation des makers face à la crise sanitaire. *Annales des Mines*, 6.

Corsini, L., Dammicco, V. & Moultrie, J. (2021). Frugal innovation in a crisis: The digital fabrication maker response to COVID-19. *R & D Management*, *51*(2), 195–210. https://doi.org/10.1111/radm.12446.

Couture, S., O'Neil, M., Pentzold, C. & Toupin, S. (2021). Free and open source software. In M. O'Neil, C. Pentzold & S. Toupin (eds), *The handbook of peer production* (pp. 155–166). Wiley. http://hdl.handle.net/1866/24878.

Cramer, F. (2019, July). Does DIY mean anything? A DIY attempt (= essay). *Anrikningsverket Journal*, *1*, 54–72.

DIN SPEC 3105–1:2020–07, Open source hardware – Teil 1: Anforderungen an die technische Dokmentation; Text Englisch (p. 13). (2020). Beuth Verlag GmbH. https://doi.org/10.31030/3173063.

DIN SPEC 3105–2:2020–07, Open source hardware – Teil 2: Community-basierte Bewertung (p. 12). (2020). Beuth Verlag GmbH. https://doi.org/10.31030/3173062.

Dougherty, D. & Karlin Associates LLC. (2012). *Maker Market study and media report: An in-depth profile of makers at the forefront of hardware innovation* (p. 35). Maker Media. https://cdn.makezine.com/make/sales/Maker-Market-Study.pdf.

Egyedi, T., & Mehos, D. C. (Eds.). (2012). *Inverse Infrastructures: Disrupting networks from below*. Eward Elgar.

Engeström, Y. (1987). *Learning by expanding: An activity-theoretical approach to developmental research*. Orienta-Konsultit.

Engeström, Y. (2000). Activity theory as a framework for analyzing and redesigning work. *Ergonomics*, *43*(7), 960–974.

Euchner, J. & Gershenfeld, N. (2015). Atoms and bits: Rethinking manufacturing. *Research Technology Management; Arlington*, *58*(5), 16–21. http://dx.doi.org/10.5437/08956308X5805003.

Fish, A. (2021). Participatory cartography: Drones, countermapping, and technological power. In M. O'Neil, C. Pentzold & S. Toupin (eds), *The handbook of peer production* (pp. 185–196). Wiley.

Geels, F. W. (2002). Technological transitions as evolutionary reconfiguration processes: A multi-level perspective and a case-study. *Research Policy*, *31*(8), 1257–1274. https://doi.org/10.1016/S0048–7333(02)00062–8.

Geels, F. W. & Schot, J. (2007). Typology of sociotechnical transition pathways. *Research Policy*, *36*(3), 399–417. https://doi.org/10.1016/j.respol.2007.01.003.

Gershenfeld, N. (2005). *Fab: The coming revolution on your desktop, from personal computers to personal fabrication*. Basic Books.

Gershenfeld, N. (2006, February). *Unleash your creativity in a Fab Lab*. https://www.ted.com/talks/neil_gershenfeld_on_fab_labs?language=en

Giedion, S. (1948). *Mechanization takes command*. Oxford University Press.

Haider, J. & Sundin, O. (2021). Wikipedia and wikis. In M. O'Neil, C. Pentzold & S. Toupin (eds), *The handbook of peer production* (pp. 169–184). Wiley. http://dx.doi.org/10.1002/9781119537151.ch13.

Handy (Jam) Organization. (1960). *American Maker*. http://archive.org/details/0380_American_Maker_M04441_11_25_14_00.

Harel, I. & Papert, S. (eds). (1991). *Constructionism: Research reports and essays, 1985–1990*. Ablex Publishing.

Hatch, M. (2014). *The Maker Movement manifesto: Rules for innovation in the new world of crafters, hackers, and tinkerers*. McGraw-Hill Education.

Hepp, A. (2018). What makes a maker? Curating a pioneer community through franchising. *Nordisk Tidsskrift for Informationsvidenskab Ok Kulturformidling*, *7*(2), 3–18. https://doi.org/10.7146/ntik.v7i2.111283

Icipriani. (2018, 22 November). *Arduino Playground will be a regular website and not a wiki – Community/Website and Forum*. Arduino Forum. https://forum.arduino.cc/t/arduino-playground-will-be-a-regular-website-and-not-a-wiki/558121.

Inês, C., Guilherme, P. L., Esther, M. G., Swantje, G., Stephen, H. & Lars, H. (2020). Regulatory challenges and opportunities for collective renewable energy prosumers in the EU. *Energy Policy*, *138*, 111212.

Iosad, A. (2020). *Digital at the core: A 2030 strategy framework for university leaders*. Emergence Education.

IPCC. (2023). Climate Change 2023: Synthesis Report. Contribution of Working Groups I, II and III to the Sixth Assessment Report of the Intergovernmental Panel on Climate Change [Core writing team, H. Lee and J. Romero (eds)]. IPCC, Geneva, Switzerland, pp. 35–115. Doi: 10.59327/IPCC/AR6-9789291691647.

Jenkins, T., & Bogost, I. (2015). *Escaping the Sandbox: Making and Its Future. Proceedings of the Ninth International Conference on Tangible, Embedded, and Embodied Interaction*, 29–32. https://doi.org/10.1145/2677199.2680558

Kelly, K. (2008, 31 January). Better than free. *The Technium*. https:// kk .org/ thetechnium/better-than-fre/.

Kulkarni, Y. (2016, 11 August). Fab Lab 0.0 to Fab Lab 0.4. Learning from running a lab in an Indian village. *Proceedings of the Fab12 Research Papers Stream*. Fab12, Shenzhen.

Liao, Y., Deschamps, F., Loures, E. de F. R. & Ramos, L. F. P. (2017). Past, present and future of Industry 4.0 – A systematic literature review and research agenda proposal. *International Journal of Production Research*, 55(12), 3609–3629. https://doi.org/ 10.1080/00207543.2017.1308576.

Liao, Y., Loures, E. R., Deschamps, F., Brezinski, G. & Venâncio, A. (2018). The impact of the fourth industrial revolution: A cross-country/region comparison. *Production*, 28. https://doi.org/10.1590/0103–6513.20180061.

Lindtner, S., Hertz, G. D. & Dourish, P. (2014). Emerging sites of HCI innovation: Hackerspaces, hardware startups and incubators. *Proceedings of the SIGCHI Conference on Human Factors in Computing Systems*, 439–448. https://doi.org/10 .1145/2556288.2557132.

Lipson, H. and Kurman, M. (2013). *Fabricated: The new world of 3D printing*. Wiley.

Määttä, A. & Troxler, P. (2011, 30 June). Developing open & distributed tools for Fablab project documentation. *Open Knowledge Conference*. http://www.academia .edu/ 1964060/ Developing _open _and _distributed _tools _for _Fablab _project _documentation.

Mack, E. (2018, 9 March). A real world "Star Trek" replicator is now possible thanks to new breakthrough. *Forbes*. https://www.forbes.com/sites/ericmack/2018/ 03/09/carbon-nanotube-membrane-breakthrough-is-real-world-star-trek-replicator -mattershift/.

Marsh, P. (2013). *The new industrial revolution: Consumers, globalization and the end of mass production*. Yale University Press.

MatterShift. (2018, 15 March). https://web.archive.org/web/20180315122354/https:// www.mattershift.com/.

maxigas. (2012). Hacklabs and hackerspaces: Tracing two genealogies. *Journal of Peer Production*, 2. http://peerproduction.net/issues/issue-2/peer-reviewed-papers/.

Mazzola, E., Piazza, M., Acur, N. & Perrone, G. (2020). Treating the crowd fairly: Increasing the solvers' self-selection in idea innovation contests. *Industrial Marketing Management*, 91, 16–29.

Meudt, T., Pohl, M. & Metternich, J. (2017). Modelle und Strategien zur Einführung des Computer Integrated Manufacturing (CIM) – Ein Literaturüberblick [Report]. http://tuprints.ulb.tu-darmstadt.de/6653/.

Meyer, M. (2021). Biohacking. In M. O'Neil, C. Pentzold & S. Toupin (eds), *The handbook of peer production* (pp. 211–224). Wiley.

National Academy of Science and Engineering – ACATECH. (2013). *Securing the future of German manufacturing industry. Recommendations for implementing the strategic initiative INDUSTRIE 4.0. Final report of the Industrie 4.0 Working Group*. acatech – National Academy of Science and Engineering.

Nayeripour, M., Mahboubi-Moghaddam, E., Narimani, M. R. & Waffenschmidt, E. (2020). Secure and reliable distribution feeder reconfiguration in the presence of static VAR compensator. *Iranian Journal of Science and Technology, Transactions of Electrical Engineering, 44*, 293–308.

Noble, D. F. (1984). *Forces of production: A social history of industrial automation*. Knopf.

OECD. (2020). *Digital Transformation and the Futures of Civic Space to 2030*. OECD Development Policy Paper, 29.

Panayotis, A. & Pantazis, A. (2021). P2P learning. In M. O'Neil, C. Pentzold & S. Toupin (eds), *The handbook of peer production* (pp. 197–210). Wiley. https://www.worldcat.org/title/p2p-learning/oclc/8908709965&referer=brief_results.

Petroski, H. (2018). *To engineer is human: The role of failure in successful design*. St. Martin's Publishing Group.

Richterich, A. (2020). When open source design is vital: Critical making of DIY health-care equipment during the COVID-19 pandemic. *Health Sociology Review, 29*(2), 158–167. https://doi.org/10.1080/14461242.2020.1784772.

Rifkin, J. (2011). *The third industrial revolution: How lateral power is inspiring a gen-eration and transforming the world*. Palgrave Macmillan.

Saadia, M. (2016, 8 September). The enduring lessons of "Star Trek". *The New Yorker*. https://www.newyorker.com/tech/elements/the-enduring-lessons-of-star-trek.

Saarikko, T., Westergren, U. H. & Blomquist, T. (2020). Digital transformation: Five recommendations for the digitally conscious firm. *Business Horizons, 63*(6), 825–839.

Scherker, A. (2013, 1 November). Penis piercings, chicken trances, parachute fails: 11 bizarre life skills you could only learn from wikihow. *HuffPost*. https://www.huffpost.com/entry/life-skills-wikihow_n_4164954.

Shaffer, G. (2021). Community wireless networks. In M. O'Neil, C. Pentzold & S. Toupin (eds), *The handbook of peer production* (pp. 254–267). Wiley.

Sher, D. (2020, 14 March). [Updating] Italian hospital saves COVID-19 patients' lives by 3D printing valves for reanimation devices. *3D Printing Media Network – The Pulse of the AM Industry*. https://www.3dprintingmedia.network/covid-19–3d-printed-valve-for-reanimation-device/.

Sipos, R. & Franzl, K. (2020). Tracing the history of DIY and maker culture in Germany's open workshops. *Digital Culture & Society, 6*(1), 109–120.

Smith, A. (2014). Technology Networks for Socially Useful Production. *Journal of Peer Production*, 5. http://peerproduction.net/issues/issue-5-shared-machine-shops/peer-reviewed-articles/technology-networks-for-socially-useful-production/.

Stratil, P. (2019, 3 May). *Svazarm* [Personal communication].

Taylor, F. W. (1911). *The principles of scientific management*. Harper.

Thwaites, T. (2010, 11 November). *How I built a toaster – from scratch*. https://www.ted.com/talks/thomas_thwaites_how_i_built_a_toaster_from_scratch.

Thwaites, T. (2011). *The toaster project: Or a heroic attempt to build a simple electric appliance from scratch*. Princeton Architectural Press.

Troxler, P. (2017). What is a Fab Lab for? In M. Menichinelli (ed.), *Fab Lab. Revolution field manual* (pp. 51–65). Niggli.

Troxler, P. (2022). Plan C – Makers' response to COVID-19. Journal of Peer Production, 15. http://peerproduction.net/issues/issue-15-transition/peer-reviewed-papers/plan-c-makers-response-to-covid-19/.

Troxler, P. & Woensel, C. van. (2016). How will society adopt 3D printing? In B. van den Berg, S. van den Hof & E. Kosta (eds), *3D printing* (pp. 205–237). TMC Asser Press. https:// www .researchgate .net/ publication/ 314578038 _How _Will_Society _Adopt_3D_Printing.

Troxler, P. & Wolf, P. (2017). Digital maker-entrepreneurs in open design: What activities make up their business model? *Business Horizons, 60*(6), 807–817. https://doi .org/10.1016/j.bushor.2017.07.006.

Trump, D. J. (2015). *Time to Get Tough: Make America Great Again!* (2nd ed.). Regnery Publishing.

Wilms, K., Meske, C., Stieglitz, S., Decker, H., Fröhlich, L., Jendrosch, N., Schaulies, S., Vogl, R., & Rudolph, D. (2017, August 10). *Digital Transformation in Higher Education – New Cohorts, New Requirements? 23rd Americas Conference on Information Systems*, Boston, MA.

Wolf, P. & Troxler, P. (2016). Community-based business models: Insights from an emerging maker economy. *Interaction Design & Architecture, 30*, 75–94.

Zott, C. & Amit, R. (2010). Business model design: An activity system perspective. *Long Range Planning, 43*(2–3), 216–226. https://doi.org/10.1016/j.lrp.2009.07.004.

Zuboff, S. (1988). *In the age of the smart machine: The future of work and power.* Basic Books. http://www.gbv.de/dms/bowker/toc/9780465032129.pdf.

7. Internet of Things/Internet of Services economies: generating social and economic value with interactive environments

Paul Manwaring and Dré Kampfraath

1.   INTRODUCTION

It is difficult to have a productive discussion about the Internet of Things (IoT), the Internet of Services (IoS), and the development of these trends as they relate to socio-economic transition without first providing some background regarding the history of the Internet itself. Despite the temptation to go into detail, we will have to be satisfied with a very brief introduction to the historical development of the Internet to the point where we find ourselves today – in a connected world where objects and people can interact in a symbiotic relationship and in ways that add value to digital, physical, social, and, therefore, economic systems.

   To begin, we will take a 20-year leap from the creation of the Internet as we know it in 1969 to 1989 when Sir Tim Berners-Lee invented the World Wide Web or "Web" at the CERN Particle Accelerator Laboratory to "enable communication among scientists, accelerate international cooperation, and advance humanity" (Jeffries, 2014). Since then, the Web has gone through four marked developmental phases commonly known as Web 1.0 to 4.0. Web 1.0 was simply "information connections" and defined as "read-only" with very little user interaction. Web 2.0 emerged gradually at the turn of the century and, in 2004, was dubbed by web pioneer Tim O'Reilly as the "Read, Write Web." Here, we see the birth of digital social media platforms and the social web where end users are able to create content and contribute to interactive platforms. Web 3.0 was first coined in 2006; this was a shift to a more "executable web" where data and content are interlinked and shared. Sir Tim Berners-Lee described this as the "Semantic Web", as if "all documents online were one big book and all the data like one huge database" (Choudhury, 2014). Then came the visual web, mobile web, smartphones, apps, ubiquitous computing, tablets, wearables, quantified self, the Internet of Things (IoT), the Internet of Services (IoS), Artificial Intelligence (AI), the Internet of Value, and more, all in rapid-fire and some in parallel as the Web grew to over 3 billion users in 2016. Now we are in transition to Web 4.0, a new phase that we are still trying to grasp, and that looks a bit like this: The Web is everywhere all the time (ubiquitous), most of us are always connected either actively or passively, but more than humans, now IoT and AI come into play and join us online to create a Web where people, places, objects, and machines are merging via data. As of January 2021, there were over 4.5 billion Internet users globally, over half the world's population. As of the writing of this chapter, it is estimated there are over 7 billion smartphone users worldwide so we can safely say that the majority of humans on the planet are "connected" (Ahlgren, 2023).

2.   DEFINITIONS AND COMPONENTS OF IOT AND IOS

The term "Internet of Things" was coined in 1999 by MIT alumnus Kevin Ashton during his work with Radio Frequency Identification (RFID) tags. Put as simply as possible, the IoT is a system of interrelated computing devices, mechanical and digital machines, objects, and animals, or people that are provided with unique identifiers (UIDs), and the ability to transfer data over a network without requiring human-to-human or human-to-computer interaction (Gillis, 2022). Today the IoT encompasses a global ecosystem of over 30.7 billion devices connected to the Internet and growing rapidly with projections reaching 75 billion by 2025 (Statista, 2016). As the IoT ecosystem grows dramatically, so does the social and economic value it generates, as we shall discuss. This relates specifically to the value we can derive from "sensing" or measuring changes in the physical world which, in turn, creates new, interactive data that leads to actionable data – data that informs processes or decisions and effects change. These elements conjoin to create generative feedback loops and provide the basis for interactive environments. Therefore, we argue that "things" in the IoT ecosystem should be:

- Non-organic, man-made objects that can generate data from the physical world and bring it into an information ecosystem via the Internet.
- Non-organic, man-made objects that can respond to data from the digital world and actuate changes in the physical world via the Internet.
- Objects that can send and/or receive data using Machine to Machine (M2M) protocols with radio transmitters and/or receivers (transceivers) or that are connected to a database via the Internet.
- Including the above, objects that have a UID can be authenticated and are, therefore, secure. These objects should be autonomous in that

they perform the functions outlined independent of human-to-human or human-to-computer interaction.

One of the problems when discussing the IoT is that of determining the autonomy of data generation and connectivity versus the isolation of a "thing" in the IoT ecosystem. For instance, if a wearable that senses your body temperature is not connected to a laptop or somehow allowed to transmit data via the Internet to a database, it is isolated. This "thing" serves its purpose locally but if it does not transmit or receive data, it is basically performing the same function as a mercury thermometer. The device senses the temperature, measures and displays the information but does not transmit that information via the Internet without human interaction, so it cannot be considered an IoT object specifically because it does not contribute data to the ecosystem autonomously. Therefore, RFID or Near Field Communication (NFC) integrated objects such as retail items including clothing that have "smart" stickers and tags, or bank and credit cards with integrated circuit chips (ICs) also cannot be considered IoT objects.

BOX 7.1   DESCRIBING IOT AND IOS

To simplify, we could say the IoT is an ecosystem; a collective of all objects and protocols that communicates information to databases via the Internet and makes possible interactive platforms that contribute to the Internet of Services.

The Internet of Services (IoS), not to be confused with the iPhone Operating System (iOS), can be simply defined as the Internet that, via interactive software platforms, supplies services. Some more familiar examples would be Airbnb, Uber, eBay, Deliveroo, and Lime. On a more conceptual level, IoS is where IoT is connected via the Internet with a Service Oriented Architecture (SOA; Moon et al., 2018) that provides a user experience (UX) based on a physical/digital/human relationship. Services, after all, are about helping or doing work for people.

As IoS is more directly related to IoT, it can be defined as those interactive software platforms that leverage the physical/social/digital interrelationships that now exist via the Internet and incorporate interactive feedback loops that generate social and economic value. Just think of the multitude and range of interactions today that create data, then have a digital, social, or physical consequence – from remotely opening a lock with a smartphone to optimising traffic flows in smart cities. To simplify the complexity of the interaction ecosystem we are discussing, Figure 7.1 illustrates these interrelationships that IoT and IoS enable. In the diagram, we see how people, data, and objects interrelate in this context. When they are enabled by IoT/IoS infrastructure these interrelationships effect changes in the Social World, the Digital World, and the Physical World. These changes contribute to the growth, thus value, of Collective Intelligence (including AI), Networked Sensing and Automation, and the Community and the Commons.

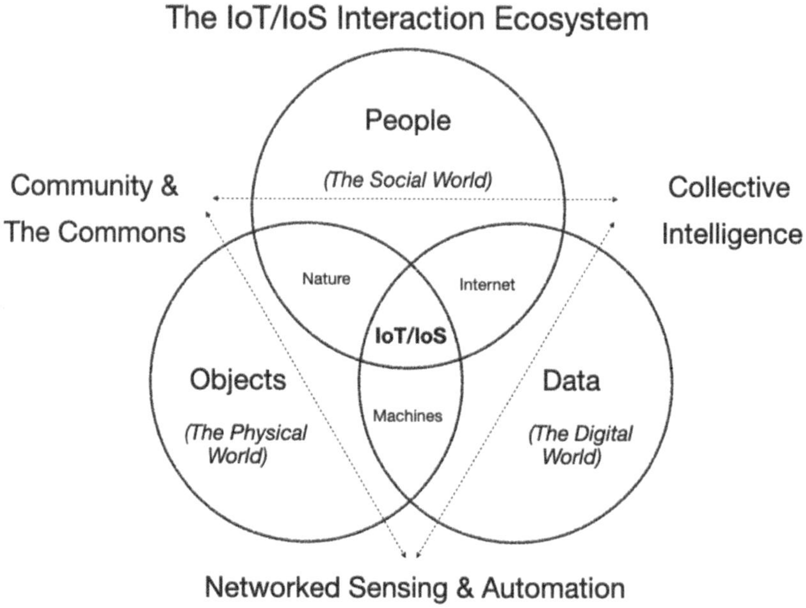

The IoT/IoS Interaction Ecosystem

Source: Authors (2021).

*Figure 7.1   The IoT Interaction Ecosystem adapted Venn diagram
with IoT and IoS at the centre of interactive environments
(Responsible Sensing Lab, 2023)*

3.   IOT/IOS ROLES IN THE CURRENT FOURTH INDUSTRIAL REVOLUTION

The convergence of emerging technologies described, the consequent growing interrelations that we have illustrated, and the resulting social and economic trends contribute to the Fourth Industrial Revolution (4IR) we are experiencing and participating in now, and the roles of IoT and IoS in this revolution are significant. The first Industrial Revolution took place in the 18th and 19th centuries in Europe and America; it was a period when mostly agrarian, rural societies became more industrial and urban. The iron and textile industries, along with the development of the steam engine, played central roles. The second took place right before the First World War and was marked by massive growth and the expansion of industries like steel, oil, transportation, and communication. For the first time, we used electric power to create mass production. Some major technological advances during this period include the telephone, the lightbulb, the motion picture camera, and the internal combustion engine. The third – some call it the Digital Revolution, some call it the Information Age – is related to pervasive computing and the rise of the Internet that began in the early 1980s. Klaus Schwab, executive chairman of the World Economic Forum, coined the term "Fourth Industrial Revolution" (Schwab, 2016) to describe the current convergence of rapidly emerging industries including IoT, robotics, AI, nanotechnology, quantum computing, biotechnology, 3D printing, autonomous vehicles (AV), and genetic engineering, to name but a few. He argued that we are at the beginning of a revolution that is fundamentally changing the way we live, work, and relate to one another as technology advances and expands at an exponential rate.

IoT, IoS, and the data they generate, the interactivity they enable, the new systems they create such as Industry 4.0, cyber-physical systems (CPS), ambient intelligent environments (AIE), smart cities, and more – what can be referred to collectively as IoT interactive ecosystems in general – are at the forefront of the Fourth Industrial Revolution. These radical changes, advances, and innovations taking place in our world today have enabled new approaches to production. Where the IoT and IoS economies emerge are in those places where new physical/ machine/digital/human interactions generate social and economic value with actionable data; data that is generated by feedback loops that enable previously unrealised insights, adaptation, participation, contribution, and change in the social, physical, and digital environments, and offer unprecedented opportunities. This relates directly to what is now commonly referred to as disruption (typically market disruption, but also social disruption) and is first about an innovation that changes the way we normally do things, then how it spreads rapidly through society because of the value generated (Rogers, 2014) until it reaches critical mass and eventually contributes to the formation of new organisational and social systems – including alternative economies (Arbib and Seba, 2020). Despite the negative connotations, disruption is a healthy and necessary reaction to failures and the negative impact of maintaining the status quo when established systems typically resist change and will not or cannot adapt in pace with organisational revolutions brought about, for instance, by technology. Understanding how IoT/IoS interactive ecosystems facilitate the diffusion of innovations, cultivate the conditions for disruption, and lay the foundations for new infrastructure, organisational, and social systems is key to understanding the formation of the future IoT/IoS economy.

3.1   On the Social and Economic Impact of IoT/IoS

Reports on the current state and potential of the IoT economy vary. In 2015 McKinsey Digital projected 3.9 to 11.1 trillion dollars a year in economic impact by 2025 (Manyika et al., 2015) which is a huge margin and, therefore, a fairly safe bet. More recently, in 2019, GSMAi estimated economic growth based on an expected increase of IoT connections from 9 billion in 2018 to 25 billion in 2025 that indicates an increase in global productivity impact from .2% GDP in 2018 to .34% GDP (Sivakumaram and Castells, 2019) in 2019. It is very difficult to get reliable reports about the potential economic impact of the IoT/IoS simply because of the lack of cohesion regarding the nature of the trends in general (e.g., definitions, inclusion criteria, impact interrelations, and crossover effects to name a few). Therefore, we will focus less on economic growth speculation and more on where and how we see transformative social value being generated with IoT/IoS interactive ecosystems and their potential to facilitate social transformation, new organisational systems formation, and alternative economies of the future.

Regardless of the accuracy (or inaccuracy) of predictions about the potential economic impact IoT/IoS could have, we can be confident that the trend is growing rapidly and the social and economic potential is and will continue to be massive. The size of the impact would also depend on how we look at IoT/IoS in the context of their contributions to innovation, disruption, and organisational shift. Although we definitely see IoT/IoS creating efficiencies and increasing productivity, what is more important is how new interactive experiences create, unforeseen opportunities in society.

What is so unique about IoT/IoS and how they will help shape future economies is that IoT is the convergence, the bridge, that joins the social and economic as well as the physical and the digital revolutions. It is a focal point, the nexus, where the Fourth Industrial revolution and Web 4.0 will merge to shape behaviour, culture, societies, and therefore economies of the future. The data generated in urban environments by IoT is not only interactive beyond the digital, it is co-creative with feedback loops that are generative (Dickson et al., 2018), and we will be able to not only gain insights into our surroundings, but act on that information in ways that will contribute data to the ecosystem, adapt our environment, and improve processes, flows, systems, organisations, and our lives in many ways that are potentially transformative. To give a simple example of this generative dynamic in play, simply think of the growth of wearables to monitor and improve personal health then expand that thinking to what IoT can do to measure the health of a city's infrastructure and what we can do with that data to improve the urban environment and our lives collectively.

As we are now in the midst of the Fourth Industrial Revolution, we must anticipate the enormous amount of data – including data sets too large or complex to be dealt with by traditional data-processing application software – what is known as big data – that will be generated as IoT/IoS interaction ecosystems distribute and scale to create seamless efficiencies in cars, homes, schools, hospitals, office buildings, factories, farms, sidewalks, streets, public spaces – basically any system that can leverage information architecture. IoT/IoS-enabled big data will create first possibilities and then momentum for new economic models by closing loops in flows for more sustainable and more circular infrastructure in communities, cities, and entire industries globally. If we can agree this is the trend, we can also see the potential influence it will have on the distribution of economic power as data production, ownership, use, reuse, and enrichment shift away from large organisations and towards objects, individuals, and communities and, therefore, become decentralised and, more importantly, networked, and resilient. How we can direct all this collectively is now a topic being discussed currently as Society 5.0 and aims to resolve various social challenges by incorporating the innovations of Industry 4.0 in a strategic approach to constant value generation. We will discuss this in more detail in section 5 (Hitachi-UTokyo Laboratory (H-UTokyo Lab), 2020).

As IoT/IoS plays an increasingly important role in the emergence of disruptive innovation in the urban environment, and if we understand the dynamics at play, we can leverage their role in more inclusive co-creation strategies that contribute to first social value for the common good, then economic value generation for sustainable futures. Further, if we hope to orchestrate positive change, we should define points of entry where this potential impact can be initiated and realised most effectively. From a business perspective, we see the combination of the physical, digital, and social worlds converging via IoT/IoS-enabled crowdsourcing platforms to create some of the most disruptive innovations this century and indicate the transformative momentum of these trends. Some of the most prominent examples would include:

- **Uber:** A crowdsourced alternative to traditional taxi services enabled by IoT/IoS where hyperlocal matching, payment processing functionalities revolve around smartphone functionalities including location tracking. Recently, we have seen Uber leveraging its market penetration and user base to expand operations to Uber Eats and other delivery services.
- **Airbnb:** Using latent resources (empty homes) to fill market demand is an important aspect of disruption and Airbnb has not only challenged the global hotel industry but it is changing the urban landscape physically and socially, both for the good and the bad. Airbnb "hosts" often use geoloca-

tion, Bluetooth Low Energy (BLE), and NFC functions of a smartphone for their guests to open locks and enable payment systems.

- **Bird, Lime, Car2Go:** Any transportation sharing platform including electric cars, scooters, blades, bikes, etc., all of these Mobility as a Service (MaaS) platforms use geolocation, geofencing, and NFC to access (unlock) and initiate use of various electronic vehicles (EVs). This would also include ride-sharing such as BlaBla and other peer to peer (P2P) platforms that matchmake and enable seamless and secure sharing like Lista, WeeShare, or even Craigslist. These platforms are huge and getting bigger by the minute.
- **Echo:** Amazon's voice-activated AI promises to be the smart home hub where you will be able to control everything from temperature to lighting, appliances, locks, security – basically, anything that can be connected and controlled – remotely or with voice commands or seamlessly with the help of AI who will optimise everything for you. This will include Google's Nest, Philips Hue, and Amazon's Ring.
- **Alibaba:** So what does Alibaba have to do with IoT/IoS? Everything actually. Without its smart warehouses that use advanced robotics and employ IoT-enabled Industry 4.0 automation principles, Alibaba wouldn't be able to deliver. Without crowdsourcing its product catalogue (inventory) via IoS platforms it would not have anything to deliver. The same goes for Amazon and eBay.

Although most of the above examples are the topic of much controversy relating to exploitative practices and questionable business ethics, we want to focus on their social and economic impact in the context of disruption and then how we must ensure social values are addressed as lawmakers play ethical catch-up with technology. Eventually, as with most innovations, governments will need to intervene to ensure social justice but, for the time being, we can benefit by examining these examples as patterns or models that could be applied responsibly to value-generating and sustainable business models in the immediate future.

If you look at different lists of disruptive companies for 2019 through to 2023 you will see a who's who of mostly IoT/IoS-enabled platforms that co-create value with feedback loops and several that use crowdsourcing and smartphones (via apps) as the keystone to build new bridges that connect the physical, social, and digital worlds. In fact, the entire app ecosystem depends heavily on IoT interactivity as the smartphone serves as a sensing, data-generating, transmitting, and receiving IoT device. The smartphone, perhaps the most socially transformative innovation this century, plays a central role by connecting human behaviour to both the physical and machine worlds. In fact, it is a key enabler that puts humans at the centre of value generation as phenomena in the physical world is measured by IoT devices and delivers sense data to the social world where humans interact with that data in IoS platforms, via smartphones and apps, the resulting behavioural data is processed and rendered into insights that generate actionable data with which humans can act upon to effect changes in the physical world.

This continuous feedback loop generates and sends data to the ecosystem that also enables machine-to-machine (M2M) interactivity. With the help of smartphones, we transmit and receive data with other IoT objects via various M2M, Internet and telecommunications protocols (e.g., MQTT, NB-IoT, LTE-M, LoRa, Sigfox, Bluetooth Low Energy (BLE), and NFC; Postscapes, 2020) that enable seamless and secure, object-oriented (hyper-local), and context-specific interactions via a spectrum of radio frequencies that enable data exchange, file transfers, payments, gate entry, media streaming, and authentications required for nearly all these platforms to function. Figure 7.2 illustrates how M2M protocols enable IoT/IoS feedback loops.

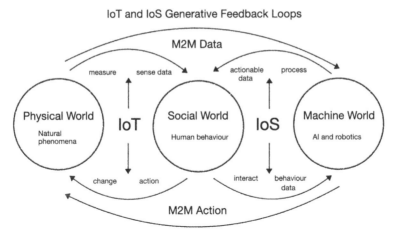

IoT and IoS Generative Feedback Loops

Source: Authors (2021).

Figure 7.2   *IoT and IoS generative feedback loops*

Of course, the examples referred to are just the tip of the iceberg. In rapidly growing, data-generating interrelationships among the physical, social, and machine worlds that enable and accelerate innovation, collective intelligence also grows and feeds more innovation. What is crucial to the development of transformative future economies is what lies below the surface – the power of disruptive platforms to incorporate, circumvent, replace, and/or transcend existing systems, thus necessitating new organisation. We can better face challenges armed with the socially transformative potential of collective intelligence and its growth is a powerful force. This is why we must examine how we can leverage all this potential and direct the power of IoT/IoS-enabled value generation towards the co-creation of innovations for sustainable systems.

3.2   The Possibility for IoT/IoS Data-driven Alternative Economies

There is a real possibility for alternative economies to emerge from all this chaos – economies which are more human-centred, social, egalitarian, sustainable, and circular. But this is not an obvious or self-fulfilling outcome. As we see most IoT-enabled interactivity taking place in the urban environment, we will focus on the city as a platform and an ecosystem where we can test, explore, and understand better how these emerging trends influence various aspects of society and generate sustainable value.

In the following sections, we will discuss in depth the generative value of IoT/IoS, their ability to create actionable data with physical/ machine/ digital/ human interactions and how that creates feedback loops and influences the urban environment. We will look at these aspects of value generation in connection with the emergence of FAB Labs, Living Labs, and smart cities that have leveraged social inclusion to disrupt the status quo and are transforming the urban landscape. We will explore how IoT Interaction Ecosystems could, in the future, become an integral part of the urban social fabric in what we call a "sensitive city" – a possible symbiotic city as a platform with AI integrated into a non-linear, networked value chain where P2P co-creation (Ikävalko et al., 2018) is brought to the forefront to realise new possibilities for social impact, thus real prospects for a new economic order that would be more inclusive, and make possible a more human-centred society.

4.   LINKAGES WITH OTHER EMERGING SOCIO-ECONOMIC TRENDS

Since the latter half of the 20th century we see that the global economy and means of production have shifted significantly from traditional supply side material extractivism, manufacturing, and distribution to intangible asset generation and enrichment. According to an article published in *The Economist* (2017), today's most valuable resource is no longer oil but data. The game changer here is that data is generative – instead of depleting with use, it multiplies. This is a radical organisational shift society is still working to catch up with. A challenge is that governments are much slower to ensure a responsible and sustainable balance of social and economic benefit than corporations are to harvest and exploit data for profit (World Bank Group, 2016).

At the same time, technological revolutions have radically democratised powerful digital and physical tools making them accessible to the public which leads to bottom-up social and economic value generation. IoT and IoS have taken a significant role in this by enabling various related trends now taking hold and becoming established cultural and social movements such as the open data movement, open source (software and hardware), the hacker and maker movements (including the emerging changemaking faction), FAB Labs, makerspaces, meetups, citizen science, living labs, urban labs, smart cities, city-making, place-making, prosumerism, crowdfunding, crowdsourcing, and various P2P platforms as discussed which in turn feed the emerging alternative economies (see Table 7.1) that are now taking form. Technological innovations in combination with democratisation and crowdsourcing trends create the necessary conditions for disruptive innovation to challenge the status quo as they replace established, linear, and centralised systems with more human-centric, participatory, networked, and, therefore, resilient alternatives. Agile methodologies, socially inclusive co-development and problem-solving approaches such as design thinking, user-centric design, rapid prototyping, and open and collaborative innovation contribute momentum to these trends and we see this manifest in the urban environment as living labs, urban labs, and smart cities become more pervasive throughout the world. These converging technologies, trends, methodologies, approaches, systems, organisations, and their applications are now part of a new global social fabric, enabling us to move forward and make ourselves more responsible and, therefore, powerful participants in human society. We can now more actively contribute to the formation of the future web, cross the bridge between the digital and the physical, and apply the power of the crowd to the formation of future cities and future economies.

Alternative economies are taking shape as organisational environments change, shift, and adapt to the global digital explosion. What is apparent is that all these trends and movements we have been discussing in the context of market disruption and social transitioning contribute momentum to the formation of alternative economies in general as they not only make these alternatives possible but unavoidable by-products of paradigm shift. The specific roles that IoT/IoS play in the formation of alternative economies are also apparent as they enable interactivity specific to driving forces behind value generation related to most emerging alternative economies. Most importantly, we should point out that without IoT-related data and IoS-related platforms combined in IoT interaction ecosystems, the generative feedback loops these economies depend on could not exist (see Table 7.1).

Where we see the most influence and potential IoT/IoS have in the formation of various alternative economies emerging today is not so much in how they exist as independent technological trends, rather how they enable all these fresh approaches to become interactive; how they, through physical, social,

Table 7.1   Table of IoT/IoS dependant emerging alternative economies,
their definition and a few examples of IoT/IoS enablers that
make them function

Circular Economy	Sharing, leasing, reusing, repairing, refurbishing, and recycling existing materials and products as long as possible to close resource loops and maximise sustainable systems	Sensing and measuring resource flows, closing loops with actionable data, tokenisation of assets, efficiencies in micro-grids, dynamic exchange algorithms
Functional Economy	Using product-service systems that charge for use only as opposed to products. Replacing the notion of selling a good with selling the usage of a good	Industry 4.0, material passport, asset tracking, urban mining, function as a service, servitisation, dynamic exchange algorithms
Bio-based Economy	Economic activity involving the use of biotechnology and biomass in the production of goods, services, or energy	Sensing the physical environment, measuring dynamic ecosystems and resource flows, efficiencies in recycling and up-cycling
Collaborative/Sharing Economy	A social economic system built around the sharing of resources where consumers rely on each other as opposed to corporations for goods and services	Deliberate asset management, geolocation and hyperlocal match-making, payment systems and P2P functionality
Self-production and Prosumerism	Economic activity taking shape around the application of digital design and manufacturing capabilities for the production of own products. It integrates the economic roles of producer and consumer into prosumer	Digital publishing platforms, including Wikipedia and social media, 3D printing, household production, solar energy and rain water harvesting, storage, distribution, exchange, use, etc

and digital participation, create feedback loops and become more inclusive specifically in the urban context. As stated before, IoT/IoS in essence are co-creative; therefore, if we add a layer of IoT interactivity to the user experience (UX) or core P2P functionality of these various emerging economies the generative links are inherent. To illustrate this, we will take a brief look at the emergence of the Maker Movement – a key element in the collaborative, sharing, and self-production economies. Then, in a progression of scale, we will establish IoT/IoS related links to the circular, functional, and bio-based economies in our exploration of the development of living labs, urban labs, smart cities, and future cities in general. By the end of this chapter, we hope to effectively demonstrate how IoT Interaction Ecosystems can enable transformative, interactive platforms that will make possible the measurement, monitoring, and optimisation of both physical/material and human/intellectual resource flows.

4.1   IoT/IoS Contributing to Social Revolution

Fabrication Laboratories (FAB labs) first started popping up around the world in 2001–2002 but their close relationship to IoT didn't develop until 2006 when open-source hardware became accessible. Single-board computers like Arduino and Raspberry Pi, and the sensors they integrated, catalysed the maker and citizen science movements. At the same time, advanced rapid prototyping tools such as 3D printers, high-powered laser cutters, and computer numerical control (CNC) routers became more affordable, compact, and easy to use. Other related digital tools and resources that emerged at this time include open-source software, cloud computing, GitHub, and other P2P collaboration platforms. The importance of crowdfunding platforms such as Indiegogo and Kickstarter that made it possible for individuals and small organisations to prototype, refine, manufacture, distribute, and sell innovative IoT related products such as Pebble cannot be overlooked.

The origins of what we now call the Maker Movement can be traced to the age-old traditions of do-it-yourself (DIY) and tinkering, but, as opposed to home improvement projects and using "what's on hand" to solve a problem, this relatively new trend is using new tools, materials, and resources previously inaccessible to the public to fabricate serious inventions or create novel and commercially viable products and services. While the "toys" we are tinkering with today have grown to significant proportions, along with the power that they have to enable individuals and communities to experiment and create social impact, current technologies allow for far more complex and complicated "things" to be made by individuals without formal training. All these various and related movements and trends combine in the mega-trend known as digital social innovation (DSI; European Union, 2015).

The first FAB lab, funded and organised by an established institution, was created at MIT in 2001 with the mission to explore how the "content of information relates to its physical representation". The goal was to enable individuals to make almost anything, including technology, normally limited to those capable of mass production. This was accomplished by making state-of-the-art, but now democratised, tools available in a small, open laboratory where people could share knowledge and skills (Ginger et al., 2012). In these collaborative workspaces, supported with some guidance, people were helped to rapid prototype their ideas into reality at a low cost. This empowering concept caught on and today there are more than 1,500 FAB labs around the world (FabFoundation, 2023).

Due to increased global Internet connectivity, the Maker Movement and DSI in general continue to distribute and grow quite evenly throughout the world. This social trend is gaining popularity and momentum because it empowers people; because it helps people express their passion in new production models and share innovations in new forms of distribution, or more specifically, in new production approaches that change the physical world and have a positive effect on people's lives – another generative feedback loop.

The Maker Movement is being lauded as a key enabler for the Fourth Industrial Revolution. "It has arrived and it will be bigger than the Web", according to Anderson (2013), former Editor-in-Chief of *Wired* magazine. A new generation of hackers, designers, artists, hobbyists, students, teachers, and entrepreneurs are all part of the rise of a collaborative DIY culture that has led to makerspaces sprouting up in innovation hubs, community centres, public schools, and libraries across the world.

In the context of IoT/IoS, we can point to the healthy factions branching off from the Maker Movement such as citizen science, and sense-making which focus on solving societal problems that put human-centric design at the centre of IoT interaction ecosystems. These factions, in turn, contribute to related emerging trends such as prosumerism, place-making, city-making, and changemaking, which are creating significant social impact and often incorporate IoT/IoS as "making" in general evolves along with increasingly accessible technology that enables participation in the collaborative, sharing, and self-production economies. The Fourth Industrial Revolution, Web 4.0, DSI – the democratisation of technology in general and the desire of individuals and communities to work collaboratively to create social impact, what is being called changemaking – are all interrelated and combining to feed each other to create conditions for "the perfect storm" which could be the beginning of a global, transformative socio-economic paradigm shift. When we look at social evolution, we can see why Society 5.0, where all these technologies, trends, and cultures combine, is an important topic.

4.2 The Impact of IoT Interactive Environments on the Urban Landscape

As the Maker Movement and its various factions became woven into the fabric of our new hybrid digital/social cultures, they also contributed to the formation of urban living labs and smart cities agendas further influencing the shape of future cities contributing even more towards social and economic impact. Originally, living labs were a sort of academic pursuit, or a label given to field labs or innovation hubs where applied research was taking place, but were not necessarily in the city itself or with public participation – mostly in university campuses and controlled environments. This seems to be where the living lab concept developed, but then the label or "brand" was adopted by industries and cities and became a bit of a hype.

There are organisations like the European Network of Living Labs (ENoLL) that have attempted to define a living lab but more for academics. There are the Open & Agile Smart Cities (OASC), an EU-funded organisation which is a global Living Lab network but more about the "city as a platform" and "experimentation as a service". While OASC focuses more on cities and municipalities, ENoLL focuses on knowledge providers and university campuses. The Amsterdam Metropolitan Solutions Institute (AMS) – a collaboration between the City of Amsterdam, TU Delft, Wageningen University, and MIT – published the *Urban Living Labs: A Living Lab Way of Working* (Steen and van Bueren, 2017), which is a pioneering resource that provides in-depth insights into what the living lab approach entails. The institute researched over 90 projects in the Netherlands and came up with some constructive insights into how living labs contribute to shape the urban environment with inclusive experimentation and co-creation. Through their empirical approach, they came to a simple, fact-based definition that *urban living labs should be seen as a safe place in the city for people to collaborate and experiment with technology.* In research we conducted as The City Innovation Exchange Lab (CITIXL) in collaboration with the City of Amsterdam with surveys and a mini-conference held in Amsterdam in 2019, the input from some 40 active living labs informed us that living labs are not necessarily a physical testing environment, but could also be a temporary pilot or experiment in both physical or digital spaces. This leads to the concept that impact begins with dynamic, inclusive, and ethical engagement and a research framework to understand how to more effectively leverage citizen engagement (Manwaring and van Arman, 2019). This empirical approach culminated in the co-creation of the Responsible Sensing Toolkit in 2022 (Responsible Sensing Lab, 2023), another valuable resource for city innovators that addresses social values when designing IoT related solutions in the city as a living lab.

Regardless of all the recent hype (see Ridley (2017) on hypes and their dynamics) and the various meanings ascribed to the concept, living labs are a sort of collective innovation in its early stages and becoming a powerful force in the urban environment – a way for individual citizens, innovators, makers, students, knowledge providers, community leaders, NGOs, public servants, governments, citizen scientists, entrepreneurs, start-ups, and corporations – any individual or organisation actually – to generate ideas, prototype potential solutions, then test, validate, and refine them with the public in practical experiments. As these solutions sometimes prove effective, the public spaces where they are implemented generate actionable data as these living labs also become IoT interaction ecosystems.

The smart cities movement has also created significant socio-economic impact and become a huge industry projected to reach 2.5 trillion dollars in 2025, and it also leverages IoT/IoS technologies to improve city services on a grand scale (PwC, 2019). In usually a "top-down" approach, the more experimental solutions provided take the form of pilots and are initiated by large organisations also known as the "triple helix" of corporations, government, and universities. Roots of the smart city approach can be traced back to Los Angeles in 1974 when the municipality's Community Analysis Bureau used computer bases, cluster analysis, and infrared satellite photography to gain insights into neighbourhood demographics. About 40 years later, the term "smart city" became a catch-all for using technology to improve city services, but it's more complicated than that. We would say that the real essence of the current smart city concept is about using technology in ways that interact with citizens, improve the quality of life, and benefit society, but also in ways that create sustainable social and economic value.

Urban innovation concepts, frameworks, approaches, and models have been called many things over the years and are related to the city as a platform, the ubiquitous city, the digital city, the data-driven city, the responsive city, and so on. They are all related, but the term "smart sity" encompasses all these, has caught on, and has stuck. Unfortunately, at the same time, it has also become a brand name for what is now a multibillion-dollar industry for multinational corporations to sell tech-driven products and services that, at times, are opposed to enabling citizen engagement and meaningful interactivity which would actually address real problems and improve lives. Definitions and descriptions of smart cities differ as well as those of living labs so, for the sake of moving on with our discussion, we offer the following, sourced from Wikipedia (2023b), that we believe covers what most would generally agree upon.

> A **Smart City** is an urban area that uses different types of electronic data collection sensors to supply information which is used to manage assets and resources efficiently. This includes data collected from citizens, devices, and assets that are processed and analysed to monitor and manage traffic and transportation systems, power plants, water supply networks, waste management, law enforcement, information systems, schools, libraries, hospitals, and other community services. The Smart City concept integrates information and communication technology (ICT), and various physical devices connected to the network (IoT) to optimise the efficiency of city operations and services and connect to citizens. Smart City technology allows city officials to interact directly with both community and city infra-

structure and to monitor what is happening in the city and how the city is evolving. (McLaren and Agyeman, 2015)

The above encompasses a good amount of what a smart city is or should be in theory and the key role that sensing the city and, therefore, IoT/IoS and IoT interactive ecosystems take. Recently, most municipalities and smart city organisations have embraced the Sustainable Development Goals (SDGs) adopted by the United Nations in 2015 as guiding principles to shape policy. These 17 goals include reduced inequalities, increased health and well-being, and responsible production and consumption (UN, 2023). This indicates an organisational shift from top-down techno-centric provisioning to fostering more collaborative, inclusive, resilient, lasting, and sustainable innovations. The SDGs and their influence on smart city agendas have a direct relationship to the significant contribution IoT/IoS-enabled interactivity makes towards circular, bio-based and functional economies in the urban environment. Many cities globally have also embraced circularity as an approach to address climate change and sustainable development (C40 Cities, 2023). Regardless of how cities of the future will form and to what extent they will embrace sustainability and circularity, smart cities are big and getting bigger. As this trend continues to grow so will digital infrastructures as cities themselves are becoming participatory platforms that generate data in massive proportions. Much of this data is and will be generated via IoT interaction ecosystems, and how it is generated, who owns it, who controls it, how it is used, reused, and enriched to contribute to the social and economic well-being of a city is of great importance.

4.3   The Three Paths Towards Data-driven Future Cities

The competitive landscape for future cities, as they relate to current and future IoT/IoS economies, seems to be playing out in three general directions. In traditional, commercial solution provision linked to the societal realm of the marketplace, we see multinationals (e.g., Cisco, Siemens, IBM, Microsoft, Google, and Toyota, to name a few) vying for the smart city market share with large-scale initiatives that provide centralised solutions to municipalities. The rise of surveillance capitalism has extended into the urban environment and the social fabric of a population via IoT/IoS to render data for exploitation, create supplier lock-in, and secure an unfair competitive advantage to increase company profits (Zuboff, 2019). The second path we see in the societal realm of the state and as a progression of the traditional surveillance state where centralised government control mechanisms employ sensing and data harvesting (IoT/IoS) to inform social engineering techniques with advanced machine learning algorithms and Artificial Intelligence. With the third path, there is a more democratic alternative, one related to the societal realm of the commons and it is gaining momentum in the new urban digital/physical hybrid environment. This more human-centred approach towards future cities addresses digital rights and social values in a productive relationship between the citizen and the city. As the digital commons rises along with open data plat-forms, and as a result of more municipal investment in public IoT/IoS-related infrastructure related to city services management and optimisation in the physical and public domains, an important feedback loop begins to co-create more government/citizen-generated, owned, and operated (open) data and so the digital commons grows. Currently, we see forward-thinking municipal leaders embracing cooperative, transparent, and inclusive approaches to socio-economic value generation in open data ecosystems that leverage the power of the crowd and stimulate citizen engagement using data as a valuable resource to promote the common good (see chapter 8 'The rise of the digital commons' in Bollier (2014)).

The first path can be illustrated with two examples found in Google Sidewalk Labs (2023) and Toyota's "Woven City" concept (Woven, 2023; Farooqui, 2018). Google, with the help of real estate developers and in cooperation with some cities, is leading the path towards pervasive surveillance capitalism with its Sidewalk Labs programme which began with a five-hectare "smart community" waterfront development in Toronto, Canada. Beginning in 2017 in what was called the "Quayside Project", Google proposed a community that would "incorporate the use of a number of sensors that gather complex data about people's movements and interactions with the neighbourhood, but it was alarmingly unclear how that data would be handled and protected" (Farooqui, 2018). The question is: When powerful multinationals like Google start to create so-called smart communities, who will own the data? The people, the cities, or the corporations? And how will the data be used? For the common good or corporate profits? Because of these ethical digital dilemmas and other issues related to the economic impact of COVID-19 the project was scrapped in 2020 (Marshall, 2020) but Google (now Alphabet) continues to promote and develop Sidewalk Labs globally as they also see the global COVID-19 pandemic as an opportunity to "remake" cities.

In Japan, Toyota announced in early 2020 they will build a city of the future completely on their own as they replace a former automobile factory with an ultra-modern corporate "community" that will house 2,000 people on 175 acres of land in their new "Woven City" (Fox, 2020). Toyota's city of the future will be a massive Living Lab where they will not only sense everything (i.e., implement pervasive IoT interaction ecosystems to collect data), includ-ing people, but they will also prototype and test underground delivery systems, smart homes, autonomous vehicles, and domestic robots – in other words, their own products and services. Like Google, Toyota sees future cities as data-generating cities and a business opportunity with huge revenue potential, and they are actively recruiting city "partners" globally to build "programmable cities" to create an "ever better way of life". Regardless of the benefits being promoted by these multinationals, and others like them, we should be aware of the risks. These approaches, in reductionist logic, could lead society in a progression of centralised control just as threatening to human freedom as digital dictatorships. Think of logical next steps such as programmable societies, communities, families, and people – resulting in dystopian scenarios – those potential threats to freedom well-known writers such as Huxley ([1932] 2014) with *A Brave New World* and Orwell ([1949] 2021) in *1984* forewarned us of long ago.

We now see this happening with the second path and on a massive scale in China (Andersen, 2020) where the central government is using data harvesting, video surveillance, machine learning, algorithms, and AI that inform advanced behaviour design and social engineering. As of late 2020, China's inescapable surveillance state employs somewhere between 170–200 million CCTV cameras (Cuthbertson, 2019) in a next-generation information architecture to monitor, recognise, report, and influence citizens' behaviour. Combined with online behaviour surveillance techniques, the end result is that the Chinese government is now watching every physical and digital move of 1.3 billion people and rating their behaviour with a "social credit score" that will reward their citizens with better Internet or limit their freedom by denying someone a visa to travel, for instance (Mozur, 2018). This is social engineering at its most advanced, using everything from special facial recognition glasses for police to instantly identify and arrest suspected criminals (Chan, 2018) to hats that sense the emotional states of workers and feed that data to employers in the name of efficiency (Fullerton, 2018). These practices, this sort of surveillance and sensing, is a violation of individual privacy rights and, by extension, our collective human dignity – an inescapable mechanism put in place not only to observe and rank but to control the masses by limiting freedoms and removing choices (Zuboff, 2019). Unfortunately, this approach is being promoted by the current regime in an aggressive and decisive strategy to distribute these practices to other countries and cities around the world, and they make no apologies as they set their sights to achieve AI supremacy by 2030 (Andersen, 2020).

The third path has strong links to the commons movement. At a more fundamental level, this pathway seems to provide a means to reinforce the democratic fabric of society and, at the same time, promote the common interest led by communities instead of a band of paladins for private companies. This approach to future cities is more democratic, inclusive, and transparent; it is debatably more promising both socially and economically as it decentralises and redistributes power in a networked approach and, therefore, generates more egalitarian, sustainable, and resilient organisational systems. We have discussed this path towards future cities previously in the context of social revolution, so suffice to say that socially inclusive approaches to urban problem-solving and solution provision are not only preferable but, also, more beneficial. Specifically, leveraging the power of the crowd in the City as a Platform approach in citizen/government value co-creation, both digitally and physically, promotes social values and stimulates economic opportunities perhaps even surpassing the traditional perspective on "economic opportunities". This path gives rise to a new economic constellation in which a multitude of values (e.g., environmental sustainability and social justice) are considered simultaneously, such as we see in Kate Raworth's Doughnut Economics approach. In cities with multiple open, transparent, and inclusive IoT interactive environments that enable public collaboration and exploration in a process of "identify – select – amplify" that mimics natural selection (Beinhocker, 2012), we, along with pioneering economists (Raworth, 2017), see an unprecedented opportunity to impact the overall socio-economic organisation in the urban environment. This third path practically extends the triple helix stakeholder concept to include communities and the environment in a quintuple helix relationship that promotes knowledge, innovation, and sustainability in a more holistic and effective concept that is becoming more accepted among theorists and practitioners today (Carayannis et al., 2012).

Regardless of the specific model, framework, or approach, understanding how IoT/IoS interactive ecosystems contribute to a more sustainable transition to future cities and, therefore, future economies is crucial to gain an overview and identify how we can introduce disruption productively.

5.   PRESENTATION OF VARIOUS CASES TO ILLUSTRATE THE TREND IN PRACTICE

What we see as the most significant and leading, emerging trends in practice that demonstrate what we have discussed thus far follow a social evolutionary progression from practical applications to revolutionary organisational shifts. This progression is linked by a chain of value added by IoT/IoS-driven interactivity and related physical/social/digital feedback loops as previously discussed. What we focus on in this section are specific cases that illustrate transformative milestones towards future economy formation in context.

5.1   IoT and Industry 4.0

In general, the application of IoT interactivity in practice can be seen very clearly in its adoption to increase efficiency in cyber-physical systems (CPS) and this is most prevalent in the manufacturing industry represented by

Industry 4.0. In essence, Industry 4.0, also known as "Smart Industry", is the trend towards automation and data exchange in manufacturing technologies and processes which include elements of IoT, CPS, Industrial Internet of Things (IIOT), edge, cloud, cognitive computing, machine learning, and AI. This is where we see IoT-enabled systems of control, including actuators and digital twinning, working effectively in purely commercial applications to create efficiencies and add value to resource flow for process optimisation. In fact, some would argue that the entire objective of CPS would be to facilitate the real-time data, adaptive functionality, insights, predictive analytics, modelling, predictive maintenance, and simulations that digital twinning interfaces provide to very controlled physical processes. This concept, and its application, goes back to the German government's economic strategy "INDUSTRIE 4.0" which was launched in 2010 as part of the Action Plan 2020 (European Commission, 2017). Industry 4.0 is a subset of the Fourth Industrial Revolution that concerns industry and includes four design principles (Wikipedia, 2023a) that support companies in identifying and implementing Industry 4.0 scenarios:

- **Interconnection:** The ability of machines, devices, sensors, and people to connect and communicate with each other via the Internet of Things (IoT) or the Internet of People (IoP).
- **Information Transparency:** The transparency afforded by Industry 4.0 technology provides operators with vast amounts of useful information needed to make appropriate decisions. Inter-connectivity allows operators to collect immense amounts of data and information from all points in the manufacturing process, thus aiding functionality and identifying key areas that can benefit from innovation and improvement.
- **Technical Assistance:** First, the ability of assistance systems to support humans by aggregating and visualising information comprehensively for making informed decisions and solving urgent problems on short notice. Second, the ability of cyber physical systems to physically support humans by conducting a range of tasks that are unpleasant, too exhausting, or unsafe for their human co-workers.
- **Decentralised Decisions:** The ability of CPS to make decisions on their own and to perform their tasks as autonomously as possible. Only in the case of exceptions, interferences, or conflicting goals are tasks delegated to a higher (human) level.

Industry 4.0 envisions environmentally sustainable manufacturing by having green manufacturing processes, green supply chain management, and green products which, of course, contribute to social and economic impact but in very industry-specific manufacturing scenarios and commercial applications (Sharma et al., 2021).

5.2   IoT-related Rural Cases

Basic CPS approaches in manufacturing have been adapted and applied to agriculture, national park, and wildlife management with the same basic principles, and have realised environmental impact. The applications have been global and the spectrum wide, so to go into a lengthy discussion here about the specifics is not possible, but we must point out a few examples with broad strokes:

- **Agriculture:** The use of ICT and satellite communications networks have benefited crop planting and harvesting for decades. More recently, the proactive use of these network capabilities to fuse with and enrich local IoT sensing data that optimise farming systems (including robotics) has enabled food production on an unprecedented level. The drawback to this increase in production can be a reduction in biodiversity. Regardless, we have seen the application of this trend begin to shift from centralised, large-scale, and unsustainable practices to more local and sustainable farming with an inclusive open data initiative by the European Space Agency which includes their ESA World Cover (VITO, 2023).
- **National Parks:** The same weather monitoring and land management applications informed by Industry 4.0 and related agricultural applications above have been applied to monitoring and managing the natural resources and complex ecosystems in National Parks. Insights regarding material flows and interactions in the natural world, environmental intervention impact measurement, and establishing important stress interactions to set exploitation limits and inform conservation policy are a few specific use cases we can point to.
- **Wildlife:** The pervasive use of geolocation and tracking devices to monitor the health of and track movements of various endangered species in their natural habitats not only for research purposes but also to reduce illegal trapping and poaching (in Africa, for example; Balsara, 2022) has created significant environmental impact. Significant contributions have been made to monitor the rapidly changing and dynamic movement, health, and changes in oceanic wildlife ecosystems related to global warming, plastic waste, and overfishing. A large-scale example would be The Ocean Cleanup (2023), a non-profit organisation that develops and scales (IoT) technologies to rid the world's oceans of plastic.

5.3   IoT/IoS-related Urban Cases

In the urban environment, IoT interactivity enables technology that contributes to more social and economic impact. Again, we can only address a few of the most significant cases as leading indicators for the greatest potential.

- **Autonomous Vehicles (AV):** The hype surrounding AV in the urban environment and the complexity of the implications for infrastructure are as large as are the social and economic impact it will make. AV will revolutionise personal transportation as we see Tesla moving forward rapidly with its S series, but there are broader applications being tested, applied, and gathering momentum. Globally, passenger trains and metro systems are being fully automated. Drones are taking to the sky with packages for Amazon and pizza for Dominoes. In Amsterdam the RoBoat is testing successfully at the "Marineterrein Living Lab" to provide autonomous garbage collection via the city canals. Made possible by multiple IoT/IoS-related sensors, crowdsourced machine learning, and cloud computing capabilities, AV will radically change the urban landscape in the near future.

- **Digital Twinning:** As city infrastructure evolves along with AV, public IoT interactive environments, various crowd monitoring technologies, and other public sensing and automation trends in the urban environment, so digital twinning of cities will become adopted as common practice and more valuable to create the same types of efficiencies and optimisations as in the Industry 4.0 CPS approach. We are witnessing this trend rapidly becoming a digital battleground also related to the transformation of future societies and, therefore, economies (Miskinis, 2019). As more cities adopt 3D modelling and the coupling of data in platforms to monitor and manage everything from street lamps to garbage bins, the more the governance of these potential system of systems (SoS) will influence the formation of future cities, societies, and, therefore, economies. Related to the three paths of future cities previously discussed, there are two paths to digital twinning – one gives more influence, control, and thus power to surveillance capitalists and surveillance states alike, and the other can serve to extend participatory democracy from the physical to the digital in future, data-driven city formation. Regardless of who creates these systems – what is important to understand is that potentially a city's digital twin could prove to integrate all physical, social, and digital activity via IoT/IoS-generated data and may well become the SoS for all future cities. Who owns and controls these system of systems is of great importance to our socio-economic future as well as human freedom and dignity.

- **City-making, Place-making, and Prosumerism:** We have discussed the Maker Movement, citizen science and other inclusive approaches to future cities. As a more specific case to illustrate the IoT/IoS trend in practice, city-making (or citymaking) is a collaborative approach that leverages sensing and making aspects of the living labs approach by actively engaging and empowering communities to test solutions in the city. Place-making is related but specific to transforming public spaces with the same approach. Prosumerism is then about the home and the individual. Its Industry 4.0 principles are applied in an optimised home as well as being more autonomous by producing what homes and individuals consume such as electricity with solar panels, rainwater capture systems and blue green roofs, urban farming, and using 3D printers to make furniture from recycled plastic bottles, for instance, or repurposing other materials for personal or household use. The applications for all of these cases relate to the circular economy and dougnut economics – how we up-cycle the city and repurpose waste as a resource and turn latent or idle resources into valuable urban solutions.

5.4   The Rise of the Global Digital Commons

The rise of the digital commons began with the free and open access to the Internet and the World Wide Web itself and continues to grow along with the global uptake and access to all things digital and data generating. Its momentum is compounded along with all these trends and cases we have been merely touching on. The use of digital platforms in our everyday lives and all the digital interaction in the urban environment and beyond creates more open data, platforms, software, hardware, collaboration, research, learning, design, etc. – in general, commons-based peer-production (Benkler, 2006). But a commons, digital or otherwise, needs more than free and openly accessible resources, it needs a community and a set of social protocols. We see a global community rising, conscious of the value it is generating with these open resources. Whether they are institutions, makers, or citizens, we see the social protocols being formed when these communities create, adopt, and use Creative Commons Licensing, or the Open Design Alliance, for example. Bollier (2014) comments on the economic potential of this IoT/IoS related trend: "The social logic of online cooperation (cheap and easy interaction among distributed users) can trump the economic logic of traditional markets (which require large amounts of capital, centralised corporate management and professional control)." The bottom line is that it is faster, easier, and more cost-effective to innovate online, and as the digital commons fuses more with the physical world via IoT/IoS interactive ecosystems the result is a profound global social revolution where alternative (as opposed to the duopoly of market/state) economic potential is only just beginning.

6. IMPLICATIONS OF IOT/IOS TRENDS FOR THE DEVELOPMENT OF VALUE CREATION AND BUSINESS MODELS

If we think of the city as a co-creative platform, opportunities for value generation and business models can and have emerged as a matter of social evolution when value-generating loops are reinforced by IoT-enabled interactive environments. What is common among these applications/businesses is that they all:

- Use IoT/IoS systems and platforms to deliver value.
- Use physical/machine/digital/human value generation loops.
- Take place in the urban environment.
- Use web apps and native apps to enable these loops.
- Are by nature of those loops co-creative business models.

IoT/IoS-enabled economies of the future, how they generate value, and any business models that can be derived are de facto co-creative and, therefore, generate more impact when they are intentionally designed to be inclusive and participatory. As more cities adopt IoT interaction ecosystems, digital twinning, computer vision, sensors, and other IoT-related technologies, and include media beyond web and smartphone apps such as augmented reality (AR) and virtual reality (VR) to facilitate interaction, they also increase feedback loops via human-generated data. These feedback loops can and should be used in mapping value creation and informing business models in a co-creation relationship for data generation, validation, enrichment, use, and reuse. In a paper entitled 'Value creation in the Internet of Things: mapping business models and ecosystem roles' (Ikävalko et al., 2018), the roles of ideator, designer, and intermediary are defined and discussed in a service exchange dynamic in which this co-creative relationship is examined, and it shows how in every case the end user is identified as the ideator. What this means specifically is that value generation in the IoT/IoS context begins with engaging those people who are most affected by solving a problem or creating an innovative opportunity. What is important for our purposes is to identify and leverage entry points for effective ideation and co-creation among actors with the City as a Platform. Deloitte (2016) describes and visualises an ecosystem of value co-creation in accordance with the processes depicted in Figure 7.2. Deloitte's ecosystem model informs these entry points where the data generation and enrichment ecosystem is a constant feedback loop.

As the urban environment evolves from a centre for trade of goods and services to a more dynamic and inclusive platform where social and economic value are co-created in a knowledge/information economy, we see opportunities for city leaders to shift their focus from providing stable organisational systems to facilitating experimentation and exploring opportunities in a participatory democracy where social and economic impact become more functional than structural, meaning generating social value first as opposed to imposing policy and provisioning top-down solutions. Tim Berners-Lee argued in 2016 that governments need to think of data as a valuable resource and an integral part of the infrastructure as important to the potential stability, well-being, and prosperity of the people as access to water, roads, power, housing, education, medical and other city services in the physical domain (Weinberger, 2016). He made it clear that politicians and leaders must ensure that data is kept open and accessible in order to promote public access to generate value as well as protect the people against market partitioning, centralisation, potential exploitation, and manipulation. If we accept this argument from the inventor of the World Wide Web as valid, then we should also consider those IoT/IoS-enabled platforms that co-create data in public spaces, provide insights to our physical environment, and facilitate interactions that contextualise and enrich that data as also valuable infrastructure to be kept in the public domain and a data commons stewardship policy becomes necessary to protect this resource and promote the common good.

6.1   The Sensitive City Concept: IoT Interactive Ecosystems for Social and Economic Value Generation

In terms of economic impact, a shift needs to take place. The entry point for all these feedback loops discussed is where the human contribution and interactions create value, and the shift is to understand that in today's digital world business models can leverage social interaction as social value generation first and then economic opportunities will present themselves.

The concept and the value of the digital commons leads us to the concept of the human-centric sensitive city, what it is and how it works. More than anything, a sensitive city is socially inclusive and empowers its citizens to take action and contribute to the common good by working with others to improve their communities. It is the city as a living lab with an open IoT sensor network, which creates actionable data using crowdsourcing, social validation, and interactive feedback loops to generate, use, reuse, and enrich that data. Eventually – when there is enough good, accessible, open, interoperable, and harmonised data – AI can be introduced to help filter that data, inform decision making, enable co-creation, and facilitate participatory democracy. This sort of inclusive approach to value generation has been validated in the marketplace with the massive success and rapid growth of disruptive companies such as Airbnb and Uber, which use latent or idle resources and the crowd to generate alternatives to the status quo. Regardless of the ethical debate surrounding the exploitative practices of these two specific companies, their business models can be generalised and applied to the City as a Platform approach to value generation. Municipalities need to embrace disruptive innovation and facilitate inclusive exploration which can lead to social and economic impact by leveraging the unrealised potential of city data in combination with interactive environments, the crowd, and socially validated AI.

As opposed to the current smart city approach – which is more about creating efficiencies by using technology to optimise verticals such as mobility, logistics, connectivity, communication, energy, health, education, tourism, culture, etc., or city services and infrastructure such as traffic, waste and water management, or large-scale solutions to perceived problems such as you see in post-modernist urban planning – a sensitive city would leverage the power of the crowd to identify the real, most impactful, social problems with citizens, explore possibilities and create opportunities using inclusive and open technology led by IoT/IoS interactive platforms. A consequence of this approach cuts across the "verticals" and demands more integral, holistic approaches in problem identification and opportunity exploration which we see emerging as a trend in recent years. An alternative approach to the technical solution providing a top-down smart city approach, a sensitive city is more like a journey than an end result, a productive exploration as opposed to a solution – a bridge. The journey to a sensitive city is actually a natural progression if we remain aware of how technology evolves in cities and if we consciously guide this evolution by using technology to experiment in socially inclusive ways that lead us towards what economist Kate Raworth calls the "safe and just place for society". In her landmark book, *Doughnut Economics: Seven Ways to Think like a 21st-Century Economist*, Raworth underscores the value of experiments as "the cutting edge – or rather the evolving edge – of economic transformation towards the distributive and regenerative dynamics we need" (Raworth, 2017). If a city evolves into a sensitive city it will be gradually, and in steps, with the help of a public engaged in active experimentation. As soon as the first steps are taken, we will see immediate progress in intangible changes that take place as we gravitate towards increased social justice, such as more ethical and inclusive policies and processes resulting in establishing trust and participation in a more engaged public. We have personally seen and participated in this process with various initiatives here in the Netherlands including the TADA (2023) data ethics manifesto and the co-creation of the Responsible Sensing Toolkit (2023) which have gained momentum globally with the Cities Coalition for Digital Rights (CCDR, 2023), for instance. Later, after problems are explored and solutions have been co-created, changes in the physical domain will become apparent. Potentially disruptive products and services will be ideated and tested, business models will be validated, value and impact will be demonstrated – innovations in general will emerge as proof of concepts, and be made robust and ready to scale. In other words, we will change our urban environment for the better because it will evolve from functional needs rather than hierarchical demands and we will know this because people's lives will improve. As those innovations become effective solutions used within communities, they can distribute and scale outside those communities in a networked approach that could extend globally, creating massive social and economic value. The spread of the digital social innovation (DSI) related trend is now beginning to materialise with organisations such as NESTA – the UK Innovation Agency for Social Good, The European Network of Living Labs (ENoLL), and Open & Agile Smart Cities (OASC) at the forefront (Nesta, 2023b; Enoll, 2023; OASC, 2023). As new IoT/IoS-enabled interactive platforms and innovations distribute and scale they will, eventually, generate enough valuable open data for the sensitive city to introduce socially validated AI as a rational filter, aid, and agent in a collective intelligence relationship that is being actively explored and researched by the Centre for Collective Intelligence Design at NESTA (2023a), for instance. Eventually, a sensitive city could become a value-generating participatory platform for innovation co-creation, but before that can become possible the power of the crowd and political economic power need to combine to create impact and move forward for the formation of future economies.

6.2   The Double Hour Glass of Urban Value Generation

If we reduce the concept of the sensitive city and how it generates value in the urban environment to a simple framework and capture its essence, we will have a clearer picture and a focused reference from which we can communicate with, refer to, and adapt as experience informs us. This framework will help us create, maintain, and share a vision that can be generalised or applied to specific problems. It will simplify complex relationships so we can get things moving in the right direction. In general, how this approach informs value generation can also inform how IoT/Ios interactivity also creates social and economic impact in parallel. We call this framework the "Double Hour Glass" and it illustrates separate elements related to social justice and social impact converging simultaneously with inclusive experimentation and co-creation in the urban context, and as they converge they create opportunities as power shifts from the city to the citizens (Manwaring, 2019).

1. Imagine the two hour glasses in a traditional state, where citizens' needs become problems over time and the city agendas will create solutions but they are separate. There is a disconnect between the city and its citizens because there is no meaningful dialogue or active co-creation.

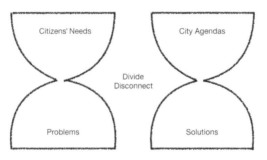

Figure 7.3   Double hour glass: divide disconnect

2. If we replace the disconnect with experimentation, when the city and the citizens begin working together to explore real problems and test possible solutions, we start building a bridge based on an active, participatory exploration of issues. Not in the traditional top-down, solution provision approach but in a side-by-side formation of ideas that can be tested.

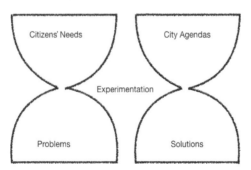

Figure 7.4   Double hour glass: experimentation

3. When we start experimenting in urban living labs the powers of the crowd and political economic power converge and create a generative loop bringing together citizens' needs and city agendas in a new, productive, co-creation relationship that shifts power into a new centre.

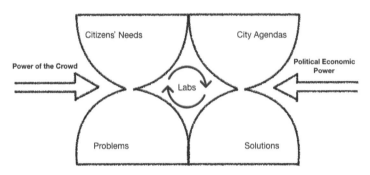

Figure 7.5   *Double hour glass: power of the crowd, politics and economics*

4. In urban living labs problems become possibilities and solutions become opportunities to be explored, tested, and validated by the public. New feedback loops are created as a new data-plus-dialogue relationship begins gathering momentum and social value generation begins to show results.

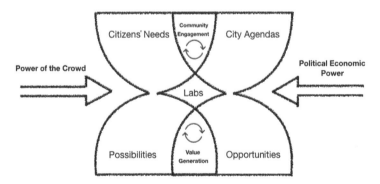

Figure 7.6   *Double hour glass: exploring opportunities*

5.   There is a spin-off effect as a result of the community engagement that occurs almost immediately, it has more of an ethical nature and can be perceived as increased social inclusion, equality, and voice. Citizens have a way to address issues in a constructive forum giving them a more powerful role in future city formation as they participate. Cities have more valid information and insight into the nature of real needs; this informs more effective policy and agendas.

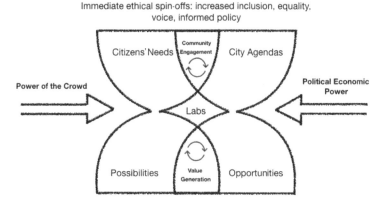

Figure 7.7   *Double hour glass: ethical spin-offs*

6.   Later, there are more visible spin-offs as the value generation loops gather momentum, and these are more related to changes in the physical urban environment resulting from the cooperative investigation and exploration into possibilities and opportunities that lead to co-creating solutions that improve the urban environment, society, the economy, and people's lives.

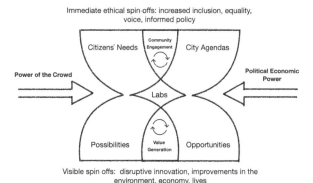

Figure 7.8   *Double hour glass: visible spin-offs*

7. These values generating spin-off elements generate momentum for over-lying positive impact in the form of increased social justice in a healthier, productive relationship between the city and the citizen, and we begin to see real social impact as conditions visibly improve in the physical domain.

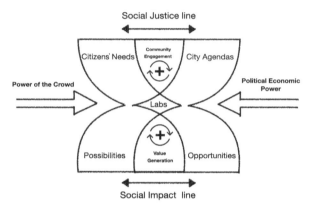

Figure 7.9   Double hour glass: urban value generation

Ultimately, the power of the crowd and political-economic power converge in the urban living lab. Over time, this practical, result-driven approach creates more and more spin-off effects for the common good. It is important to note that glass is both transparent and fragile. Open resources and inclusive design principles are critical. In this illustration power shifts as a result of a balanced co-operative engagement, not converged by force. Hopefully, this visual metaphor helps us understand better the value urban living labs can generate and points out the fact that the relationships involved are fragile and time is ticking away.

6.3   Impact of the Trend Regarding Societal and Economic Transformation

As we discussed in Section 4: Linkages to Other Trends, IoT/IoS have already contributed significantly to societal and economic transformation as they have been at the forefront of Web 4.0 and the Fourth Industrial Revolution. Now we add Society 5.0 (Deguchi et al., 2020) that builds on this innovation momentum to direct the potential of IoT, big data, AI, machines (including robotics), and alternative economies to shape the next phase of social evolution. Again, as outlined in the first section of this chapter, we find ourselves in a world where people, places, objects, and machines are merging. We described the possible application of IoT/IoS interactive ecosystems in a hypothetical sensitive city and how that could contribute to social and economic value generation with the double hour glass illustration. The next step is to explore specific applications of IoT/IoS-enabled functionality that contribute significant momentum to transformational systems we see as real possibilities to catalyse and form not only future cities but also future economies.

6.4   IoT/IoS and the Internet of Value

A new topic, what is being called the Internet of Value or the Internet of Value-Exchange (Deloitte, 2016), has emerged and encompasses all Peer-to-Peer (P2P) platforms, and is related to commons-based peer-production(CBPP) and distribution IoS trust networks (characterised by exchanging goods and services via cryptocurrency, smart contracts, or tokens) are gaining traction as they enable any quantum of value to be transferred or converted as quickly and fluidly as information is today. This is characterised by:

*   Decentralised Processing Networks.
*   Distributed Ledger Technologies (DLT).
*   Digital Signatures (Smart Contracts).
*   Programmable Logic.
*   Open-Source Software (Including Blockchain).

The potential for the Internet of Value to disrupt the financial status quo is revolutionary and we need to better understand tokenisation and how IoT/IoS contributes transformational value in effective token economy design (Kim and Chung, 2018). Next to the cloud itself, the emergence of DLT in general is arguably the most significant contribution IoS has made to enable transformative future economies as they can be adapted to scale over time and networked in such a way to enable a resilience and robustness that could eventually supersede traditional fiat currency exchange and trading systems globally. This trend is as complex as it is controversial and it is beyond the scope of this chapter to dive deeply into the topic but we must outline the relationship between the Internet of Value and IoT/IoS and touch on how this could contribute to social and economic transformation in context.

6.5   The Tokenisation of Assets in IoT/IoS Interaction Design

Decentralised ledger technology (DLT) in general has emerged and has become synonymous with blockchain, cryptocurrency, and bitcoin, but there is more to DLT than what we see in the news, and it is much more than blockchain. In a report issued in August 2017, the Netherlands Central Bank (DNB) stated that there are limitations of DLT that include inefficiency caused by high energy consumption, lack of full certainty that payments are completed, and capacity shortages, but saw potential in cross-border payments, tokenisation of assets, and smart contracts (Canellis, 2019). While the instability and sustainability challenges of Blockchain technology is a cause for concern, and its long-term potential is still in question, more sustainable DLT software is emerging such as IOTAs Tangle (IOTA Foundation, 2023) and other permissions-based P2P applications such as Hashgraph by Hedera (Hedera Hashgraph LLC, 2023) which uses less energy-hungry computational, mathematical and cryptographic approaches (Markus, 2019). In the end, DNB did recommend further experimentation and investment in DLT in combination with AI – a relationship that is not only promising but could be revolutionary (Canellis, 2019).

Tokens are a specific application of DLT and differ from cryptocurrency in that they have wider functionality beyond making "payments", which include additional attributes like permissions and triggers embedded in smart contracts. These are IoS-enabled technical (software) applications of mutual agreements in multiple egalitarian decentralised value exchange (P2P) networks creating incorruptible and transparent records – basically, digital execution of age-old bartering practices with a quantum twist – they transcend previous physical limits of time, distance, and scale.

Tokens, in the form of clay coins, first appeared in human history in the transition from nomadic hunter-gatherer societies to agricultural societies, and the expansion from simple barter economies to more complex economies has become the stuff of history (Schmandt-Besserat, 1996). Beginning in the 1800s, token economies have been used to influence or change behaviour with reinforcement techniques in controlled settings and were proven very effective (Hackenberg, 2009). It is important to note that systems of exchange, trading goods and services, and bartering are such age-old practices engrained in the human experience; it is such a universal propensity because these are social activities that not only leverage and create collective intelligence but which in turn stimulate innovation in the exponential curve we are now attempting to understand, control, and hopefully direct towards the common good and a sustainable planet (Ridley, 2011). It is possible that we could intentionally direct the emerging Internet of Value to contribute to an organisational transition, but we need to be conscious of the pitfalls and mitigate risks by focusing on long-term goals that revolve around social values including transparency, inclusivity, and sustainability as opposed to traditional revenue-generating opportunities. Regardless of the details, new systems of P2P value exchange can be designed to contribute to sustainable social and economic transformations. What is important for our purposes is to explore effective token functionality in the context of IoT/IoS interaction design for positive social impact and test how we can leverage physical/machine/digital/human interactions to effectively circumvent the decaying traditional financial systems and replace them with sustainable, value-generating systems.

Function as a Service (FaaS; IBM, 2023) is already being used as a business model for software and cloud services architecture where you pay only for the resources you use when you use them. If we apply FaaS principles and adapt current tokenisation of assets (Laurent, et al., 2018) practices in a micro-economy, it would be possible to generate value specific to material and intangible exchanges and flows to optimise feedback loops for positive social and ecological impact. This could lead us to a new sort of digital currency – a next generation, hybrid currency, with memory, purpose, and meaning – what we have coined a "Currency with a Conscience". To illustrate, when a token is created it can be assigned various attributes that bind that token to an action in the digital world that can be connected to an action in the physical world. This is how we can insert tokenisation of assets functionality to IoT/IoS interaction design by assigning a specific function of a physical resource like water or a non-tangible asset like time (labour), an idea or consumables like energy and food token generation, ownership, or exchange and create a digital relationship among objects or assets in a token economy where contextual value generation is the function. We could, for instance, optimise positive actions related to each of the 17 UN Sustainable Development Goals (SDGs) by adapting the sensitive city to include the tokenisation of assets. Regardless of the asset or goal, wherever there are resources and resource flows there are possibilities to design tokens into the functional design of systems that incentivise several layers of value generation across any vertical.

6.6   Circularity and Tokenised IoT/IoS Functionality

In a circular economy the most essential (physical) assets we need to manage are energy, water, food, and reusable materials with the goal to design systems that close loops to eliminate all waste. This relates to the aspect of IoT defined as sensors and actuators connected by networks to computing systems that can monitor or manage the health and actions of connected objects and machines (Manyika et al., 2015). In this context, IoT has the ability to collect information generated by sensors and connect stakeholders across the value chain to eliminate waste. Metals are a compelling example because they all have strong intrinsic recycling potentials. In his review of digitalisation of the circular economy (CE), and its importance for the field of metallurgy, Reuter (2016) argues that IoT can help inform CE models as dynamic feedback control loops. Moreover, IoT provides a fundamental basis for evaluating the consequences of the actions of various stakeholders throughout the life cycle of physical products. This is related to the concept of the "Material Passport" (Van Capelleveen et al., 2023), which is gaining significant attention in the construction industry in the context of addressing CE considerations. Salminen et al. (2017) corroborate the importance of IoT for the circular economy, as management and analysis of data coming from various sources is routed through data-to-service processes, leading to business co-evolution of the circular economy. Kim and Chung (2018) demonstrate how an initial coin offering (ICO) generated growth and sustainable value by incentivising voluntary and informed participants to create that growth and value. Basically, if you behave in a way that benefits the community then you are rewarded with a token that rises in value because the value of the community grows. What they call crypto-economics can influence human behaviour through participatory incentive design by the community for the community (the common good) and solve a range of problems related to sustainability. In the system of crypto-economics, the value of the network is linked to that of the token and, as the network expands, the value of token incentives – distributed to initial participants – increases, making it possible to provide sufficient benefits to participants. Applying this design approach to link behaviour and related incentives to specific functions and flows (value exchange) in a circular economy could create multiple feedback loops of contextual value generation and participant-directed social and economic impact to achieve transformative momentum.

7.   AN INFORMED, YET PERSONAL INTERPRETATION OF THE "SUSTAINABILITY" OF THE TREND IN QUESTION

As stated earlier, if you talk about the Internet of Things more than one definition is possible. In this chapter, when we talk about IoT, we talk about the concept of a network of objects that exchange data, which can be generated through sensing the physical world.

Thinking about the relationship between IoT/IoS and sustainability, the first thing that comes to mind is the often-presumed clear relationship between knowing and acting. If you know the figures and the facts, rational acting is the next step. But we know that in real life, this is not a law of nature. On the other hand, when you want to act, it is a great help if you have good information. One of the main qualities of IoT is that it is generating data: data often from the physical world. Good data is a great ingredient of good information. And with good information you can make better decisions. A special quality of the data IoT can generate is that it comes directly from the physical world through sensors. Another quality is that it can send and receive information through a network independently of human interaction. These qualities give us great possibilities and we see how the world is embracing this trend; the estimated

26.66 billion IoT devices we have now, with the estimation of 75 billion by 2025, shows how rapidly.

So, what is the impact of this important technology trend for sustainability? Some things seem clear. IoT will help to inform us better, it will give not just more information but quality, more precise information and therefore deeper insights so we can make better decisions. If a company, city, or country wants to be more sustainable, then they need the right data to measure the impact of their actions. Since it is the specialty of IoT to generate quality data directly from phenomena in the physical world, it is no discussion that IoT will have an important place in the toolkit of any organisation or company that wants to become "greener". Clear, but that holds a lot of presumptions.

Looking around, you see a great variety of applications for IoT-generated data in the urban environment, from parking place alerts to complete infra-structure monitoring, maintenance, and control. The possibilities for sustain-able impact are many, they are growing at a high speed, and they will help us find new solutions.

IoT and IoS as technical trends are not by definition sustainable nor do they contribute to sustainability. In many cases for material or resource flows, it can help because it can support being more efficient and precise. With IoS as a platform enabler, it can be a great tool for recycling, reusing, and up-cycling, for instance, and that can contribute to sustainability. That is just one example of hundreds, but all are potential cases in which the sustainability comes as a by-product of the sort of efficiencies that IoT/IoS enable. At the same time, IoT interactive environments come with the risk of compromising privacy and freedom.

As a tool for reaching sustainable goals, we see a lot of potential. But the first step has to be the decision to formulate a sustainable goal. The moral decision that lies underneath is not a question of data. Once an organisation or a government has taken that step, it can start with the use of these tools.

We think that real momentum towards more sustainable strategies comes from public opinion, and since IoT-related equipment has become so acces-sible potential IoT-enabled applications and solutions are now in the hands of the Maker Movement, and the citizen scientist, and, with IoS, you can add all the 3.8 billion people with a smartphone. All these tools give us power to measure what is happening around us and the ability to check the information governments or companies provide. These abilities give the green movement and an increasingly concerned public in general extra empowerment to con-tribute to a more sustainable society.

The citizen movement is the starting point of a variety of different initiatives to make the city more sustainable. A city that will be "sensing" where the exchange of data between man and machine and machine and machine (M2M) will open enormous new possibilities, with many changes to make the city more sustainable. And these possibilities and power will increase when IoS (Internet of Service), AI, and DLT are brought in.

To capture the essence of what we have seen and where it can lead us is not such a difficult task if we think of how often, in this chapter, we have referred to social value generation as a starting point along with the central place human interaction commands in all value generation we have discussed. We, and how we choose to participate, are at the nexus of all of this. IoT is about how we measure sense data that is important to us. IoS is how we interact in platforms that make that data actionable. AI is a next phase of collective human intelligence with the machines we create as a tool to augment our capabilities. DLT is how we freely exchange those resources that are valuable to us in P2P networks. The concepts of IoT interactive ecosystems, living labs, sensitive cities, and the tokenisation of assets in our progression from IoT/IoS technology to possible future cities and economies is all contingent upon how we choose to use technology and participate in platforms. All of these potentially transformative innovations, trends, and emerging economies depend on us as ideators, problem owners, stockholders, experimenters, testers, users, and solution providers in the co-creation that is inherent in IoT/IoS value generation.

In the end, what is being expressed with all the incredible technological developments we, as humans collectively, have been creating and using as tools to improve our ability to improve our lives is a simple equation – the more we interact with our environment and each other either, the better.

8.   SUGGESTIONS FOR FURTHER RESEARCH: FUNDAMENTAL AND APPLIED

It is clear that we are at the beginning of a new era with a dazzling number of new technologies. In this chapter we placed IoT/IoS and AI together with the value-generating possibilities of DLT with people at the centre. We are very aware that (1) we only see the beginning of these disruptive and transformative technologies; (2) we, in these writings, can only scratch the surface of the possibilities that could be realised in the near future; and (3) the dynamics of this time of singularity make it very difficult to make accurate forecasts. Regardless, we pointed out several possibilities and – in combination with the smart city initiatives and living lab experiments we were personally involved in or know from the global community – some risks and problems we foresee. To move forward and take advantage of these possibilities and to mitigate these risks, the transformational potential of these technologies needs to be researched but in a very practical way. A problem we see is the choice between inclusive experimentation in living labs or the more rigorous scientific approach of universities and institutes. How do we resolve the grassroots "learning-by-doing" approach with traditional applied research? The pace is much faster, the agile methodologies used are based more on Lean Startup principles and less on rigorous science. There is a disconnect between experimentation and the learning-by-doing approach in living labs and structured traditional research approaches – this presents a dilemma. While, in this chapter, we have pointed to various topics, areas, and directions for future research and experimentation, we would recommend more attention be directed at resolving complexities regarding data regulation, privacy issues, wisdom of the crowd, strategies, forms of interactive, participatory value creating social ecosystems, and related ethical dilemmas.

The opportunities for transformative social and economic impact led by IoT/IoS in the context of the Fourth Industrial Revolution, Web 4.0, and Society 5.0 are nearly boundless. The challenge we face is that we need to look at the breadth and width of so many technologies that are now converging to form the IoT/IoS economy as tools – things beyond the incredible advances of hardware and software needed to make sensors – things like: high-speed connectivity (5G) and global networks, ubiquitous computing, massive bandwidth, processing power and storage, big data, the cloud, smartphones, apps, AI, cognitive computing, quantum computing, even bio-tech and nano-tech, among dozens of more emerging technologies. All those emerging technologies that combine to create the Fourth Industrial Revolution need to be examined in the context of IoT/IoS and the role they play to contribute to and enable interactivity, actionable data, and feedback loops in a more human-centric approach to social and economic value creation. There is a danger that if we allow all these emerging technologies to develop in non-inclusive, non-participatory ways led by multinationals, those multinationals will create market partitions to control those technologies more for profit rather than for the common good. Understanding better how to leverage the power of the crowd for egalitarian, disruptive value generation with participatory platforms will help us create sustainable futures, so we must ensure IoT and IoS and even AI and the algorithms they use remain as open, accessible, and inclusive as possible while addressing social values. It is this inclusive path towards transformative social and economic impact that we need to guide our efforts.

8.1   AI, Collective Intelligence and Empathic Urban Design

In order for more egalitarian and sustainable alternative economies to compete with the status quo, we not only need to introduce participatory IoT interactive environments, we also need to start seriously testing the symbiotic decision-making capabilities of individuals and communities aided by the cognitive computing power of AI as soon as possible. This is a specific and relatively new aspect of collective intelligence that is just now being explored (e.g., Nesta, 2023a) yet shows significant potential to accelerate sustainable social and economic progress. To safeguard against centralised power and the potential abuse of that power, we must ensure open and transparent systems, processes, and governance that are first and foremost controlled by humans then aided by AI – not the other way around. We must mitigate the risks and work together to create AI-enhanced intelligent, IoT/IoS-enabled interactive environments (closely related to ambient intelligence; Aarts et al., 2006), that help us make sense of the complexity of a given problem and inform us of the implications of choosing path or solution A over B, or coming up with a better alternative C in an effective modelling approach. In the context of this chapter, we see the need to make very complex data related to urban problems and sustainability more accessible and, therefore, more actionable. We recognise that some fear the destructive potential of AI. Rather than focusing on the dangers of powerful technology, we should be more concerned with keeping AI open and accessible so it can be used as a tool for the common good. Regardless of the practical and ethical problems inherent in creating a symbiotic relationship with man-made machines, we must also realise that in the long run, the benefits far outweigh the risks.

8.2   Tokenisation of Assets to Enable Circular Economies

To remain dedicated to the aspects of sustainability related to social justice, we need to explore how we can increase value in new economies based on collective participation and egalitarian P2P distribution and how they can scale production and exchanges of resources relating to the essentials of energy, water, food, and materials (waste) through recycling, reuse, and redistribution.

Why not take all these trends, technologies, and approaches to the next logical step and explore how the tokenisation of assets can inform systems of flow and enable circularity in general? No doubt we would benefit from researching and experimenting with the tokenisation of essential assets such as water, energy, food, shelter, transportation, time, labour, knowledge, etc., in circular communities for collective value generation. On a small scale we have seen this approach prototyped in Amsterdam, specifically in De Ceuvel (2023), a circularity living lab, but we know of very few examples outside of our own experience. We are currently working on a comprehensive IoT-enabled water infrastructure management platform that we plan to incorporate with smart contracts to enhance efficiencies among municipalities and vendors for predictive maintenance as one use case. At the same time, we have seen see the rise of prosumerism in more sustainable communities, and how important the home is to solar energy harvesting, and how tokenisation facilitates feeding excess energy into micro-grids. There are many experiments now being conducted with large apartment dwellings and office buildings with blue green roofs that capture otherwise wasted rainwater and contribute to CO2 reduction in the urban environment. These are some approaches to increasing circularity and sustainability that we can point to specifically that are being tested in Amsterdam, a city that has a serious commitment to being 100% circular by 2050 (Gemeente Amsterdam, 2020). But Amsterdam is not alone; many cities are participating in organisations and initiatives such as C40 Cities (2023) and The EU Circular Cities and Regions Initiative (European Commission, 2023). And as we have discussed, wherever there are asset flows, IoT and tokenisation can enable asset management.

We should not only focus on material assets though, but should realise the massive value of participation and contributions of human assets such as time, knowledge, and expertise to community-driven projects or to increasing efficiencies. Regardless of the specific approach, the more we learn about the special interactive qualities and the impact we could realise with IoT/IoS interactive ecosystems both large and small, the value generated, the problems solved, and the transformative opportunities would be realised more rapidly, and, therefore, would gain economic momentum and political legitimacy by generating both ethical and visible social and economic value, which in turn increase social justice, social impact, and more evenly distributed economic impact to ensure sustainable futures.

REFERENCES

Aarts, E. H. L., & Encarnaçao, J. L. (2006). *True visions: The emergence of ambient intelligence*. Springer-Verlag.

Ahlgren, M. (2023, 6 July). 100+ Internet statistics, facts and trends for 2023. Website rating. https://www.websiterating.com/research/internet-statistics-facts/.

Andersen, R. (2020). The panopticon is already here. *The Atlantic*, September. https://www.theatlantic.com/magazine/archive/2020/09/china-ai-surveillance/614197/.

Anderson, C. (2013, 2 May). 20 years of *Wired:* Maker movement. *Wired*. https://www.wired.co.uk/article/maker-movement.

Arbib, J., & Seba, T. (2020). *Rethinking humanity: Five foundational sector disruptions, the lifecycle of civilizations, and the coming age of freedom*. RethinkX.

Balsara, S. (2022, 22 April). LoRaWAN-enabled IoT being used to save Africa's endangered wildlife from poachers. IT World Canada. https://www.itworldcanada.com/article/lorawan-enabled-iot-being-used-to-save-africas-endangered-wildlife-from-poachers/480322.

Beinhocker, E. (2012). New economics, policy and politics. In T. Dolphin & D. Nash (eds), *Complex new world: Translating new economic thinking into public policy* (pp. 134–146). IPPR. https://www.researchgate.net/publication/234720011_New_Economics_Policy_and_Politics.

Benkler, Y. (2006). *The wealth of networks: How social production transforms markets and freedom*. Yale University Press.

Bollier, D. (2014). *Think like a commoner: A short introduction to the life of the commons*. New Society Publishers.

C40 Cities. (2023). C40 cities. https://www.c40.org.

Canellis, D. (2019, 1 May). Dutch central bank tested blockchain for 3 years. The results? 'Not that positive' [Technology news]. *The Next Web*. https://thenextweb .com/news/dutch-bank-blockchain-dlt-cryptocurrency.

Carayannis, E. G., Barth, T. D., & Campbell, D. F. (2012). The Quintuple Helix innovation model: Global warming as a challenge and driver for innovation. *Journal of Innovation and Entrepreneurship*, *1*(1), 2. https://doi.org/10.1186/2192-5372-1-2.

CCDR. (2023). *Cities coalition for digital rights: To protect and uphold digital rights at the global and local level*. Cities Coalition for Digital Rights. https://citiesfordig italrights.org.

Chan, T. F. (2018, 12 February). Chinese police are using facial-recognition glasses to scan travelers. *The Independent*. https://www.independent.co.uk/news/world/asia/ china-police-facial-recognition-sunglasses-security-smart-tech-travellers-criminals -a8206491.html.

Choudhury, N. (2014). World Wide Web and its journey from Web 1.0 to Web 4.0. *International Journal of Computer Science and Information Technologies*, *5*(6), 8096–8100.

Cuthbertson, A. (2019, 2 October). China invents super surveillance camera that can spot someone from crowd of thousands. *The Independent*. https://www.independent .co.uk/tech/china-surveillance-camera-facial-recognition-privacy-a9131871.html.

De Ceuvel. (2023). *Welcome to De Ceuvel*. https://deceuvel.nl/en/.

Deguchi, A., Hirai, C., Matsuoka, H., Nakano, T., Oshima, K., Tai, M., & Tani, S. (2020). What is Society 5.0? In Hitachi-UTokyo Laboratory (H-UTokyo Lab.) (ed.), *Society 5.0* (pp. 1–23). Springer Singapore. https://doi.org/10.1007/978-981 -15-2989-4_1.

Deloitte. (2016). *Blockchain: Enigma. Paradox. Opportunity*. Deloitte. https://www2 .deloitte.com/ch/en/pages/innovation/articles/blockchain.html.

Dickson, R., Lisachuk, H., & Cotteleer, M. (2018, 8 March). Growing Internet of Things platforms [Company blog]. *Deloitte Insights*. https://www2.deloitte.com/us/ en/insights/focus/internet-of-things/iot-ecosystem-platforms-value-creation.html.

Enoll. (2023). *European network of living labs*. European Network of Living Labs. https://enoll.org.

European Commission. (2017). *Germany: Industrie 4.0* [Digital Transformation Monitor]. European Commission. https://ec.europa.eu/growth/tools-databases/dem/.

European Commission. (2023). *Circular cities and regions initiative*. European Commission CCRI. https://circular-cities-and-regions.ec.europa.eu.

European Union. (2015). *Growing a digital social innovation ecosystem for Europe: DSI final report*. Publications Office. https://data.europa.eu/doi/10.2759/448169.

FabFoundation. (2023). *Fab lab network*. FabFoundation. https://fabfoundation.org/ global-community/.

Farooqui, S. (2018, 14 August). Sidewalk labs reveals latest plans for Toronto "smart city" development. *The Globe and Mail*. https://www.theglobeandmail.com/ business/article-sidewalk-labs-reveals-latest-plans-for-toronto-smart-city/.

Fox, A. (2020, 7 January). Toyota will build a "prototype city of the future" in Japan. *The Hill*. https://thehill.com/changing-america/resilience/smart-cities/477129 -toyota-will-build-a-prototype-city-of-the-future-in/.

Fullerton, J. (2018, 30 April). "Mind-reading" tech being used to monitor Chinese workers' emotions. *The Telegraph*. https://www.telegraph.co.uk/news/2018/04/30/ mind-reading-tech-used-monitor-chinese-workers-emotions/.

Gemeente Amsterdam. (2020). *Amsterdam circular strategy 2020–2025*. Gemeente Amsterdam. https:// projects2014 -2020 .interregeurope .eu/ rumore/ news/ news -article/8759/amsterdam-circular-strategy-2020-2025/.

Gillis, A. S. (2022, March). *What is the internet of things (IoT)?* [IoT Agenda]. TechTarget. https://www.techtarget.com/iotagenda/definition/Internet-of -Things-IoT.

Ginger, J., McGrath, R., Barrett, B., & McCreary, V. (2012). *Mini labs: Building capacity for innovation through a local community fab lab network.* Fab8NZ, Wellington, NZ. https:// www .academia .edu/ 2822723/ MINI _LABS _BUILDING _CAPACITY _FOR _INNOVATION _THROUGH _A _LOCAL _COMMUNITY _FAB_LAB_NETWORK.

Hackenberg, T. D. (2009). Token reinforcement: A review and analysis. *Journal of the Experimental Analysis of Behavior, 91*(2), 257–286. https:// doi.org/ 10.1901/ jeab .2009.91-257.

Hedera Hashgraph LLC. (2023). *The open source public ledger for everyone.* Hedera. https://hedera.com.

Hitachi-UTokyo Laboratory (H-UTokyo Lab) (ed.). (2020). *Society 5.0: A people-centric super-smart society.* Springer Singapore. https://doi.org/10.1007/978-981-15-2989 -4.

Huxley, A. ([1932] 2014). *Brave new world* (Special 3D edition). Vintage Books.

IBM. (2023). *What is FaaS (Function-as-a-Service)?* [Cloud]. IBM. https://www.ibm .com/topics/faas.

Ikävalko, H., Turkama, P., & Smedlund, A. (2018). Value creation in the Internet of Things: Mapping business models and ecosystem roles. *Technology Innovation Management Review, 8*(3), 5–15. https://doi.org/10.22215/timreview/1142.

IOTA Foundation. (2023). *IOTA.* https://www.iota.org.

Jeffries, S. (2014, 24 August). How the web lost its way – and its founding principles. *The Guardian.* https://www.theguardian.com/technology/2014/aug/24/internet-lost -its-way-tim-berners-lee-world-wide-web.

Kim, M., & Chung, J. (2018). Sustainable growth and token economy design: The case of Steemit. *Sustainability, 11*(1), 167. https://doi.org/10.3390/su11010167.

Laurent, P., Chollet, T., Burke, M., & Seers, T. (2018). The tokenization of assets is disrupting the financial industry. Are you ready? *Insight, 19*(October), 62–75.

Manwaring, P. (2019, 21 June). *The double hour glass for urban value generation.* Urban Living Lab Summit, Amsterdam. https://www.ams-institute.org/events/urban -living-lab-summit-deep-dive-ams-urban-living-lab-way-working/.

Manwaring, P., & van Arman, T. (2019). *Amsterdam Living Lab new years resolution.* CitiXL: City INnovation Exchange Lab. https://www.citixl.com/livinglabresolution/.

Manyika, J., Chui, M., Bisson, P., Woetzel, J., Dobbs, R., Bughin, J., & Aharon, D. (2015, 1 June). *Unlocking the potential for the Internet of Things.* McKinsey Global Institute. https://www.mckinsey.com/capabilities/mckinsey-digital/our-insights/the -internet-of-things-the-value-of-digitizing-the-physical-world.

Markus. (2019, 26 June). IOTA a sustainable cryptocurrency [Blog publishing system]. *Medium.* https://medium.com/@markusgebhardt/iota-a-sustainable-cryptocurrency -a50a52018eaa.

Marshall, A. (2020, 7 May). Alphabet's Sidewalk Labs scraps its ambitious Toronto project [Transportation]. *Wired.* https:// www .wired.com/ story/ alphabets -sidewalk -labs-scraps-ambitious-toronto-project/.

McLaren, D., & Agyeman, J. (2015). *Sharing cities: A case for truly smart and sustain-able cities.* The MIT Press.

Miskinis, C. (2019, January). How digital twins will be utilized to create smart cities [Technology]. *Challenge Advisory*. https://www.challenge.org/insights/digital-twins -and-smart-cities/.

Moon, I., Lee, G. M., Park, J., Kiritsis, D., & von Cieminski, G. (2018). *Advances in production management systems. Smart manufacturing for Industry 4.0*. Springer.

Mozur, P. (2018, 16 July). Looking through the eyes of China's surveillance state. *The New York Times*. https:// www .nytimes .com/ 2018/ 07/ 16/ technology/ china -surveillance-state.html.

Nesta. (2023a). *Centre for collective intellligence design*. Nesta. https://www.nesta.org .uk/project/centre-collective-intelligence-design/.

Nesta. (2023b). *We are next: The UK's innovation agency for social good*. Nesta. https://www.nesta.org.uk.

OASC. (2023). *Welcome to open & agile smart cities, or OASC for short*. Open & Agile Smart Cities. https://oascities.org.

Orwell, G. ([1949] 2021). *1984* (William Collins paperback edition). Collins Classics.

Postscapes. (2020, 1 February). *IoT standards and protocols*. Postscapes Tech. https:// www.postscapes.com/internet-of-things-protocols/.

PwC. (2019). *Creating the Smart Cities of the future: A three-tier development model for digital transformation of citizen services*. PwC. https:// www .pwc .com/ gx/ en/ sustainability/assets/creating-the-smart-cities-of-the-future.pdf.

Raworth, K. (2017). *Doughnut economics: Seven ways to think like a 21st-century economist*. Chelsea Green Publishing.

Responsible Sensing Lab. (2023). *Step 5: Data collection, processing, visualisation*. Responsible Sensing Lab. https://responsiblesensinglab.org/step-5.

Reuter, M. A. (2016). Digitalizing the circular economy: Circular economy engineering defined by the metallurgical internet of things. *Metallurgical and Materials Transactions B*, *47*(6), 3194–3220. https://doi.org/10.1007/s11663-016-0735-5.

Ridley, M. (2011). *The rational optimist: How prosperity evolves*. HarperCollins.

Ridley, M. (2017, 12 November). Amara's law [Blog]. *Matt Ridley*. https:// www .mattridley.co.uk/blog/amaras-law/.

Rogers, E. M. (2014). *Diffusion of innovations*, 5th edition. Free Press.

Salminen, V., Ruohomaa, H., & Kantola, J. (2017). Digitalization and big data supporting responsible business co-evolution. In J. I. Kantola, T. Barath, S. Nazir, & T. Andre (eds), *Advances in human factors, business management, training and education* (Vol. 498, pp. 1055–1067). Springer International Publishing. https://doi .org/10.1007/978-3-319-42070-7_96.

Schmandt-Besserat, D. (1996). *How writing came about* (1st abridged edition). University of Texas Press.

Schwab, K. (2016). *The fourth industrial revolution* (1st US edition). Crown Business.

Sharma, R., Jabbour, C. J. C., & Lopes De Sousa Jabbour, A. B. (2021). Sustainable manufacturing and industry 4.0: What we know and what we don't. *Journal of Enterprise Information Management*, *34*(1), 230–266. https://doi.org/10.1108/JEIM -01-2020-0024.

Sidewalk Labs. (2023). We build products to radically improve quality of life in cities for all. Sidewalk Labs: Part of Google. https://www.sidewalklabs.com.

Sivakumaram, M., & Castells, P. (2019, April). *The contribution of IoT to economic growth: Modelling the impact on business productivity* [Business presentation]. https://data.gsmaintelligence.com/api-web/v2/research-file-download?id=41091146 &file=2749-240419-IoT-Productivity.pdf.

Statista. (2016, 27 November). *Internet of Things (IoT) connected devices installed base worldwide from 2015 to 2025*. Statista. https:// www .statista .com/ statistics/ 471264/iot-number-of-connected-devices-worldwide/.

Steen, K., & van Bueren, E. (2017). *Urban Living Labs: A living lab way of working*. Amsterdam Institute for Advanced Metropolitan Solutions (AMS).

TADA. (2023). *Tada! Data disclosed: With data we make cities smarter. But also wiser?* Tada. https://tada.city/en/home-en.

The Economist. (2017, 6 May). The world's most valuable resource is no longer oil, but data: The data economy demands a new approach to antitrust rules. *The Economist*. https://www.economist.com/leaders/2017/05/06/the-worlds-most-valuable-resource -is-no-longer-oil-but-data.

The Ocean Cleanup. (2023). *The largest cleanup in history*. The Ocean Cleanup. https://theoceancleanup.com.

UN. (2023). *Make the SDGs a reality* [Sustainable Development]. United Nations Department of Economic and Social Affairs. https://sdgs.un.org.

Van Capelleveen, G., Vegter, D., Olthaar, M., & Van Hillegersberg, J. (2023). The anatomy of a passport for the circular economy: A conceptual definition, vision and structured literature review. *Resources, Conservation & Recycling Advances, 17*, 200131. https://doi.org/10.1016/j.rcradv.2023.200131.

VITO. (2023). *Worldwide land cover mapping*. ESA. https://esa-worldcover.org/en.

Weinberger, D. (2016, 10 August). *How the father of the World Wide Web plans to reclaim it from Facebook and Google*. Digitaltrends. https://www.digitaltrends.com/ web/ways-to-decentralize-the-web/.

Wikipedia. (2023a, 23 July). *Fourth industrial revolution* [Online encyclopaedia]. Wikipedia. https://en.wikipedia.org/wiki/Fourth_Industrial_Revolution.

Wikipedia. (2023b, 25 July). *Smart city* [Online encyclopaedia]. Wikipedia. https://en .wikipedia.org/wiki/Smart_city.

World Bank Group. (2016). *World Development Report 2016: Digital dividends*. World Bank. https://doi.org/10.1596/978-1-4648-0671-1.

Woven. (2023). *Our vision*. Toyota Woven City. https://www.woven-city.global.

Zuboff, S. (2019). *The age of surveillance capitalism: The fight for a human future at the new frontier of power*. Profile books.

8. Conclusions on the future of the economy

Sjors Witjes and Niels Faber

1. INTRODUCTION

Current society is faced with challenges the magnitude and urgency of which is greater than ever. A changing climate, a closing-in on running out of natural resources, as well as loss of biodiversity, combined with social unrest and growing inequalities have generated an exciting and contradictory but also energetic and promising world that is increasingly 'ramshackled' with a confusing number of developments reinforcing and simultaneously counteracting each other.

In this book we addressed a number of 'slow' and enduring economic and societal trends that have embodied the potential to reshape our economy in the past and present and will most possibly do so in the near future. This final chapter provides a critical analysis of the discussed trends, their impacts on society, and the implications for organising collaborative and collective human activities. We discuss societal developments that are considered as forming the undercurrents of the set of trends. In this discussion, we will return to the birth of the economic field, during the Renaissance, where, among others, Greek philosophy was translated into the main economic principle of an equal distribution of and access to resources. The original Greek concept of *oikos nomos*, signifying the management of a household, had been adopted and transformed into what is currently understood by the term economics: the study of production, distribution and consumption of products within and between nation-states. With the current crises showing that nowadays the economic system deviates from the principle of equality, we consider the six economic trends that are identified in this book as intentions to transform our society towards one with more equal distribution of and access to resources.

Taking a bird's-eye view and looking back over the narratives on the six trends provided in preceding chapters, we notice the following. First and foremost, the trends we address in this volume do not stand in isolation but are heavily intertwined and are in pursuit of resolving the inequality and detrimental environmental effects of economic activity in one way or the other. In this fashion, each of the trends – circular, functional, bio-based, sharing, self-production, digitalisation and Internet of Things and Services – together shape a close-knit network of actors and activities supporting each other.

Second, digitalisation and the Internet of Things and Services seem to form a densely crafted digital foundation for all other trends. This digital fabric offers a plethora of services with regards to product characteristics, usage patterns, wear and tear, life cycle stages, autonomous and intelligent application, logistics, et cetera.

Third, we see a shift in focus, changing the gaze from merely providing products to an integral focus on the product life cycle. In particular, this concerns the various forms and values a product takes during its life cycle for both humans and non-humans to which it relates.

Fourth, and extending from the previous observation, we see a shift towards a growing sense and manifestation of shared responsibility and accountability across all stages of a product's life cycle or even wider society by the actors involved. This shift towards shared responsibility and accountability may be the prelude to a more fundamental shift of the economy's role in society, where the future of the economy will not be actor focused but society focused in relation to its natural environment. It will be a household to keep up our *oikos* as a whole, consisting of humans and non-humans together, as participants on an equal footing. This implies that participants carry the burdens of shared responsibility and accountability. Consequently, the concept of value for all becomes broader, across a wider array of actors.

Fifth, the six trends seemingly feed into a common understanding that individual actors are no longer in the 'economic game' for mere self-interest. Instead, the key question for any actor becomes what s/he may contribute to the whole.[1]

Sixth, a common denominator for all of the six trends seems to be that they all challenge principles fundamental to the current fabrics of our economies and societies. For starters, the trends question the principle of ownership. For example, the sharing economy trend operates on a form of hybrid ownership, and the circular economy stretches this principle, pushing the envelope of transactions from transfer of ownership towards service delivery (e.g., Product as a Service solutions). Next, the issue of value is challenged. This

---

[1] This aligns with the historical words in J. F. Kennedy's Inaugural Address on 20 January 1961: 'Ask not what your country can do for you – ask what you can do for your country' (Kennedy, 1961). Also, this principle forms the basis of the Swedish social system, sharply contrasting with the individualistic perspective of the Anglo-Saxon system.

is most salient in the principle of value retention around which the circular economy takes shape. Furthermore, the relation between mankind and nature is challenged, navigating between the subjection of nature as a resource for human needs versus perceiving them as equals or humans seen as subordinate to nature. Additionally, the principle of competition that rules in current economic thinking is challenged, inspired by mankind's ability to achieve synergies in collaborations. Also, the growth paradigm is heavily contested by degrowth and post-growth movements, inspired by the notion of 'Limits to Growth'. Subsequently, the blind trust in technological advancements as the principal force of economic development, dominant ever since the Industrial Revolutions, seems unfit to address current societal challenges. Finally, the traditional economic roles of producers and consumers are becoming obsolete because new technologies enable individuals to combine both roles. This change in roles has shaped the self-production economy.

Finally, the discussed trends seem to indicate that the economy of the future is not in the future but can already be found in parts of the present world, especially the non-Western parts.[2] The idea and ideal of an 'economy for all' was the basis of many indigenous societies in the past, resonates in the now, and hopefully will be so in the future. Interestingly, these 'other' economies have found ways to provide for all, while simultaneously keeping their works within planetary boundaries. Up to now, we seemingly went to great lengths to overlook, ignore or subconsciously divert our gaze from these non-Western societies and economies, either because of our general ignorance of their existence, or our inability to understand how these operate or reconcile with their underlying principles. Given the current dominance of Western economic thinking in global institutions, the failure to overcome differences and incompatibilities with 'outsiders' goes beyond the superficial. Possibly this is fuelled by a deeply rooted belief of human superiority in Western axiology, resonating in its perspectives on economy and society, that has been refined and enhanced ever since the Industrial Revolution (Burchett, 2015). Or perhaps this dominance stems from the blinding conviction that rational approaches that have shaped our societies and physical environments are the only way for society to progress. Whatever the explanation is, dominant economics has brought prosperity for some, but at great costs for others (including nature). At this moment, its global impact is already exceeding five planetary boundaries

---

[2]   Escobar (2005) already addresses the opportunities for inspiration and learning across cultures, specifically when this takes shape between developed and developing parts of the world. In particular, the solutions chosen in developing parts may provide novel approaches to addressing societal challenges en route to a sustainable development.

(IPCC, 2023), affecting Western and non-Western societies. Swift and drastic interventions are needed (IPCC, 2023).

In the remainder of this concluding chapter, we will explore the consequences of these six shared conclusions from the chapters of the book from an ontological, epistemological and methodological perspective towards crafting the economy of the future. We finish with an agenda for academic institutions as these have an important part to play in crafting the economy of the future.

2.   ONTOLOGICAL CONSIDERATIONS: FLATTENING THE LANDSCAPE

While we have gradually been weaving this new economic fabric (as we have shown in this book), two fundamental issues have emerged and re-emerged ever since the start of the debate on sustainable development. The first concerns the position of nature in relation to economic thought. From the outset, nature has been considered merely as a passive resource, to be exploited by societies through entrepreneurial activities. In other words, mainstream economic thinking regards humans and nature not as equals, with the interactions between them always favouring humankind. The second issue has to deal with the interactions within society and how these are valued. In short, not all interactions between people are valued in similar ways; in fact, only those interactions that are framed within the confines of economic thinking are valued. Through the process of commodification (e.g., Appadurai, 1986), these interactions are brought into the frame of transactions around the delivery of goods and services. The consequence of both issues is that the current economic ways of thinking do not provide means to balance between matters that are in and outside of the economic system. It is the restoration of such balance that lies at the heart of sustainable development (e.g., Raworth, 2017; Rockström et al., 2009; WCED, 1987). Seeking ways to reconcile both nature and mankind, and the appreciation of the possible multitude of interactions, assuring that they move forward on an equal footing, requires economic reconstruction from the ground up.

The need for a reconsideration of how humans and their natural environment are positioned to one another is addressed in the discourse on progressing from the Anthropocene towards the Symbiocene (Albrecht, 2014). In the Anthropocene, human behaviour shapes around human interests alone, without paying much respect to other beings in their environment. This results in the human dominance over non-humans we currently observe around the world. In contrast, the Symbiocene takes shape around the notion of the restoration of the relationship of humans with their natural environment and the beings it houses. Various perspectives on the relationship between society and nature have gradually emerged, presenting alternatives to the man-over-nature

premise. Inspired by Latour's (2004) *Politics of Nature* and other social theorists, Raffin et al. (2021) have developed the 'flat ontology' concept. The
flat ontology challenges the prioritisation of human agency in common social
thinking (including economic). Instead, it accepts 'humans, things, plants,
animals, feelings, and concepts ... [as equal beings that coexist, which] ...
express themselves through their ... associations with other beings' (Raffin
et al., 2021, p. 4). Some scientists put this equal relationship between humans
and non-humans as a means with the survival of the human race as a final
goal: for example, the late James Lovelock. He presented the Gaia theory in
which, taking a systems perspective, human society is seen as a sub-system of
nature. Abiding by the rules of the super system nature allows humans in their
equal relationship with non-humans to ensure survival. The insight to consider
humans and non-humans as equals has also given rise to a reconsideration
of the stakeholder concept (e.g., Starik, 1995). The emphasis on relations
between human and non-human beings in relation to the super system nature
shows resemblance with Capra's (2007) ontological perspective in which the
importance of the 'relation' concept is emphasised.

In addition to the foundations of a flat ontology, Raffin et al. (2021) provide
a method to put this ontology into practice, making use of the mechanism of
spokespersons (see also Latour, 2004) to give voice to those beings that are
unable to articulate their own positions. Experiments using this approach
indicate that it may yield novel ways to design and intervene in social contexts,
more deliberately seeking balance between humans and non-humans involved
in issues of sustainability.

To complement the means part of giving humans and non-humans a voice
in the process of reaching an equal relationship, the articulation of the goal
has been worked on in several fields. Where the Sustainable Development
Goals tend to define set goals for a sustainable future, the goals do not go far
enough, are inconsistent (Swain, 2018), or even are developed from a dominant Western perspective. As an alternative, in Sweden, governmental and
private organisations are taking the four system conditions established in The
Natural Step, developed by Karl Henrik Robert and his team, as the main goal:
in the sustainable society, nature is not subject to (1) systematically increasing
concentrations of substances extracted from the Earth's crust, (2) increasing
concentrations of substances produced by society, (3) ongoing degradation by
physical means, and, (4) in that society, human needs are met worldwide. We
suggest a wider exploration of alternative ontological perspectives in which
humans and non-humans and their interactions are included from the outset is
fundamental to obtaining a more profound understanding of sustainable development, and provides a solid basis for the elaboration of future economies.

Taking a closer look at how people within society interact, we observe the
inclination to increasingly commoditise or economise these interactions, and

consequently consider only these interactions relevant from the economic perspective. Over the course of the past centuries, more and more of these interactions have been subject to economic dynamics, including the framing in terms of supply and demand, pricing and scarcity. Mazzucato (2019) elaborates on these shifts in perception of human interactions. She argues that the ways these are valued have gradually shaped the economy as we know it. What is considered productive (i.e., the creation of value) and non-productive (i.e., the extraction of value) lies at its heart. Through the centuries, the perspective on productive activities has moved from only soil-bound activities (i.e., agriculture and mining), to the incorporation of industrial labour, the inclusion of services, and lastly the emergence and acceptance of the financial sector as part of the economy. Activities related to household and government have been systematically considered receivers and thus as non-productive (e.g., Mazzucato, 2019, p. 51). The divide between productive and non-productive no longer only applies to activities, but moreover is used as a qualification of people, even stretching as far as, for instance, the criminalisation of poverty (see, for instance, Hitchcock, 2018; de Clercq et al., 2018),[3] or at least creating a divide between the haves and have-nots of capital. Mintzberg (2015) notices an imbalance in society that has emerged in parallel to the changing perspectives on productivity. He specifically elaborates on the imbalance of power that has emerged between the three pillars of society: public, private and 'plural'[4] (Mintzberg, 2015, pp. 27–29). He argues that the position of the private sector (i.e., corporations) benefited unjustly in this process, being awarded various privileges and liberties that have historically been for people exclusively. This, for example, materialised in the recognition of 'corporations as persons' (Mintzberg, 2015, p. 3) and the extension of their privileges thereafter (Mintzberg, 2015, pp. 9–10), tipping the scale in their favour. For example, they have been allowed to devolve responsibilities to society (e.g., pollution and waste) hiding behind the principle of externalities (see Coase, 1960).

Mazzucato and Mintzberg both call for a change of heart in the ways society is perceived and organised. Mazzucato (2019) pleads for a revival of the debate on value at the core of economic thinking, while Mintzberg (2015) suggests the restoration of balance between the private, public and plural realms. In effect

---

[3] Conversely, Herring et al. (2019) mention the institutionalised ways in which the criminal justice system assures people are stuck in their poverty.

[4] Mintzberg introduces the notion of the 'plural', which emphasises the plurality that is found in civil society. It consists of 'cooperatives, nongovernmental organisations (NGOs), unions, religious orders, and many hospitals and universities' (Mintzberg, 2015, p. 29).

these are two sides of the same coin. Value theory dictates what activities and actors are of value, which relates closely to how the three realms of society are balanced. Mazzucato (2019, pp. 270–271) reflects on this matter, questioning whether perceiving entrepreneurs and businesses as the sole creators of wealth is justified. Mintzberg's (2015) imbalance may be a direct consequence of such a kind of thinking. It awards the private realm with a preferred position in relation to the public and plural, possibly leading to a form of 'predatory capitalism' (Mintzberg, 2015, p. 62). The call for the restoration of both the value debate at the core of economics and the balance between the private, public and plural realms, seems to align with the notion of sustainable development. At least it allows for a fundamental reconsideration of the way society is organised and what interactions between people are considered valuable.

To conclude, and in alignment with Mazzucato's (2019) suggestion, we argue that it is time for a fundamental reconsideration on how we reshape the link between empirical reality and economic thought. This immediately implies re-establishing the discussion on value theory at the core of the economic discourse. More precisely, we call for the careful crafting of such value theory, in close connection with how value takes shape in empirical reality. While the latter may seem abstract, mankind has been able to make judgements on what is of value from the moment they started roaming and populating planet Earth. Clear enough at least to build stable communities and larger societies. Given the state of our ecological and social environment, a reconsideration of this idea of what we value and how we construct an economy around this is unavoidable, starting with a broad recognition of actors, including non-human, and how they are related.

3.   EPISTEMOLOGICAL AND METHODOLOGICAL CONSIDERATIONS: CRITICALLY AMENDING THE ROLE OF ACADEMIA

Academic institutions play a special role in the development of societies and how societies face challenges as they prepare future decision-makers, and generate knowledge on decision-making in society, organisations and institutions (Snelson-Powell et al., 2016; Ng, 2022). As such, academic institutions can be seen as one of the most influential institutions as they enhance the welfare of the nation, economically, intellectually, socially and culturally (Lambert & Butler, 2006; Pelikan, 1992). Jantsch stressed the need for collaborative forms of science that successfully contribute to solving societal issues by adapting universities 'as a means of increasing the capability of society for continuous self-renewal' (Jantsch, 1972, p. 12). Collaborative forms of science can be framed by the concepts of multidisciplinarity, pluridisciplinarity, crossdisciplinarity, interdisciplinarity and transdisciplinarity, and have been part of critical

debates in sociology of science/philosophy of science on the role of universities in society focusing on the need to create collaboration between natural
sciences, social sciences and humanities. This collaboration in science justified
the normative approach in scientific work and 'education for self-renewal'.
With the various (mono-) disciplines all separately focusing on certain aspects
of the real-world phenomena related to the physical and the social world (Ng,
2022), multidisciplinarity refers to the connecting knowledge in approaching
an issue, using various perceptions of a range of disciplines, while each discipline works in a self-contained manner with little cross-fertilisation among
disciplines, or synergy in the outcomes. Interdisciplinarity refers to a form of
coordinated and integration-oriented collaboration between researchers from
different disciplines (Hirsch Hadorn et al., 2006; Mauser et al., 2013).

Transdisciplinarity (TD) as a research approach is aimed at bridging science
and society and is widely recommended for academics willing to contribute
actively to societal issues (Lang et al., 2012). Transdisciplinary research
approaches have emerged as an integrating field of science, as well as in a wide
range of disciplines contributing to the analysis and problem solving of the
many interrelated issues covered by the concept of sustainable development
(Vermeulen & Witjes, 2021). 'If you want to have an impact in the real world,
you must take your work beyond the academic publications and bring it to the
world of practice' (Hoffman, 2021).

TD research brings about methodological challenges and recent trends
towards greater disciplinary integration (Fahy & Rau, 2013) responding to
the call for more engaging and interdisciplinary science (Franklin & Blyton,
2013), but is, at the same time, depending and building on outcomes of disciplinary, interdisciplinary and multidisciplinary approaches. TD approaches are
increasingly argued to benefit from analytical treatment of social-ecological
systems (e.g., Ahlström et al., 2020) to understand the role of social actors
and related values in societal change processes while being confronted with
new knowledge or developments (e.g., technologies) (Söderbaum, 2009).
As a result, the individual researcher is likely to face epistemological and
methodological dilemmas when operationalising TD questions and projects
as TD approaches walk the thin line between meaningfulness for practice and
science (Lang et al., 2012). The close collaboration between academic and
non-academic actors while applying TD approaches needs reflections on the
implications of multiple knowledge systems (see, e.g., Cash et al., 2003; Tengö
et al., 2014; Polk, 2015) created by multi-actor collaboration, as well as on the
different roles that each actor can have in the collaboration. While academic
roles in TD include acting as 'a facilitator', 'a self-reflective scientist', 'change
agent' and 'knowledge broker' (e.g., Wittmayer et al., 2014; Milkoreit et al.,
2015; Cockburn, 2021; Sellberg et al., 2021), there is a lack of debate on how
to handle these roles: what does TD research imply for each actor involved in

a TD approach and how should they be trained or prepared? (see, e.g., Care et al., 2021). These different roles require specific competences and attitudes, such as negotiation skills, the ability to translate between disciplines, openness, and so on. Enhancing the understanding of these personal aspects of TD supports the goal of capturing real-world challenges experienced by TD academics and promotes reflexivity (Sellberg et al., 2021).

In addition, the attempts of academics to contribute to societal challenges have seen the development of a collaboration between academics and non-academics forming so-called triple helixes of private and public organisations, and academic institutes (Carayanis et al., 2016). Consequently, research on academic institutions contributing to societal challenges is taking communities' perspectives like communities of practice (e.g., Wenger, 2009), organisational ecosystems (Moore, 1996), etc. One of the conditions necessary for the co-production of knowledge between academics and non-academics harks back to the initial focus that universities should have on their deeper underlying capabilities, or as it is called within the context of a university, academic skills. Universities are often consulted or deployed as bridge builders due to their independent role, critical thinking and objective way of assessing situations (Dentoni & Bitzer, 2015; Hoffman, 2021). However, when universities actively participate in societal communities, they become engaged scholars (Hoffman, 2021): by leaving their ivory towers as they choose to bridge the worlds of theory and practice, while getting connected and involved in specific cases.

International accreditation schemes such as UN PRME, AACSB, EQUIS and AMBA require the scientific output of, in this example, academic schools of management to be published in high-impact academic journals as well as to foster quality, locally relevant management education and impact development for local business communities and public institutions (Urgel, 2007). For academic institutions at large, this means that educational activities aimed at enhancing capabilities, as well as research activities aimed at the contribution to the production of knowledge, are a means to the impact of an academic institution. As other actors or institutions in society, academic institutions also have to determine how best to contribute to the development of society or societal challenges by using capacity and knowledge development for societal interventions (Van Hoof & Witjes, 2024).

With the world being complex and dynamic, TD approaches enable academic institutions not only to contribute to society, but they also enable students in their development towards their future role in society by connecting education to TD approaches of research with academic institutions being grounded in society. With critical reflection on the meaningfulness for practice and science of the outcomes at the heart of TD approaches, the close collaboration between academics (i.e., researchers and students) and non-academics means that all actors are learning on the potential of the process as well as the feasibility of the outcomes. Consequently, education and research output are merging while TD approaches are aiming for intervention output in the societal realm, resulting in a triple pronged output as the basis for TD approaches (see Figure 8.1). A collaboration with universities of applied science and practice-based education is necessary to teach students from these educational institutes already within their education programmes how to collaborate and work to generate synergy. Specifically at an educational programme level, this implies education on fact knowledge being mixed with methodology courses on, for example, system thinking and team-based learning on the application of the knowledge and methods in real-life cases. Academic institutions can, therefore, have an enhanced impact by combining capacity building (i.e., education) based on experience-based learning while producing knowledge (i.e., scientific output) based on abductive logic while contributing to innovations (i.e., impact) based on consultancy (see Figure 8.1; Van Hoof & Witjes, 2024):

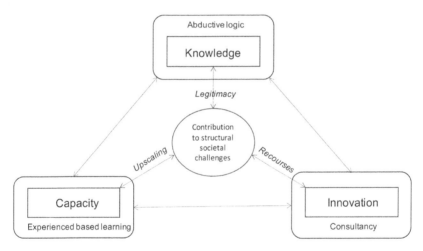

Figure 8.1   *The triple-pronged output of academic institutions aiming for contribution to society*

The collaboration for TD research approaches depends on the focus and aim of the TD research project (Vermeulen & Witjes, 2021). While striving for a contribution to societal challenges, TD approaches can be diverse in their aims leading to a wide variety of TD research configurations. Some scholars have reflected on the implications of multiple knowledge systems (see, e.g., Cash et al., 2003; Tengö et al., 2014; Polk, 2015) created by multi-actor collaboration as is necessary to contribute to societal challenges, as addressed earlier in this chapter, as well as the different roles that researchers can have in this collaboration.

To avoid major biases in finding the right balance between knowledge production and interventions, TD should be applied consciously and cautiously (Macintyre et al., 2021). The role of the different research participants (i.e., academics, students and non-academics) has a direct influence on the independence of the research and critical orientation or interpretative analysis of the research outcomes. The objectivity of the researcher and the research results could be in jeopardy when also aiming for meaningful outcomes for practice, re-emphasising the ethical dilemma. This may create friction in the collaboration between TD members (Schaltegger et al., 2013). In practice, TD leads to tensions, i.e., contradictory demands as perceived by the involved actors (Vermeulen & Witjes, 2021; Macintyre et al., 2021). This typically involves diverging interests between scientists and the more practice-oriented actors (Sellberg et al., 2021; Thompson et al., 2017). Thus, the collaborative setting in which TD takes place plays a vital role (Laasch et al., 2020).

In sum, academic institutions applying TD approaches in search of a direct contribution to societal challenges should acknowledge that researchers can and should consider power dynamics between the actors in the TD collaboration. An ethical and political stance is demanded if the TD researchers are to reach a contribution to societal challenges. In order to do so, TD researchers need a set of skills, e.g., communicating and negotiating with actors, in addition to balancing interdisciplinary tensions, and the tensions between knowledge production and intervention development. It is thus important to critically explore these roles when executing the diversity of TD approaches and to effectively navigate trade-offs when co-producing solutions for a better society.

4.   CRAFTING THE FUTURE OF THE ECONOMY

The deeper analysis of the six trends shaping the economy of the future, as addressed in the chapters of this book show that the social contract between state, market and civil society in an era of transition is being questioned. Among the reflections of the different actors in society on their contribution to the welfare of all, also institutions, public and private organisations especially are being urged to rethink their functioning within wider society. For example, the debates on corporate sustainability, with a focus on reduction of negative output of commercial activities, via debates on corporate social responsibility, focused on how firms create social value, are emerging into something that could be called corporate societal responsibility. Organisations have to externalise their responsibility for the welfare of societal actors, humans and non-humans. In countries like the Netherlands this can be seen with companies being forced to comply with environmental legislation since the 1980s focused on the control of the input and output of corporate processes, via current legislation which explicitly addresses companies controlling their impact on their context or the Extended Producer Responsibility (EPR) legislation forcing market actors to define responsibilities in reducing the impact of a product during its life cycle. The upcoming Corporate Sustainability Reporting Directive (CSRD) legislation has been strengthened by governments. This will lead to an enforcement on companies for making their impact on society transparent. Transparency has already been an aspect of the search for a sustainable development of society since its beginnings. For example, the need for transparency of the inputs and outputs of processes entailing the life cycle of products is needed to calculate the environmental impact of a product throughout its life cycle. With the first Life Cycle Assessment (LCA), as the overall method to quantify the environmental impact of a product throughout its life cycle, being carried out in the 1960s, it was in Agenda 21, launched during the COP in Rio in 1992, that LCAs were defined as one of the main tools for sustainable consumption and production. Since then, the need for transparency has been one of the main barriers to a greater uptake and use of LCAs. The current EPR and CSRD legislation is underlining the importance of transparency, this time transparency of organisations in their impact on the welfare of society. In both cases (i.e., LCA and CSRD), transparency is meant to support communication and collaboration between actors in society to address responsibility and trust on the contribution of each actor.

The current growing urgency to take action to contribute to societal challenges has resulted in more societal actors flocking together in so-called communities of practice (Wenger, 2009): actors from different backgrounds but with a shared goal who can achieve that goal while collaborating. With the development of the Symbiocene and the added goal for a sustainable society, as discussed earlier, these communities of practice can be seen as a collaboration of a mix of human and non-human actors aiming for a contribution to a sustainable society. Communities of practice also make clear that solving current challenges is not possible for individual actors or isolated organisations in society: we need to collaborate to contribute to the welfare of all.

For organisations, the collaboration needed to contribute to societal challenges brings along the strategic challenge of a single organisation on how to link this collaboration to inter-organisational activities: how can organisations adjust their regular organisational processes based on what is being developed in collaboration with other actors in these communities of practice? Debates on the concept of organisational ambidexterity have already been addressing strategy formation of organisations as a process of synching internal and external organisational activities. The growing need for organisations to be transparent about how they take responsibility for their contribution to societal challenges urges organisations to prioritise outcomes from corresponding communities of practice.

This prioritisation can also have a downside as some companies are proactively starting or joining communities of practice aimed at the resilience of a specific sector or supply chain. For example, companies have ensured their intake of primary resources by setting up strategic collaborations. The enhanced awareness of resource loss has urged companies to take more control of resource supply. In the plastics producing sector, for example, big companies are adding waste treatment activities to ensure supply, as supply of virgin plastics is becoming scarce and prices are rising. The added waste treatment by plastic producing companies will give them first contact with recycled content as well as an energy source that will come in handy in uncertain times due to energy transitions.

Challenges arising from the transition to a more sustainable energy production have resulted in several vehicle-producing companies being engaged in intra-organisational collaboration. With transport having a national and, especially in a small country like the Netherlands, an international impact, national and supranational governments have been added to these collaborations in their attempt to steer the developments towards 'fair for all'. Unfortunately, also in this case, companies prioritise their own survival above the welfare of all in society and have initiated communities of practice to control and steer certain developments. For example, several truck-producing companies have grouped together to find companies for long-haul truck transport in Europe based on the development of electric trucks. With European public debates on truck transport relying on hydrogen as the energy source, this private initiative enables a big shift forward as the collaboration company is ensuring a network of roads, charging stops and separate energy production, but that is finally an alternative to developments coming from collaborations among other actors in society on this topic. Besides, and in this case specifically, the off-the-grid production of electricity to ensure sufficient energy to charge trucks during their stops prioritises energy for long-haul truck transport over other energy necessities in society (e.g., industry, housing, etc.). Thus, intra-organisational collaboration aimed at societal challenges could be a great vehicle for creating synergy between the contribution of societal actors, but there is a need for high-level coordination to ensure that these developments contribute to a society that is fair for all or will generate well-being for all.

REFERENCES

Ahlström, H., Williams, A. & Vildåsen, S. S. (2020). Enhancing systems thinking in corporate sustainability through a transdisciplinary research process. *Journal of Cleaner Production, 256*, 120691.

Albrecht, G. A. (2014). Ecopsychology in the symbiocene. *Ecopsychology*, *6*(1), 58–59. https://doi.org/10.1089/eco.2013.0091.

Appadurai, A. (ed.). (1986). *The social life of things: Commodities in cultural perspective*. Cambridge University Press. doi:10.1017/CBO9780511819582.

Burchett, K. (2015). Anthropocentrism and nature: An attempt at reconciliation. *Teoria*, *34*(2), 119–137.

Capra, F. (2007). Sustainable living, ecological literacy, and the breath of life. *Canadian Journal of Environmental Education*, *12*, 9–18.

Carayannis, E. G., Campbell, D. F. J. & Rehman, S. S. (2016). Mode 3 knowledge production: Systems and systems theory, clusters and networks. *Journal of Innovation and Entrepreneurship*, *5*(1). https://doi.org/10.1186/s13731–016–0045–9.

Care, O., Bernstein, M. J., Chapman, M., Diaz Reviriego, I., Dressler, G., Felipe-Lucia, M. R., Friis, C., Graham, S., Hänke, H., Haider, L. J., Hernández-Morcillo, M., Hoffmann, H., Kernecker, M., Nicol, P., Piñeiro, C., Pitt, H., Schill, C., Seufert, V., Shu, K., Valencia, V. & Zaehringer, J. G. (2021). Creating leadership collectives for sustainability transformations. *Sustainability Science*, *16*(2), 703–708.

Cash, D. W., Clark, W. C., Alcock, F., Dickson, N. M., Eckley, N., Guston, D. H. , Jäger, J. & Mitchell, R. B. (2003). Knowledge systems for sustainable development. *Proceedings of the National Academy of Sciences*, *100*(14), 8086–8091.

Coase, R. H. (1960). The problem of social cost. *Journal of Law and Economics*, *3*, 1–44.

Cockburn, J. (2021). Knowledge integration in transdisciplinary sustainability science: Tools from applied critical realism. *Sustainable Development*, 1–17, https://doi:10.1002/sd.2279.

de Clercq, K., van den Broek, M., van Nieuwpoort, M.-A. & Albers, F. (2018). *The colonies of benevolence: An exceptional experiment*. Koninklijke Van Gorcum, the Netherlands.

Dentoni, D. & Bitzer, V. (2015). The role(s) of universities in dealing with global wicked problems through multi-stakeholder initiatives. *Journal of Cleaner Production*, *106*, 68–78.

Escobar, A. (2005). *Más allá del tercer mundo: globalización y diferencia*. Bogotá, Colombia.

Fahy, F. & Rau, H. (2013). *Methods of sustainability research in the social sciences*. SAGE Publications. USA.

Franklin, A. & Blyton, P. (2013). Researching sustainability: A guide to social science methods, practice and engagement. Routledge.

Herring, C., Yarbrough, D. & Marie Alatorre, L. (2019). Pervasive penality: How the criminalization of poverty perpetuates homelessness. *Social Problems*, *67*(1), 131–149.

Hirsch Hadorn, G., Bradley, D., Pohl, C., Rist, S. & Wiesmann, U. (2006). Implications of transdisciplinarity for sustainability research. *Ecological Economics*, *60*(1), 119–128. https://doi.org/10.1016/j.ecolecon.2005.12.002.

Hitchcock, D. (2018). 'Punishment is all the charity that the law affordeth them': Penal transportation, vagrancy, and the charitable impulse in the British Atlantic, c.1600–1750. *New Global Studies*, *12*(2), 195–215. https:// doi .org/ 10 .1515/ ngs -2018-0029.

Hoffman, A. J. (2021). *The engaged scholar: Expanding the impact of academic research in today's world*. Stanford University Press.

IPCC. (2023). Climate change 2023: Synthesis report. A report of the Intergovernmental Panel on Climate Change. Contribution of Working Groups I, II and III to the Sixth

Assessment Report of the Intergovernmental Panel on Climate Change [Core Writing Team, H. Lee and J. Romero (eds)]. IPCC, Geneva, Switzerland.

Jantsch, E. (1972). Inter- and transdisciplinary university: A systems approach to education and innovation. *Higher Education, 1*, 7–37.

Kennedy, J. F. (1961, 20 January). *John F. Kennedy's inaugural address.* Inaugural address, Washington DC. https:// www .jfklibrary .org/ learn/ about -jfk/ historic -speeches/inaugural-address.

Laasch, O., Moosmayer, D., Antonacopoulou, E. & Schaltegger, S. (2020). Constellations of transdisciplinary practices: A map and research agenda for the responsible management learning field. *Journal of Business Ethics, 162*(4), 735–757. https://doi.org/10.1007/s10551-020-04440-5.

Lambert, R. & Butler, N. (2006). *The future of European universities. Renaissance or decay.* Centre for European Reform, London, UK.

Lang, D. J., Wiek, A., Bergmann, M., Stauffacher, M., Martens, P., Moll, P., Swilling, M. & Thomas, C. J. (2012). Transdisciplinary research in sustainability science: Practice, principles, and challenges. *Sustainability Science, 7*(S1), 25–43. https://doi .org/10.1007/s11625-011-0149-x.

Latour, B. (2004). *Politics of nature.* Harvard University Press.

Macintyre, T., Witjes, S., Vildåsen, S. & Ramos-Mejía, M. (2021). *Embracing transdisciplinary tensions on the road to 2030.* In M. Keitsch & W. Vermeulen (eds), *Transdisciplinarity for sustainability: Aligning diverse practices.* Routledge. http:// transgressivelearning.org/.

Mauser, W., Klepper, G., Rice, M., Schmalzbauer, B. S., Hackmann, H., Leemans, R. & Moore, H. (2013). Transdisciplinary global change research: The co-creation of knowledge for sustainability. *Current Opinion in Environmental Sustainability, 5*(3–4), 420–431.

Mazzucato, M. (2019). *The value of everything: Making and taking in the global economy.* Penguin Books.

Milkoreit, M., Moore, M.-L., Schoon, M. & Meek, C. L. (2015). Resilience scientists as change-makers – Growing the middle ground between science and advocacy? *Environmental Science & Policy, 53*, 87–95.

Mintzberg, H. (2015). *Rebalancing society: Radical renewal beyond left, right, and center.* Berret-Koehlers Publishers.

Moore, J. F. (1996). *The death of competition: Leadership & strategy in the age of business ecosystems.* HarperBusiness.

Ng, F. (2022). *A guide for independent-minded scientists.* Forest Research Institute Malaysia, Kuala Lumpur, Malaysia.

Pelikan, P. (1992). The dynamics of economic systems, or how to transform a failed socialist economy. *Evolutionary Economics, 2*, 39–63.

Polk, M. (2015). Transdisciplinary co-production: Designing and testing a transdisciplinary research framework for societal problem solving. *Futures, 65*, 110–122. https://doi.org/10.1016/j.futures.2014.11.001.

Raffin, J., Rolland, Y., He, L., Perus, L., Mangin, J. F., Gabelle, A. ... & de Souto Barreto, P. (2021). Cross-sectional and longitudinal interaction effects of physical activity and APOE-ε4 on white matter integrity in older adults: The MAPT study. *Maturitas, 152*, 10–19.

Raworth, K. (2017). *Doughnut economics: Seven ways to think like a 21st century economist.* Chelsea Green Publishing.

Rockström, J., Steffen, W., Noone, K. et al. (2009). A safe operating space for humanity. *Nature, 461*, 472–475. https://doi.org/10.1038/461472a.

Schaltegger, S., Beckmann, M. & Hansen, E. G. (2013). Transdisciplinarity in corporate sustainability: Mapping the field. *Business Strategy and the Environment*, *22*(4), 219–229. https://doi.org/10.1002/bse.1772.

Sellberg, M. M., Cockburn, J., Holden, P. B. & Lam, D. P. M. (2021). Towards a caring transdisciplinary research practice: Navigating science, society and self. *Ecosystems and People*, *17*(1), 292–305. https://doi.org/10.1080/26395916.2021.1931452.

Snelson-Powell, A., Grosvold, J. & Millington, A. (2016). Business school legitimacy and the challenge of sustainability: A fuzzy set analysis of institutional decoupling. *Academy of Management Learning and Education*, *15*(4), 703–723. https://doi.org/10.5465/amle.2015.0307.

Söderbaum, P. (2009). Making actors, paradigms and ideologies visible in governance for sustainability. *Sustainable Development*, *17*(2), 70–81. https://doi.org/10.1002/sd.404.

Starik, M. (1995). Should trees have managerial standing? Toward stakeholder status for non-human nature. *Journal of Business Ethics*, *14*, 207–217.

Swain, R. B. (2018). A critical analysis of the sustainable development goals. In W. L. Filho (ed.), *Handbook of sustainability science and research* (pp. 341–355). Springer.

Tengö, M., Brondizio, E. S., Elmqvist, T., Malmer, P. & Spierenburg, M. (2014). Connecting diverse knowledge systems for enhanced ecosystem governance: The multiple evidence base approach. *Ambio*, *43*(5), 579–591. https://doi.org/10.1007/s13280-014-0501-3.

Thompson, M. A., Owen, S., Lindsay, J. M., Leonard, G. S. & Cronin, S. J. (2017). Scientist and stakeholder perspectives of transdisciplinary research: Early attitudes, expectations, and tensions. *Environmental Science & Policy*, *74*, 30–39.

Urgel, J. (2007). EQUIS accreditation: Value and benefits for international business schools. *Journal of Management Development*, *26*(1), 73–83.

Van Hoof, B. & Witjes, S. (2024). Schools of management making an impact: Operationalization mechanisms and methods for contributing to organizational change. In P. Shrivastava & M. Starik (eds), *Sustainable universities and colleges: Leading or following society toward resilience*? Edward Elgar.

Vermeulen, W. & Witjes, S. (2021). *History and mapping of TD research*. In M. Keitsch & W. Vermeulen (eds), *Transdisciplinarity for sustainability: Aligning diverse practices*. Routledge.

WCED. (1987). Report of the World Commission on Environment and Development: Our Common Future. United Nations General Assembly document A/42/427, New York, USA.

Wenger, E. (2009). Communities of practice: The key to knowledge strategy. In *Knowledge and communities* (pp. 3–20). Routledge.

Wittmayer, J. M., Schäpke, N., Steenbergen, F. & Omann, I. (2014). Making sense of sustainability transitions locally: How action research contributes to addressing societal challenges. *Critical Policy Studies*, *8*(4), 465–485.

Index